PETER LENNON

Foreign Correspondent

Paris in the Sixties

PICADOR

First published 1994 by Picador

a division of Pan Macmillan Publishers Limited
Cavaye Place London SW10 9PG
and Basingstoke

Associated companies throughout the world

ISBN 0 330 31911 6

Copyright © Peter Lennon 1994

3 5 7 9 8 6 4 2

A CIP catalogue record for this book is available from
the British Library

Typeset by CentraCet Limited, Cambridge
Printed by Mackays of Chatham Plc, Kent

ACKNOWLEDGEMENTS

My thanks are due to the *Irish Times*, which first published the FLN interview in 1960, and to the *Sunday Times* magazine which published, in 1988, a piece by me on the 1968 student revolt from which I have drawn for the chapter on May 1968. I would like to thank Faber & Faber for permission to quote from T. S. Eliot's 'The Love Song of J. Alfred Prufrock' (*Collected Poems 1909–1962*).

I think (without being soppy about it now that I am back there) that I do have to thank the *Guardian* and its freethinking denizens for (often unwittingly) making it possible for me, over the years, to have some rewarding experiences.

One

My first journeys to work were not to a newspaper office but by way of a number 15 double-decker bus to a Dublin bank. I was seventeen. From the very outset I noted, with foreboding, that the Dublin Savings Bank in Lower Abbey Street was on the site of the old morgue. The words City Morgue were still to be seen cut into the sooty grey stone above the high pillared entrance.

As far as my mother was concerned getting into the bank was like being deposited in a secular monastery which would provide security right up to a pensionable old age. The very title 'bank clerk' was liveried in respectability. I harboured a bemused version of this belief myself. When she told my father she sat close to him in the kitchen, her voice becoming reverent and musical as it did in times of great contentment. She spoke very clearly to him as to a child. He was drunk. 'You are going to be very proud of your son,' she told him. 'Peter has been accepted for a job in the bank.'

My father swivelled a dangling head towards me and something shifted in his slurred eyes. I think it was fear. He must have sensed forces at work in his family beyond his already wobbly control. His expression was now clearly wary as if I had become a stranger. Could one of his sons really have turned into a banker?

He was a tender man really, perplexed by an inadequate control of his own life. I recognized this in innocent childhood and came to recognize it again in late manhood. But in my teens I saw him only as an authoritarian without authority. My brothers and I only showed him respect as part of the charade for helping to keep him off the booze. Another method was hiding his trousers.

I cannot blame my mother for her obsession with respectability and keeping up appearances. Appearances were about all we possessed to keep up. We lived in flats but only in good-class areas. We were stowaways in first-class roads deferring to landladies' instructions to display the same patterned lace curtains so that passers-by would not realize the house had been let in flats. We had moved seven times by the time I was seventeen, debt or spectacular public demonstrations of my father's affair with drink provoking our landladies to move us on.

Although my father came of a respectable wine merchant family, with six properties in Dublin at one point, booze had got to the business by the time we three boys were born. When his father died of it, my father left a junior clerical job in Cosgrave's Free State Civil Service to help his brother drown the business. The properties were gradually sold off, profits devoured by shadowy solicitors and family squabbling. I was born in the stern old family Georgian house in North Frederick Street (now a hotel), but by the time I was four, we had already backed into a semi-furnished flat in the slummier end of Donnybrook.

For the rest of his life my father was a freelance salesman living on paltry commissions. He was a buyer and deal-maker for an Italian named Boni who had a National Cash Register and a Milner's safe franchise. But they mostly dealt in second-hand furniture and fittings, my father hanging around the auction rooms on the quays, stitching up deals. I don't know how he learned these quayside skills, nor indeed why he chose to, coming from a different class. My mother never worked – neither her religious convictions nor the customs of the time permitted it. She gave up her job in the Post Office when she married: her place was in the home.

So my father had the frightening task of singlehandedly edging us four dependants along, like an itinerant with a handcart full of humans. He would gain a few feet here and a few yards there with a fiver, or very occasionally a tenner, no sum ever taking him more than five or six days into the future. I sometimes imagine the terror in which he must have lived, without a steady income or a particular talent, trying to keep us all alive. But my mother, who came of impecunious small but ferociously honourable and respectable Tipperary farmers, never allowed us to feel for an instant that we were one of the Poor. Refinement was her refrain and it came to her naturally. Piety was another, but it was not without humour. We indulged, on our knees, in sweet, deeply emotional recitation of the rosary on bad nights and had frothy cream buns to celebrate good days. Whenever possible we went to the pictures to get our share of the glories of life that had been so sluggish in coming our way.

Every now and then my father would drink himself down a kind of yellow brick road of temporary freedom, and for weeks our days and nights would be beset with dismay and tension, my mother in a state of collapsing despair or false lightheartedness as we waited for him to come home so we could search his pockets for money.

The whole thing outraged me because of its grotesque similarity to a Victorian temperance playlet. I often had to hang around pub doors downtown to get money from him. This was just one of the crosses that, as my mother put it, along with what she called 'torture of mind and body', we had to bear. Though, to be fair, my father was never violent; it was his enervating loquaciousness, when he'd come home half-drunk and keep the family up until the early hours, which created the physical torment.

As we three boys edged towards self-reliance, his effect on our lives lessened, if only because of the capacity of adolescents to be so devoured by their own porridgy needs.

The bank job was seen as the family's first access to a secure world. But, surprisingly, instead of financial security becoming an obsessive goal I realized I had gained a kind of immunity to crippling insecurity. Having very little was such a familiar state, I had built up a resistance to it; like taking a poison routinely until it had no effect. There could be no better training for a future exile. Institutions could not hold me in bondage with promises of long-term security.

So, although I did not realize it at first, the morgue had little hope of holding me.

My first shocking revelation about adult working life, a revelation

3

as profound as any in sexual initiation, was that establishments such as banks, presented as central to the well-being of the community, were baleful machines that robbed you of a lifetime's daylight hours. It was a fact that, curiously, everyone else appeared to accept as natural. But I remember my panic when it struck me that the morgue would never allow me to see daylight for five and a half days a week for the rest of my life.

The building, a single vast hall bisected by a long counter, had no windows, only a high, blurred skylight. The manager, Mr Coniffe, occupied what must have been the corpse-washing room, now turned into an intimidating bureaucrat's sanctuary. We stood with the ledgers behind the counter in the area where the corpses must have been laid out. I was paid twelve pounds a month.

I suppose I could have become resigned to the theft of my days, since the eight pounds a month I handed up hugely boosted the peace of mind of the family, but for two factors. The first was my dislike of the petty-minded mentality these money warehouses breed. We were just a plain savings bank, no foreign exchange, no financial services. It was largely a facility for small family businesses, poor grannies and Friendly Societies. The staff was never more than ten with one two-man branch up in the slums near the Coombe.

Since there was no substance to our work, our energies were directed unwholesomely towards professional parochialism, spurious issues of status. Officially the bank affected the severe airs and posturing of the great international banking world. We had to wear ties, of course, but also we were not allowed to wear sports shoes in summer, even though our feet were not easily visible to the customer. We were only allowed three-quarters of an hour for lunch and that behind a folding screen in a shadowy corner of the hall.

Within our mausoleum, territories were guarded with aggrieved watchfulness. A territory would just be a high stool placed in a particular spot and not removable without permission of the owner. It was not even a fixed spot. Only the four cashiers had their forehead-high, fenced-off enclosures for which they had keys. Clerks carried their stools to whatever position they were temporarily working and generally did not have time to sit on them anyway during opening hours. But the stools were our only individual possession, and we kept a vigilant watch on them.

The most alert to infringements of status were the Intermediate Senior Officials, youths of about twenty, newly promoted clerks. One of them tried to persuade me of the importance of acting 'for the good of the bank'. Even then I found the proposition laughable. My instinctive resistance to official institutions must have been atavistic, adapted from my mother whose youth had been dedicated to hostility against institutions which then happened to be British. (When she worked in a post office by the Kildare Street club, headquarters of the British forces in Ireland, she purloined army wireless despatches for the Republicans.) I transferred this defiance to the principal symbol of authority in my life, namely the Dublin Savings Bank.

The second hindrance to my making a successful career in banking was a talent for creating clerical errors of such mathematical ingenuity that it took the team of annual auditors a full extra week to discover them before balancing the books.

After three years of this the manager called me into his office one day and told me that I was 'not showing signs of permanency'.

It was Bob Johnson, a cashier from the bank and music critic of the *Irish Press* in his spare time, who sidled me into journalism. He decided I had literary skill because of my passionate arguments with my colleagues about the power of literature, the value of art, and the nobility even of 'dirty' writers such as James Joyce. (I had only read *Portrait of an Artist* at that stage.)

Johnson, who was about ten years older than I, was an endearing man. He had a nervous manner which took the form of laughing aloud at almost anything anyone said. To emphasize this rather ingratiating hilarity he would contort his body in the manner of someone dying to scratch his scrotum but unable to go the whole way for reasons of decency. After making clawing motions around his hip he would suddenly straighten up with an expression of extreme gravity. It was not always clear why he had either reaction. But he was a transparently good-natured man.

He had one serious affliction for a newspaper critic: he couldn't write – attempting to put two sentences together brought on an

almost physical infirmity. So when it came to producing full paragraphs he resorted to a unique technique. He kept back-numbers of
Musical Opinion and other English music journals and in writing
about, say, a Stravinsky revival, he would search his magazines for
published reports on a similar concert in Britain, snip out useful
phrases and paragraphs, paste them together, and then retype this
jigsaw, with small modifications, for his article. It was agonizing
labour for him but his reward was access to the social life of Dublin's
theatre bars, which he loved.

Johnson had been made music critic for the daily because he was
also a weekend church organist and occasionally gave brief concerts
on Radio Eireann. Up until then he could just about string together
standard clichés about colouring, exquisite phrasing and attack. But
the arrival of international companies such as the Bolshoi or the
Munich State Opera (Dublin was a staging post for London) made
painful demands on his talent. He asked me to help him out. The deal
was he would bring me to the events and give me the full one guinea
fee if I wrote them up under his name.

This worked a treat. Bob had even more time to enjoy the
conviviality of first nights; allowing me one drink, he shooed me off
to write the piece. Then he could saunter into the office with it in
time for the city edition. His articles began to get more and more
prominent display and we even took on book reviews. This productiv-
ity was greeted with heavy sarcasm by the newspaper. Dublin was too
small a town for such an arrangement to remain a secret for long but,
in any case, Johnson was without guile and too good-hearted to want
to deceive anyone – except, of course, the readers. Soon he was
reluctant to leave the theatre bar at all, and let me take in the copy.

The news editor, a pal of his, had no objection to the scam. He
couldn't make me music critic since I had no academic background
and I couldn't even play the fiddle. The pieces were readable. It was
not too difficult for me to build an article around stock musical
clichés. The first requirement of a journalist is the ability to become
an expert on anything at a day's notice (he then completely forgets
what he has learned, since there are no foundations to his knowledge).

6

So with a readable piece signed by a plausible name the paper was quite content.

The arrangement had advantages for me. I got practice in writing for newspapers (previously I had been labouring with grim short stories) and I was getting to know the newsmen of the town. Not only did Johnson honourably pass on the full fee (sometimes as much as two guineas): conscious-stricken about how he was making use of me, he introduced me to all the editors he knew. The introductions had a mysterious tinge because while Johnson would whisper that I was a promising journalist neither of us could offer proof.

I decided not to wait any longer and, to the consternation of my family, left the bank to make myself available for freelance work. Through Johnson, I got Saturday shifts on the *Sunday Press*, the sabbatic edition of De Valera's *Irish Press*. The night's pay was nearly as good as a week at the bank.

Through Johnson's influence I also got casual 'markings' covering the children's and suburban courts for the *Irish Press* and the *Evening Mail* (long since defunct). This was an unorthodox way into journalism, indeed a backward route. It was the route by which alcoholic journalists on the skids normally faded into oblivion. The usual pathway in was an apprenticeship in the provinces; but my apprenticeship years had been wasted in the bank. The other was swanning into the *Irish Times* from Trinity College. Even if we could have afforded it, the Archbishop of Dublin, John Charles McQuaid, did not allow Catholics to go to 'Protestant' Trinity.

So every day, neatly turned out, I would join the soup-kitchen queue of Dublin's scribbling drunks waiting for markings, paid at the rate of fifteen shillings a half day. These artists are not to be confused with Dublin's staffed alcoholics who drew their own chalk line through their career and tiptoed along it with aplomb. The most celebrated of these was R. M. Smyllie, the convivial, reclusive (he chose his pub company fastidiously), erudite, occasionally berserk, editor of the *Irish Times*.

Two of my colleagues in the queue, Arthur MacGann and Andy Stewart, had, when sober, or half-drunk, an extraordinary facility for turning out pieces, even lengthy features. I learned as much from their desperate deftness and skill in minimizing workloads, essential to those with an effective working day of less than three hours, than I ever did later from settled colleagues. As is often true of such cases, they loved words and were as skilful with them as W. C. Fields was with a billiard cue. But, like the character in Beckett's *Molloy*, they only got cash when they had filled the sheet of paper.

My task was to work my way up backstream to a full-time job. I managed to add night-time casual subbing on the *Irish Times* to my activities. Fully occupied with my own zigzagging schedule I had to neglect Johnson. He gradually resorted, without rancour, to the scissors again and his pieces shrank to their former size. Occasionally I would do a book review for him for old times' sake.

I had persuaded the features editor of the *Irish Times*, Jack White, a sensitive and talented man, to let me do a Court Notebook. These were weekly sketches, based on characters, incidents and verbal exchanges in the Dublin District criminal courts with the names of the participants changed to allow some of the liberties of fiction. For about a year these sketches of drunks and tinkers, foreign motorists engaged in nightmare altercations with Dublin bowsies or acts of heart-stopping desperation provoked by poverty were a central attraction of the Saturday edition. Then, restless for more complex material, I sat in on the civil courts.

There I came across the case of a Dublin butcher prosecuted for mixing a chemical into mincemeat to give it a bright appearance. There is little human detail in these civil actions, no insights into character, so I had imaginatively to reconructt the original encounter: the apparently finicky customer who asked for three-quarters of a pound of mincemeat and then demanded it be divided up and put into three separate containers. I guessed at the sardonic reaction of the butcher as the doggedly officious customer sealed the three containers. He then gave one to the butcher, held the other and announced that the third would be sent for analysis.

This case revealed the hazard of straying from classic petty crime. The facts were unique, therefore the characters easily identifiable. The

8

judge was the father of a friend of mine and recognized himself with amusement. The Corporation Health Inspector was not so beguiled.

My piece had speculated on the kind of mentality which could, day after day, carry out these stealthy raids on fellow citizens and endure their obloquy in officious silence. I decided he must be a reformed drunk.

Unfortunately he was a zealous teetotaller – one of the centurions of Father Matthew, Apostle of Temperance, who throughout my childhood extended his bronze hand from a plinth in O'Connell Street in perpetual rebuke to Mooney's pub. The inspector, sporting the Pioneer Pin of Total Abstinence (which I should have spotted), threatened to sue for libel.

My first intimation of trouble was when, on the bus home from work, a fellow I knew from Dublin Corporation, but didn't normally speak to, plonked down beside me in a state of malicious agitation and said: 'I know a geezer who is going to sue you!' The corporation inspector claimed he had been held up to 'ridicule and contempt' by his colleagues, who had easily penetrated the fictitious cover.

Destiny's cloak now revealed a denser material. It was approaching the end of an era for the *Irish Times*: Bertie Smyllie was dying (of drink) and I attribute the terminal fatigue of this odd and original figure to the fact that the *Irish Times* behaved with considerable unfairness towards me.

Official-looking strangers appeared in the corridors of the paper and there was an out-of-court settlement. I was never consulted; the column was suppressed without explanation. This was the kind of total capitulation I associated more with Catholic papers, habitually collapsing before a stroke of the crozier. The Protestant *Irish Times* (I was the second Catholic ever employed and then not staffed) had previously seemed to me of aristocratic authority. To discover that it dared not risk future, unspecified dangers, let alone stand up to a minor challenge, reinforced a belief that my country was sloughing me off.

Jack White now indirectly handed me my ticket for Paris. My features editor, considering that I had been unfairly treated, became reckless on my behalf. When the paper's circulation manager, a Mr Turner, told him he was looking for someone to relaunch his dead father's provincial weekly, instead of recommending an established journalist, Jack White suggested me.

I was appointed editor.

I hurriedly got a friend to teach me to drive. Lessons consisted of him taking me out to the Phoenix Park in a hired Ford Anglia and leaving me there after half an hour to bump around, scattering the deer or bucketing up and down with the handbrake on, alarming lovers in their cosy nooks in the Furry Glen. You could get a licence, at that time, without being able to drive; my cousin who worked in the licence bureau brought it to me when she came to tea one evening. By the time I got to Longford I was able to drift down the middle of a road without hitting anything and, since most of the cars on Longford roads would be horse-drawn, I did not anticipate any sudden emergencies while I was polishing my driving skills.

If you were to choose a town which most comprehensively scuppered the stereotype of Ireland as a place of magical landscapes and literary wits having great gas in gorgeous old pubs, Longford was it. It was a downcast little place in apparent perpetual convalescence from some disabling history. The sky constantly leaked, the landscape slurped underfoot, the pubs smelled of carbolic soap and were populated by catatonic old men served by distrustful barmen with pulpy voices. On Fair Day the main street ran with shit.

These midlands people were not so much slow as disinclined ever to get started. In my short stay – the Turner enterprise was doomed from the start – my main source of insight into the inhabitants was the courtroom. It was in Longford that I discovered why, at the end of the rosary, my mother regularly prayed that we be protected from 'schemes': 'Bless and protect us from thieves, schemes, heresy and sudden death.' Judging by the courts, the people of Longford were a collection of feuding, barn-torching, spell-laying, litigious rascals very high in the art of scheming.

The Turners were agreeable people but they were actually job-lot printers who I think had the notion that producing a weekly newspaper was little different from putting out flower-show catalogues. I managed to produce the first dummy, but when the second-hand linotype machines necessary for full production arrived from England no one could get them to work. The Turners lost their nerve, or recognized the risks in the enterprise, and abandoned the project. My contract allowed me five weeks' pay. I decided to take a look at Paris.

Two

It was my first time outside Ireland. It never occurred to me that this visit to Paris would lead to exile from my native country. I saw the trip as an unexpected gift, the kind of thing rich men in books gave to their sons as a twenty-first birthday present. I was possessed of the need to have some special experience; I could not bear the thought of living an entire lifetime without some attainment, even if it was only having spent a month in a foreign city. I had discovered that journalism too had its recesses in which reporters mooched away their lives in spiritless routines. I anticipated a future life in some such marginal role in journalism, a life led at a dead unchanging pace on the night subs' desk perhaps. Before such incarceration I would grab this interval of freedom.

The deal with the Turners of Longford was that they would pay me eight pounds a week redundancy money for five weeks, on the understanding that if I got a job I would stop drawing the money. They were a bit miffed to find themselves subsidizing what must have looked like a long frolic in Paree.

The day I got my passport I bought a return boat and train ticket to Newhaven and a single, Dieppe to Paris. This was a characteristic balance of recklessness and prudence: I was willing to take risks if there was a lifeline. If things went really badly, I had my return ticket. But there was a jaunty flourish in not having my Paris–Dieppe return.

The journey, by mail boat, a vomit-splashed exiles' steamer that plied between Dun Laoghaire and Holyhead, and then by a comfortless train (the English made no attempt to ease the journey of Irish immigrants) to London was one of profound misery. I was surrounded by dejected immigrants, girls and lads, their normal animation drained by the loss of Ireland which many of them would take as a kind of punishment. They were more like convicts than emigrants, being sent to a neighbouring hostile island. Few would make enough spare money to make the modest return journey for at least a couple of years. This was the late fifties, a period when the young middle class were trooping after the traditional labourers into exile – to Canada, America, Australia, or flooding in desperation to England. Everyone knew someone going away.

Sean O'Faolain was already writing about *The Vanishing Irish*. It was predicted that, at the current rate of immigration, within thirty years the country would be drained of life. This period had some similarity to the draining of the population and the extinguishing of hope that went with the Great Hunger of 1845–7. The blight this time was on jobs; public starvation was not so obvious. The crude and incompetent patriots had created a lethargic climate; the Church a population of emotionally apprehensive, deluded people.

I broke away from the emigrants' trail at Euston and took the train for Newhaven. This vehicle showed signs of some slight consideration for the comfort of the English travelling class.

It was not until the boat pulled out into the deep, cool, sunlit waters of the Channel that I had my first full sense of being abroad. I stood on the deck and watched the white tumbled wake of the ship stretching away softly to the mainland. I remember that on the line of the horizon there were two ships, plain black outlines, like models on a flat imitation sea, facing in opposite directions, the thread of smoke from their funnels crisscrossing high in the sky. I had the impression of being part of something fictitious.

It was very quiet on the French boat; a few people leaned on the rails speaking in low voices. I got talking to a young Frenchman from the Swiss border who had been teaching French in Manchester, and a girl returning to a hotel in Cannes after three months' perfecting her English. Neither of them knew Paris well, but they spoke encouragingly of the friendliness of the people. It was not necessary to know French, they assured me, many people spoke English and you could pick up the essential phrases very quickly. Very soon, they said, the sound of French would convey some sense to me. I felt proud, already anticipating such expertise.

It was intimidating to realize that, for the first time, I would have to speak in a different and peculiar way to make myself understood. We learned Irish at school, but only with the aim of avoiding a thrashing. In Dublin, it was never considered seriously as a way of talking to someone.

I took out a phrase book; we all three leaned on the rails and they began to teach me French. She repeated the words clearly and advised how to establish connections with English so that a phrase would stick in the mind. But soon they grew tired of the lesson and looked silently at the heaving, empty sea. I put away the phrase book and we chatted at random.

I arrived at the Gare St-Lazare late at night and immediately went down into the rattling Métro; it was gratifyingly foreign, shadowy and suggestive. I got out at St-Michel.

I stood in the place St-Michel, with its obligatory postcard Parisian fountain, suitcase in hand, gaping up the boulevard. It was a good two hours after pub closing time at home but everywhere was streaming with people. It was more like a fairground than a street, the ever-replenishing crowds visiting the terraced cafés as if they were sideshows.

I turned into the rue St-Jacques, a long crooked road parallel to St-Michel, which also stretched as far as the edge of Montparnasse. I had been given the name of a cheap hotel on this street by a languid, university-educated leader-writer in the *Irish Press* who spoke fastidious French, or spoke an imitation French fastidiously, and claimed to have met Françoise Sagan.

St-Jacques was so long and crooked that it had the character of three or four streets: a ragged *place* with dank laneways and jutting decayed houses at the junction with the Seine (it took time for me to adjust to the fact that what would be a slum building at home could be an honourable and ancient bourgeois block of apartments here). The street became a sedate cobbled stretch as it skirted the Sorbonne; further along, crossing Gay Lussac, little groceries and bakeries appeared. I felt I was in genuine Balzac territory. Finally it came up to the sweaty, dull grey front of the church of St-Jacques across from which was my hotel, the Dagmar.

It was much further up than I had anticipated and tottering to a standstill I took what they offered: a small room, top back, for 750 (old) francs a night, without breakfast. At the rate of exchange that was about 70p. But if I were to last five weeks on eight pounds a week I would have to do better than that. An African student I spoke to next morning when I went to get a drink (the sickly Pschitt orange) in a café told me of a cheaper hotel on the rue Cujas, just around the corner. I moved there that day. The room was almost a replica of the first, conspicuous neglect bringing the price down to 550 francs a night, about 45p. But I was determined that there would be no premature cash haemorrhage to cheat me out of as much as one day of what I anticipated would probably be my only trip abroad. (There were no cheap package tours then and Irish newspaper bureaux did not go further than London; New York was the only exception.)

I discovered that there was quite a free and easy exchange of information in the cafés among students, not just French but Swedish, Americans, Germans and even Chinese, who spoke good English. From one of them I got the name of an even cheaper hotel further up towards Port Royal – the grandly titled Hôtel du Maréchal Ney. I was in there on my fourth day.

A skinny building, trim as a wardrobe, high and bright, my tiny room cost 350 francs a night. My window looked down into the narrow rue Henri Barbusse, but through a gap in the buildings opposite I could see the tapering end of the Luxembourg Gardens and beyond the roof-rops of Montparnasse. I had halved my accommodation costs within three days; now I had to trim eating costs.

The Capoulade, on the corner of the rue Soufflot and the Boul. Mich', with Le Maiheu, were the principal Sorbonne students' hangouts. I spent hours sitting there, watching student life, squinting at the fountain and imagining the sunny destinies of the students strolling into the Luxembourg Gardens with their girlfriends: work seemed to be very brief interludes in their day. (In fact, they overworked to the point of nervous breakdown.)

The Capoulade appeared to be the information exchange of the Quarter. Here I learned about a cheap self-service restaurant, the Foyer St-Geneviève, around to the right of the Panthéon; you could get a skimpy three-course dinner there for 180f, about 20p. Beer *à la pression* was 30 francs; in a café it would be fifty. Then there was the Foyer Franco-Lebanese further on at the rue Lhomond, a subsidized restaurant for students where they were lax on checking cards: you could eat there for 200 francs. To supplement a daily restaurant meal you went to the markets for fruit or bread and cheese.

I was surprised to discover that the Eiffel Tower was on the Left Bank and not straddling the Champs-Élysées, as I had somehow imagined. I did not like the dryness of the Tuileries nor its rigid design. I missed the lusciousness of our parks.

I was fascinated by Americans in Paris. They sat, family groups, in cafés in a sort of trance. They seemed to be guarding their Americanism like something precious: as if on one level it had to be put on display and on another they were afraid it might be snatched from them by the foreigners. Nationalities were gloriously identifiable in those days before international homogenization of dress. As they wandered from monument to museum I noticed they had a curious disinclination to listen to one another: the women commented on everything with a deadly, calculating enthusiasm; the men bestowed a laconic benediction in ball-game Americanese on a *Mona Lisa*, a Champs or a fillet steak.

Living an underfed over-excited existence, disorientated by the absence of any familiar snugness, almost afraid amongst such strangeness, I wanted to convey to someone a sense of what I was experiencing. Jokey postcards home were not enough after the first two weeks, so I wrote, my first literary letters, to Jack White.

I announced grandly that I was learning something about Paris and about Europeans and 'because I now have something to set up as a comparison I am beginning to understand certain things about Dublin and the Irish'.

It has been said [I wrote solemnly] that Paris does not belong to the French but to the world. That is true in the sense that the world has moved in and claimed it, like a public claiming a national theatre. Because of this, Paris, which is the stage, and the Parisians, who are the actors, have inevitably absorbed something from their possessive public – their vulgarity, their notion of what Paris should be. Paris knows what is expected of it and it can be depended on to produce the trivial, vicious, depraved, dramatic or beautiful things which its public demands. But it also has genuine splendour, a splendour of artistic and intellectual achievement so much greater than the bizarre displays of tourist 'art' and antics everyone is familiar with.

The real life of Paris is outside all this, among the genuine artists, the students and scholars and the French families living a regular, normal, slightly prudish life. It is the genuine animation, the sense of 'life' which leaves the deepest impression on me. I have lived in Ireland all my life reading about 'life', now for the first time I see 'life', cosmopolitan people playing the great game of life.

In the evening when I walk along the embankment of the dark, mirror-still Seine by the Tuileries Gardens a memory of Ireland comes to me and it is like the remembrance of a dream in which I plough on leaden feet by weak-smiling, tired people, discontented people, frustrated people, tortured by puritanical restrictions, deafened by the ceaseless, senseless shout of inept and insincere patriots – a country with its future in the hands of people who think in terms of the past.

It is a characteristic of my countrymen that even the most intelligent can collapse into obscurantism when they approach too dangerously near the borders of true revolt. At this point in my correspondence I found myself taking a dive into orthodoxy. I wrote: 'I realize that there is a lot that has to be explained away [about Paris]. Pigalle could be blamed on the tourists, but the immorality of the gentle, charming Frenchwomen is a social weakness. Surprisingly, such complete freedom from convention does not seem so desirable now, because it is a freedom gained at the cost of some necessary quality.'

I wince when I read that now. From callow literary heights I tossed myself into a holy water font of evangelical platitudes. In practice, of course, I had favoured no such puritanical notion ever since I had given up going to confession a couple of years previously. But there were still fault lines in my mentality which opened up every now and then and into which I would occasionally stumble and wallow.

I have a suspicion that I was being, partly unconsciously, dishonest. There was some element in this of cramming in a morsel of what was expected of me – but surely not expected by Jack White who was not even Catholic? It was probably also a cowardly way of exonerating myself, establishing that I had remained respectable; making a virtue, indeed, out of failure. What would I have written if I had succeeded gloriously in sinning? Erotic success at home was usually ingloriously furtive.

Throughout that first visit, both to exercise my few words of French and in a scatter-gun tactic to make contacts, I forced myself to talk to everyone I sat down beside in a café; I mostly chose to sit next to girls. My need for information helped me overcome my bashfulness. These were cheering or at least consoling encounters: the girls, who generally had sufficient English to construct a makeshift conversation, were always friendly after I had established my authenticity as a foreigner. I had no notion then that French girls were habitual slayers of advances from importuners, of which the Latin Quarter had battalions. Recognizing my innocence they were helpful in a limited way. But the encounters mysteriously never led to anything.

I suspect there was something in my technique which impeded development. Not wishing to be thought, even by strangers, to be attempting a pick-up, I was probably too thorough in convincing them that all I wanted was information. I hated the idea of anyone spotting that I needed companionship and I believed that if I did have physical designs on these foreign girls I had to keep it a deadly secret.

Befuddled in my motives I tended to end up with a nice girl who then produced a helpful boyfriend (students were often living together, from which I got my glimpse into general immorality). These were settled young couples who had the time to guide my material needs and repair my geographical and historical ignorance.

But they absorbed valuable hours that I realized should have been spent in misbehaving.

There was also the question of finance: I did not have any money to 'take a girl out'. At home you needed at least enough for a couple of cinema tickets and, later, coffee and ice cream. I did not catch on that the young French girls did not expect to be treated. If they liked you, a cup of coffee was enough to ensure companionship, if not more, and even then students often insisted on paying their share to preserve their independence.

In my last letter I recovered my intellectual élan. 'I discovered', I wrote, 'that there are ways of life very different from the pattern of life accepted in our country; that the world is not dominated, or even affected by the mentality which dominates Ireland; that Ireland has a place in the world – a small place,' I said boldly, 'when it forgets its parochial preoccupations.'

On the fifth week I had to go back to those parochial preoccupations, completely broke.

I was full now of a determination that I kept as secret as if it were a clandestine love affair, to get back to Paris and live there.

My fugue to Paris had not been regarded initially with much approval by senior men in the *Irish Press*. In those days Paris was just another word for 'dirty' and I was suspected of having gone there simply to be able to sin in comfort. It would be the comfort part that would upset them: discomfort was an obligatory part of sinning. Indeed I might not have got my part-time job back on the *Sunday Press* were it not for a providential scoop on the way home.

While coming back to Ireland on a Saturday across the plains of Normandy our train hit a flour lorry at a level crossing. The flour puffed high into the air, drifted down tranquilly, spread along the roof of the stationary train, and whitened the faces of nervous passengers sticking their heads out the windows. Many of them were Irishwomen returning from a pilgrimage to Lourdes.

'Isn't it a miracle we weren't all killed?' they cried. 'Miraculous escape of Irish pilgrims to Lourdes,' I phoned from London the moment we arrived and the *Sunday Press* splashed the story next morning, names and home villages scrupulously listed – a certain circulation boost. (No one was injured except for the unfortunate anonymous French lorry driver who was of no interest to an Irish paper.)

I could not have returned in more triumphal raiment. That one deed reaffirmed my loyalty to the paper and my alertness to Catholic values. I had had also that rarest of scoops: a story that existed in a vacuum, a vacuum without any lines to normal contacts – police, hospitals, railway companies, news agencies. The French agencies did not know, or care, about the Irish pilgrims. The rival papers at home were totally baffled in their attempts to discover the source and follow it up.

My plan was to save a little money and head off within a few months for the adventurous life of a foreign correspondent in Paris. England had no appeal for me; its anaemic films of the fifties suggested a musty community surviving on brittle gentility and bogus cheerfulness. Anyway, my politics disdained the place, although my taste revered its literature.

Since I knew no French (I had taken 'science' instead at school) and had no money, nor much promise of any, my plan was one that could only have been hatched by a youthful mind; that is, one free from encumbering experience and in a state of demented impetuosity.

I managed a dozen or so French lessons from a distracted Toulousian at five bob a time, but made little headway with this undemanding teacher and, since our home circumstances were so straitened, none either in saving money. Paris began to shrink even in my imagination. Frightened that time would undermine my resolve I decided to borrow from a money-lender and get out while the energy of my ambition was still alive. I borrowed £30, Bob Johnson, rather nervously, going security. I made shaky arrangements with the *Press* and *Irish Times* to take articles.

The inexplicableness of my conduct made it impossible for my family to put up any persuasive objections to my disappearing abroad.

20

They were bewildered by what I was doing, but with little to offer they no doubt felt they had no right to command. So one evening, escorted by my brother and a friend I prepared to take the boat again from Dun Laoghaire. As I climbed the gangway they waved me off, when I think that what I wanted was to be rescued.

I cannot now explain the tumult in my brain that got me to that precipice and beyond. I was not a compulsively adventurous type, yet here I was, virtually penniless, supported only by unreliable promises, setting out to live and work in a country whose language I did not speak and where I knew no one. If I failed I had no comfortable home to retreat to; so failure was not to be contemplated.

The compulsion to get away blurred everything; a mysterious force was at work that I have never fully understood. No doubt sex had something to do with it.

The boat that took me across that dark Irish Sea seemed to be sailing into delirium. The pleasures of Paris appeared suddenly flimsy; foreignness was still a palpable and vaguely menacing entity; I was delivering myself irrevocably into its power. I felt nothing but fear. I could not restrain an undermining longing for family love; the folly of companionship wilfully discarded rose unchecked in me like soft waves of seasickness. I felt like an invalid fleeing across England by train, nothing supporting me.

The manoeuvres of alighting and re-embarking at Newhaven, of getting on a boat that already had some memories helped dissipate my apprehension and soon, in daylight on deck, my imagination gave itself over to the adventure before me.

I again made the Hôtel du Maréchal Ney my headquarters. Although cheap, the daily rate would swallow up all my borrowed £30 within six weeks without providing a single meal. I needed urgently to get a private room by the month where I could live on boiled potatoes. My feverish research on survival in Paris the first time meant that I already knew many of the routines for finding cheap nourishment. Now I learned that enrolment in the Alliance Française language school on the boulevard Raspail provided a student card and access to their

21

accommodation notice board. An ad in *Le Figaro* would, when I had a room to receive some pupils, bring in a dribble of income. That would keep me going until I had learned enough French to begin to function as a journalist, milking the local press.

But the Alliance Française enrolment cost me another few days of food money. In addition the student card proved to be of limited value; it did not give access to the Sorbonne student restaurants where meals were half the price of the cheapest chop house. But there was still the Foyer Franco-Lebanese.

I had also arrived at the wrong time: it was late September and all the students were back, looking for new or better rooms. I was competing with those more knowledgeable about short cuts to accommodation, and soon accepted I would have to look outside the Latin Quarter. My days and nights became long treks across the river, my financial calculations continually undermined by the necessity of having to eat where I found myself, unable to get back in time to my cheap Foyer.

I noticed now a quality of dryness in the air of Paris which I had never experienced in moist Dublin. My lungs felt scoured. Left alone I was not much of a drinking man then, even if I had the money; my instinct was to be sober in the face of testing situations. But my brain ached, my gritty socks burned my feet and I felt a terrible absence of sea or hills. I longed for that constant view of wistful Dublin mountains and the busy winds which keep Dublin freshly stirred.

Late one night going home up the Boul. Mich' I checked my finances and realized I had passed the half-way mark and still had no prospect of a private room. So long as I had shelter I could get bits of food – the first pupil at ten bob an hour would give me the price of a couple of meals. But without rent money, without a proper base, I was finished. In a few days there would not be enough to meet the month's rent in advance that any landlady would demand. At that point I would be defeated.

I had an attack of panic which was like a seizure. My insides buckled; I visualized my whole adventure collapsing into something ludicrous, foolish and shameful. There was nothing to be got from my family; indeed my departure had already impoverished them further. Going back broke with poor job prospects would only burden their life even more.

I moved around in a sickly state. Paris as a noble and elegant setting for an exhilarating future had already become tarnished by the acid of a thousand mechanical, unpromising transactions. I slogged around the city sullenly aware that some kind of beauty was piled up around me like a backdrop in a film; but it was not intended for my participation.

Occasionally I would allow myself to live passively and stroll purposelessly along the Seine from the Pont des Arts to the graceful back and shoulders of Notre Dame. George Brassens had recently brought out his Banc Publique and the whole sunny city conspired to support that notion of the banks of the Seine as the natural home of courting couples. Sometimes in the evening, sitting at ease alone on a bench on a boulevard, my mood would change. Free of glances which at home had the force of interdiction, released from the pressure of being known; the air perfumed with odours of flowers, dust and Gauloises, the pavements brimming with life that at midnight and beyond showed no signs of obeying any law of fatigue or any rule that things must come to an end, optimism was restored and I remembered I had come to the right city.

I got a room. I was standing by the notice-board in the Alliance Française as the card was put up and immediately went into the office for the address. It was rue Beaubourg in the 3rd *arrondissement* by the Hôtel de Ville. Although only fifteen minutes' walk from Odéon, being across the river it seemed way out of the Latin Quarter. It was what they called a *quartier populaire*, where the squat, dark-faced workers on the edge of Les Halles went to toil at 7 a.m. and to bed at 10 p.m.; people for whom Montparnasse was a foreign, and a foreigners', village. No hint then of the architectural conceits which were to bury Beaubourg and Les Halles.

The room was only £7 a month. It was spacious, on the second floor: it contained a double bed, honourable old wardrobe, a sink, a small gas stove. There was a hole-in-the-floor toilet in the hall just outside my door. I had two fine high windows, but one looked out on to the slime-encrusted piping of a wall a foot away and the other stared down into a continually dim triangle of courtyard. A shaft of sunlight reached across to my window around midday, turned to cold yellow by two o'clock and dirty grey for the rest of the afternoon. But with the shutters closed, the soft curtains drawn and a red bedspread thrown over the gas stove, the high-ceilinged room was a not unstylish boudoir. (When the pupils came I could drape a sheet over the sink.)

Having paid the huddled and apparently servile old couple who owned the place a month's rent in advance, I closed the door and sat on the broad bed with a deep sense of salvation. I was secure for an entire month.

I put an ad in *Le Figaro*: 'Jeune prof. donne leçons d'anglais.' I caught myself putting '*prof anglais*' but changed it: I did not mind lying about my professorial status but I was not prepared to lie about my nationality. I was meticulous then in limiting my dishonesties.

I began to make calculations. Ten bob an hour for lessons. With a newspaper of the circulation of *Le Figaro* I could get maybe a hundred replies. Well, let's say fifty, of which only twenty actually took lessons. I liked to be realistic in my fantasies; it was more comforting. Well, twenty pupils coming twice a week meant £20 a week, without counting what I would soon begin to earn as a freelance foreign correspondent.

A thousand a year already! I had a wonderful sense of relief and then of luxury as I further calculated that some of them might come in pairs even in groups of four and my teaching week could be reduced to maybe twenty or even ten hours a week, leaving plenty of time to work on my journalism. This did not seem an unreasonable hope. Indeed, I allowed myself a few moments to contemplate my own reasonableness with deep approval.

The ad produced five pupils. One pair of girls came to my room; two others, a middle-aged lady and a young man, lived in diametri-cally different parts of Paris and chose times in the middle of the day

which meant that, with travelling, about five hours a day was devoted
to two lessons. The fifth, a restless fellow who worked in an office
and who did not seem to know why he was taking lessons, went on
holiday after the second lesson and never came back. None of them
wanted two lessons a week. So the income – with a reduction for
teaching a pair – worked out at a potential £57 a year. About three
and a half cheap meals a week.

I decided that while I still had a little cash I would call on a girl I
had met on the boat on my way back to Ireland that first time. Annick
Cabioc was a young secretary who was going to Ireland to improve
her English. I had taken her out a couple of times while she was in
Dublin, so she definitely owed me a meal.

She was *bretonne* and I had confided in her my secret intention of
going to live in Paris. In my mind, this established a special
relationship between us, gradually introducing a tenderness which
was more a tribute to her sincere decency than any real erotic
attraction. But as I didn't have a girlfriend at that time, a sentimental
involvement mechanically started to develop on my side. At that stage
of my life I interpreted the absence of an overwhelming sensual charge
as evidence of the genuineness of a relationship with a girl – we
would be partners in a sinless life. This ill-conceived approach, which
in no way reflected the outlaw needs that galloped through my brain
from dawn till dawn, were to lead me into some barren encounters.
Fortunately these respectable girls generally spotted my sinfulness at
an early stage and either recoiled from me in distaste or got fed up
waiting for my true nature to speak and abandoned me. In the end
not too much time was wasted. Those I met in cafés later who
manifestly did not subscribe to Victorian Catholic morality got better
value.

My room was on the east side of Les Halles; Annick's apartment
was about five minutes' walk away on the rue Étienne Marcel, the
northern edge of the markets. She lived with her widowed mother
and brother who worked as a steward in Air France.

Although Étienne Marcel took a considerable overspill of prostitutes from the rue Saint-Denis across which it cuts, Annick's was a
thoroughly respectable, even pious, Catholic family. It would have

been impossible for a decent Irish family to live right alongside a brothel and maintain a reputation for respectability, even supposing we admitted to having such areas in Ireland. I remained tactfully silent while working out just what the Cabiocs' attitude to, or indeed relations with, the local prostitutes could be. One of them was even reclining against Annick's street door on my first visit and gave me a polite *Bonjour* as I went in.

I was discovering the compartmentalized way the French could live. Annick did refer to the rue Saint-Denis around the corner as a 'bad' area which her mother did not like her going into. But I got the impression that it was the customers who offended her mother more than the girls. Perhaps, I decided, they accepted prostitutes in the way we accepted drunks.

The Cabiocs put on the traditional French lavish display of food; I left secure in having a contact with a decent French family. But when I followed up the visit a few days later, dropping in unannounced on a Saturday as I would at home, there was an unmistakable rigidity in the response of all three, as if I had done something catastrophic. They seemed to be waiting for me to go from the moment I came in. The mother suggested a glass of wine but disconcertingly accepted my first polite refusal. I sat there empty-handed, labouring against intermittent silences which were clearly telling me to go. Annick appeared unaffectedly friendly so I made cheery preparations for meeting her at the weekend and left.

The next morning I received a *pneumatique* from Annick. I loved to receive those letters that shot across Paris through the post office tube system; delivered like telegrams they arrived crumpled and hot like something from a bakery.

Annick wrote that I must not call at the house or telephone; if I wished to see her I must write care of the Louvre *poste restante*. While baffled I was not displeased by the romantic implication of the arrangement. But when we eventually met and strolled briefly along the rue du Louvre Annick told me she could not see me again. Her mother was terrified she would marry a foreigner, abandon her and live abroad; I must understand how a widow felt. When I had called that second time, as if by right, her mother had become terribly upset.

Annick said she had already deceived her mother by meeting me like this but she could not bear the thought of continually lying. We must never meet again.

I thought this a bit extravagant. Since I lived within five minutes' walk of their apartment, 'never again' seemed rather hard to carry into practice so I went off assuming things would eventually cool down. But I was to discover that while in Dublin all roads led inescapably back to re-encounters, in a great metropolis if your trajectory was south (mine was to the Left Bank) and the other's west (her place of work was on the Right Bank) your paths might never again cross. They never did.

Annick's guillotine set me free to concentrate on establishing myself as a foreign correspondent. The first problem was to get a *carte de séjour*; without it my time in France was limited to three months. I had less than two months left on my original visa. The police were very active on the Left Bank in catching foreigners with out-of-date visas and slinging them out. I was not eligible for a *carte de travail* without a normal job and without a *carte de travail* you could not get a *carte de séjour*.

Foreign correspondents had a way out. If you were a representative of your paper you automatically got a *carte de séjour* for a year. It is the Ministry of the Interior, not the journalists' union, which provides press cards in France. At the end of that period you produced cuttings to confirm your status and got your card renewed. The difficulty was that the *Irish Times* already had a gent who for years had supplied a Letter from Paris and his own residence permit depended on it. Desmond Ryan was a stylish writer but often produced nothing for months, and all his dispatches had copious references to drinking.

Once again Jack White came to my aid. He gave me a letter declaring I was *a* correspondent of the *Irish Times* rather than *the* correspondent. I went with this letter to see Ryan in his rather grand apartment on the rue Molière. He was already nervous about the consequences of my arrival.

Ryan and his household at first glance represented all that was what we called 'West Briton', colonial even. He was a Trinity (Dublin) man speaking in a very anglicized accent and with literary affectations, I thought. His entourage was out of Somerset Maugham. I had the impression of an indeterminate number of ex-wives and ex-mistresses. He also had an incalculable number of children, ranging from Trinity students to infants by his current companion, a silent, nervous woman who worked for the OECD. Places such as Nice and Ascot figured frequently in Ryan's conversation.

He invited me with great grace to sup with them in his library dining room.

'Have some more soup,' Desmond suggested, after we'd both consumed what was in our bowls. He waved a world-weary hand towards the elegant porcelain tureen.

'No, thank you,' I said politely.

'You had better,' he said. 'There's nothing else.'

Ryan, so far as I could make out, lived on an allowance from an aunt in Canada who was supposed to own half of the Canadian railroad; between cheques his companion's wage spread sparsely over the children's needs. His obligations to wine merchants dictated the route by which he would escape out of the rue Molière. On prosperous days he could go boldly into the rue de Richelieu; in fallow periods he would have to back off into the avenue de l'Opéra.

When I had convinced him it was not my intention to take over his Letter from Paris he allowed his generous nature full rein. He escorted me to the Press and Communications Office of the Ministry of the Interior, then on the rue Lord-Byron off the Champs-Élysées, and introduced me to Monsieur Pravard, who presided over it. I was terribly impressed by Ryan's ceremonious French and unselfconscious use of the *passé simple*, a circumlocution which had been pointed out to me by my uncouth Toulousian teacher as an antiquity used only by eminent scholars.

Monsieur Pravard agreed to provide me shortly with a press card with the obligation of producing cuttings as proof of my activities. We celebrated my official installation by stopping at a few cafés on the stroll back to the rue Molière, me pressing booze on the impecunious Ryan and thereby souring my relationship with his companion from the outset.

Three

Interviewing English-speaking celebrities in Paris was one of the ways of marking time until I was linguistically equipped to tackle a great French intellect in his (we did not think then so much about 'her') own language. Professionally I was outside the Parisian circus tent peeping in, panhandling any stray anglophones for a bit of material. One of the first attempts was on Edmund Wilson who I had seen from the *Herald Tribune* was briefly in town. I rang his hotel from a public phone.

When I started out in journalism I assumed that no self-respecting, internationally famous person would give me an interview. Why should the rich, famous and powerful submit to telling *me* about their lives? What authority had I? I was to discover that celebrities to whom I was totally unknown would confide in me without any investigation of my educational or journalistic credentials. I thought it demeaning that they should submit to my questioning.

Edmund Wilson was the only one who fulfilled my high expectations, ever. His hefty scholarly voice filled my ear as I stood holding the phone by a smelly toilet in a café: 'Why', he demanded, 'should I let you write an article about me when I can do it better *and* get paid?'

He waited courteously for a reply. I leaned on the telephone shelf and pondered. This was not only a very reasonable attitude, it was one I shared; it was right he should demand an interlocutor of his own stature. (Of course, if everyone were to follow such a code few journalists would get interviews.)

I thanked him and hung up.

I had the impression he was a trifle disconcerted by my prompt and heartfelt agreement with his principles.

There were a couple of English-speaking celebrities on my door-step, or café step: Richard Wright, and Chester Himes. Himes, who was going with an English girl named Leslie, sloped into the café Tournon from time to time. But a Paris-based Harlem funky thriller writer was difficult for me to decipher then. In any event I was still at the stage where I assumed that 'serious' writers were more valuable journalistic copy, so I chose Wright.

Richard Wright lived on the same street as the Monaco, a little café at Odéon I had made my headquarters, and occasionally came into the café Tournon late at night. Then fifty-two, the author of *Native Son* and *Uncle Tom's Children* was a respectable and respected figure in Paris, not yet eclipsed by James Baldwin.

I conducted this interview, for the *Irish Times*, in his study in the rue Monsieur Le Prince with all the diligent earnestness of a liberal provincial who had never had anything much to do with black people but who had been well tutored in sympathy for their distress-ing predicament. Apart from Himes, whom I never interviewed, about the only other two 'negroes' familiar to me were film actors Stepin Fetchit and Jack Benny's Rochester. The term was in common use then, and did not seem to offend Wright at the time, but I can hardly bring myself to recollect its appearance in my introduction.

'His features are not noticeably negroid,' I innocently told my Irish readers, 'and his skin hardly more than a deep nut-brown. His voice is slightly high with few of the customary negro slurring and dragging on words, but he has the very negro trick, when laughing, of laying his tongue out on the underlip and laughing from the back of an open throat.'

I knew that Wright, born on a Mississippi plantation, had run away from school at fifteen so I thought it would be useful to get his public support of my private hope that not only was university education not essential for a writer it could even be a disadvantage.

'In frontier societies perhaps it is not essential,' he said. 'Most of our writers, as you know,' he added, courteously conferring some extra scholarship on me, 'are really self-educated. But in a place like France the best way to absorb the past is by university education. America has no past, really.'

I had a preference for freedom fighters and overt champions of causes so I was a bit taken aback when this great champion of the Negro cause said that he did not consciously feel that he was championing any cause. 'I chose the subject before I realized its importance,' he said. 'It comes from the inside and then becomes part of something external and social.'

I suggested that racial discrimination in the northern states was no stronger perhaps than class snobbery in England; no worse than the disapproval in southern Ireland which kept Catholics from mixing with Jews. (Ireland, being neutral during the war, and ever wary of 'British propaganda', took a long time to accept the truth of the Holocaust.) Wright's response was to offer me a little homily on the nature of racial discrimination.

Wright had married a white woman in New York and his French-born children were American citizens. With the simple-minded intolerance of idealistic youth I began to feel he had sold out; abandoned the Cause for comfort. He explained that he did not want his children to go to the States until they were educated and had developed a sense of values; he was afraid of the danger of personality damage, which, after the tolerance of Paris, exposure to American racism would bring.

I wondered if he had had any trouble taking the Pledge of Allegiance to the USA, to the American way of life which caused blacks such hardship.

'I don't think it has caused me much hardship,' he said surprisingly. 'I live quite comfortably. [It was here that he displayed the difference between himself and the unforgiving, more analytical Baldwin.] I had to take the Pledge, of course, for my passport,' he said. 'But you know that we American Negroes are the most vociferous defenders of the Constitution.'

31

I wanted to know what conditions would be necessary to setting the Negro free. He told me the expression was 'integrate' not 'set free'.

Was Paris more free of discrimination against the Negro than other cities?

Distinctly so, he thought. 'There may be very occasional sporadic outbursts, like Jeune Nation thugs beating up a Negro in St-Germain recently, but that is not at all typical.'

I sent a copy of the piece to Wright and for years remembered him as a rather chill individual, deducing this from the lack of cordiality in his greetings when we met on the street later. At the time I put this coldness down to his being a Negro whose natural Negroid ebullience had been diluted by respectability. Now the memory of that introductory paragraph makes me fold with embarrassment.

The American black always got special treatment in Paris. This was partly snobbery: American Negro meant jazz musician or writer – Sidney Bechet, Bud Powell, Wright, Baldwin were all resident in Paris at various times in the late fifties, early sixties. An American black I met later had a different slant on Parisian tolerance: he liked Paris because the Parisians were indiscriminately nasty to everyone, he said.

But there was an area of French racism still to be uncovered: the attitude to Arabs, particularly Algerians.

I was considerably hampered in my scrambling around for news features in that I could barely decipher the opening paragraphs of stories in the newspapers. A radio (if I had had one) would have been useless; meaning still galloped ahead of all comprehension.

I began to labour with the dictionary. I was calmed by my earlier lesson that newspapers got news from other newspapers, rarely from unminted mines so I did not tire myself in desperate pursuit of flour-drenched trains. I paddled in what shallow puddles of information were available to me, sustained Oriental-like on handfuls of fees from private lessons. I patiently awaited the day, as one might a win in the

Sweep, when all those French papers would eventually yield up their treasures.

I had presented my credentials, such as they were, to Conor Cruise O'Brien, Counsellor at the Irish Embassy. We had a guarded exchange of civilities and I left it at that. I couldn't see what the Irish Embassy had to offer (except copious libations on St Patrick's Day). At Aer Lingus in my first week I had come across an obliging Frenchman who later allowed me to penetrate a couple of hundred yards further than usual, into the runway area at Le Bourget where I gazed at the plaque which marked the spot where Lindbergh dropped down in 1927. I turned this less than momentous experience into living drama for the *Irish Press* readers – with what convincing phrases I can't imagine. I suspect it was the pictures which really sold this soft feature, although I remember them as dumb company photographs of dead-on-the-ground aircraft.

From this somnambulistic report I received, a couple of weeks later, a cheque in the post for £4, minus bank charges. It was the first time the connection between scribbling on my own in a foreign country and real money was made concrete.

I celebrated by crashing a party in the Left Bank that Saturday night, using a bottle of wine as a pass. All the ardour I felt for the future, all the sense of having been admitted into the circus ring of life I unleashed over a startled young French Canadian; pretty as a postcard, insipid as a pear. The crowded Parisian studio, the wet gabled roofs, French voices everywhere, all cried out for more clichés. I carried her around on my hip in a foxtrot and whispered in her ear, 'Je vous aime.'

At home I would have scrupulously avoided making such a false declaration. In any case, it was a ridiculous phrase; if you are in love you don't 'vous' but 'tu' your adored one. But I wasn't ready to pay attention to such niceties, nor to any of the thousand inhibiting regulations which had hitherto undermined me. I had plucked money from the Parisian skies; now I must pluck, so to speak, *une petite amie*.

At the party I had been d'Artagnan with a bottle and, to my own amazement, I was still able to keep up this uncharacteristic swash-buckling performance when I called at the girl's hotel room the following Sunday afternoon. Since we had nothing to say to each other we celebrated the Sabbath by falling on the bed and fumbling into love-making. It was swifty stuff, like bathing in champagne froth without savouring the contents. But I trotted home as frisky as a terrier.

I was by now convinced that Destiny was my escort and on my side. The whole thrust of my recent activities, the escape from Ireland, the availability of Paris (Rome was the city generally made easily accessible to my countrymen), the achievement of a new lifestyle were all arrived at, it seemed, in partnership with this approving Fate. I was doing my best; my musketeer leap into bed should surely have met with continental Fate's approval.

And what did I get? She gave me a dose of the clap!

That was the kind of lesson any Dublin parish priest would have been happy to prescribe. I was clearly not to be permitted to go too easily into the playground of sin. Sex certainly looks evil in the dank, hot-lava form given it by the clap. But a couple of visits to the American Hospital where cheery English nurses stuck needles into my bum suggested that this was a routine experience for young men in Paris.

There was an awkward duty still to be performed. The doctor told me I should tell the girl: women don't always immediately recognize the symptoms, he informed me. Apparently it was up to me to head off a plague.

When I called at her hotel room my briefly loved one was in bed with a symptomless 'flu'. A young German was prancing around the room attempting to jolly her back to health, manifestly for his own ends. When I said I wanted to speak to her privately she looked decidedly reserved. The Teutonic swain professed manly tolerance, which, however, did not take him out of the room.

I sat on the edge of her bed; like a hypnotist I stared into her eyes, and mouthed the words 'You are *malade. Maladie! Compris?*' She just stared back, her wary expression making it clear she knew what I was talking about.

When he realized I was making no attempt to stay, the German youth put on an obnoxious display of yodelling camaraderie. But two minutes in my former chamber of love was enough for me. I did not feel my duties extended to warning him.

The whole experience slayed me for a time. The connection between sin and scalding retribution was too evident for a man with a national disposition for spotting spiritual portents. The notion that you will pay for your illicit pleasures had been well instilled into me; on that brief prod of pleasure a skyscraper of obligations and foul consequences had fallen on me – just as the Christian Brothers hinted they would. It was too much for any penis to carry. There was clearly more to liberation than turning off the conscience and storming ladies' hotel rooms with a bottle.

But, the clap symptoms gone without complications, I soon returned to the usual pursuits which generally involved an endurance test of sitting out rivals in the Tournon, a café at Luxembourg, until the early hours.

Now I made energetic assaults on French newspapers. I was able to identify quickly the two papers, *France Soir* and *Paris Presse*, where gold dust, or at least copper dust, would lie: stories of sanguinary human interest; tales of tragedy and triumph; tales of sudden wealth. I was soon able to produce a trickle of anecdotal reports for the *Irish Sunday* and *Evening Press*. *Le Figaro* was always too po-faced for me; too full of barren propriety. *Le Monde*, with its labyrinthine style, seemed beyond me. Later I realized *Le Monde* writing was quite lucid, but I could not extract sense quickly enough from its curlicued prose, which its journalists rode like a four-in-hand. I preferred *France Soir*'s plain donkey-cart.

As I harvested appetizing stories of misfortune and misbehaviour it was a surprise to discover how many people were living in sin in France. At first I thought it was a misprint when Philippe *Lenoir* and Giselle *Pantin*, protagonists in a tale of miraculous escape from death, seemed to be living at the same address and indeed sharing the same bedroom from which they escaped unscathed when a monoplane landed at the foot of their bed. The next time I came across a couple with the same address, but not the same surname, I caught on.

This put me in a quandary. If Jacques and Jacqueline were living together out of holy wedlock, they were not fit to appear in an Irish paper, even if Jacqueline's father had suddenly reappeared after a twenty-year absence in the Foreign Legion and discovered his lost child when she knocked him down with her bicycle. Equally if Georges and Michelle, in the Auvergne, had lost their life's savings when a goat (which they then ate) had eaten their cardboard money box they had only got what they deserved by failing to go to the altar. Certainly none of these persons was entitled to prominence in a Dublin paper. From then on I was as busy as a curate marrying these people in preparation for delivery to Ireland. (Some years later I was railing in the *Guardian* against the kind of voluntary lay censorship which prevailed in Ireland. I had a graduate's knowledge of how it worked by then.)

I was soon transferring my abridged version of a *France Soir* story directly into my typewriter without rewriting. This speedy method led to some gaffes. There was the case of the Prix de la Courage. Every year the city of Paris awarded the prize to a simple citizen who had displayed exceptional fortitude or ingenuity in overcoming misfortune. The laureates were presented with cash and a scroll at a ceremony at the Hôtel de Ville. On this occasion one of the winners was a young woman, deaf and dumb from birth who had been supporting her paralysed widowed mother with secretarial work. She then went to night school and graduated with top marks in an accountancy course.

The French had a way of giving vital statistics in their reports: in describing this blonde girl *France Soir* noted her exceptional height, nearly 2 metres. They described her climbing the steps of the Hôtel de Ville to be greeted by the Mayor. I dashed this one off in a hurry, adding some colour to the scene on the steps of the Hôtel de Ville. I was gratified to discover how successful my descriptive writing must have been. The *Sunday Press* editor rated the story a lead page spread.

But it was not my purple prose which won this position, nor was it the child's devotion to her mother. In tossing the piece into the typewriter I had done some absent-minded translation of 2 metres and it was the heroic scaling of the Hôtel de Ville's steps by a 2-foot midget which had astounded and gratified the editor.

Tales of stage and screen were also profitable, although Billancourt was not as fertile as Hollywood; not many French actors were known at home. There was Brigitte Bardot, of course, but I found the gossip about her love life tedious. There was Jeanne Moreau, Jean Gabin and Jean-Louis Barrault. Everyone in Dublin had heard of *Les Enfants du Paradis*. Young Françoise Sagan, still in her twenties, was a kind of literary BB and worth a story when she crashed her car, which, fortunately, was frequently.

Someone of the stature of Jean-Paul Sartre would have been too heavy for the *Irish Press*. And I did not know who would be interested in a peculiar Irish fellow, writing very obscure stuff, Samuel Beckett. I decided that the fact he was writing in French disqualified him sufficiently from general Irish interest.

Four

My rent was two weeks overdue. Monsieur Lapineau, my landlord, and his wife had begun to confront me in nervous tandem at my door when I arrived home at night. At first they appeared to be more embarrassed than I, and accepted with relief stories of cheques being in the post and money orders on the way from Ireland. But by the end of the second week I could not think of any more excuses. I stood before them, wobbly with shame. I felt like a shoplifter, publicly exposed. Debt was a delicate matter at home, since we were always in it, a condition we went to extraordinary lengths to conceal. I thanked God that at least the neighbours could not understand what was being said. Then I realized, of course, they could – they were French too. But if this was not home all the feelings of disgrace and humiliation came directly from home.

Returning to my own room one day I carried my assumed insouciance too far by attempting to pass Monsieur Lapineau in the corridor with a casual wave. But since he was standing at his door at an acute angle to me I had practically to shoulder him aside to put my key in the lock. Insouciance was not exactly the appropriate demeanour.

While I stooped to fumble with the iron key he began to rain 'ce-n'est-pas-correct's on the back of my unprotected neck. At first there was disappointed reproach in his voice and then provoked by my dumbness he became more frenzied. When I did look at him I caught a beseeching look in his eyes. But I could not think of any fresh excuses and became sullen.

Madame Lapineau had a squint. My compassion for her affliction, which had initially prompted me to be particularly courteous to her, turned to spontaneous distaste in the face of my persecution. I became convinced that the squint was the outward revelation of her inward crookedness. I decided I despised the pair of them, for being both ugly and excessively foreign.

At increasing intervals Madame Lapineau would let her husband out through the door at me, like a dog. She would hold the door ajar and then scoop him back swiftly when he had gabbled a few reproachful sentences, sticking her nose out of the closing door to mouth, *'Voleur!'* at me.

The collapse of my entire adventure appeared imminent when one morning Monsieur Lapineau thumped on the door and in a state of unlovely agitation told me that if I did not pay the rent that night I would be put out on the street. Madame peered from their door, her eyes glittering with a kind of fearful excitement, like someone watching an indecent act. She kept sentry in the background while Lapineau shouted: 'L'argent ce soir ou partez! Partez ce soir. Fini! Fini!' Then he vanished back into their apartment, his wife swiftly swinging the door shut as if fearing I might take a leap at them.

I went out, furious that these comic creatures could be the cause of the degrading failure of my brave adventure abroad; how could such creatures have the power, in one night, to reduce me to the state of a tramp obliged to camp in some doorway?

I could already detect the softening of will which would turn me into a beggar and felt the marks of dereliction crimping my features. It was, of course, obvious, I told myself, that there was nothing in me of the true adventurer. I had none of the thoughtless bravado of the buccaneer who ploughs his way to fortune, indifferent to the criticism of others. Anyway, I did not believe I had the stamina of a professional exile; it needed a strain, too, of callousness about those you had left behind which I did not think I had. Nor, still being virtually illiterate in French, did I have the confidence that I could ever be on a par with the Parisian. How could I? At the first real test I had been bested by a pair of dwarfs.

I could already visualize my reception at the Irish embassy, arriving disgraced, a mendicant. I felt the street where the embassy stood well named: rue Rude. All the triumphant intolerance, the instinct for fingering others for puniness, the smugness, the morbid piety, everything which sickened me about Ireland gathered like a fog about the official building I would soon have to go to for sanctuary. I would go home, I realized, publicly disgraced and live my days defeated, like a reformed alcoholic.

What was infuriating was that, though I admitted I had no talent for the role of a buccaneering exile, neither was I in any way cut out to be a tramp. I was much too intimidated by the requirements of respectability to be able to exist in comfort as a layabout.

I walked all the way to the Métro to conserve the last few tickets in my *carnet*. It was a bitterly cold October night. I counted my resources: in all I had to hand enough money to pay for a few skimpy meals. The income from the four private lessons I would give that week would take survival into the beginning of the next week. But no further.

As I crossed the Seine at the Pont au Change my rage centred on the pair of pudding creatures who would be the direct cause of my disintegration, Monsieur and Madame Lapineau. If I were being felled by the hand of an aristocrat it would have been easier to stomach and better to relate. But that stumpy couple! At first they had been brimming with cloying goodwill, but they soon turned, as is the way of their ilk (I told myself), into ratty little predatory merchants. My whole being looked down on them with impotent scorn.

Of course, virtually the only Frenchmen I had come in contact with were waiters and landlords; I had not yet encountered the peerless Frenchmen for whom this graceful edifice, Paris, had been raised. Now I would never get a chance to shake their hands and call them *amis*.

Hope was rekindled when I saw Will Wills sitting alone on a stool in the deserted café Monaco at Odéon. Will was a resting, indeed a convalescent, architect from Tennessee; he represented the upper echelon of prosperity in the café. I had known him to be able to borrow *five thousand francs* at a time (about £5).

He and Bill Marshall, an Australian freelance illustrator who drew the 'Le Crime ne paie pas' strip cartoon on the back page of *France Soir*, were the only ones I had ever come across dealing in such sums. Five thousand was a good two-thirds of my rent; it suddenly looked as if I might, after all, be able to raise enough to placate the landlord. Wasting no time on preliminaries I told Will of my coming eviction. He bought me a beer to mark the special importance of my anecdote. I was not too reassured to see that he put it on the slate.

Will, who was about thirty, specialized in folksy avuncular philosophizing, not of the hillbilly kind but of the Southern gentleman school. His engaging courtesy, however, had not protected him from a disastrous experience. When coming out of the nearby Odéon Métro one evening he had walked into revved-up riot police during a skirmish with students. He was clubbed senseless despite crying, 'Je suis Américain!' arms folded over his skull. As a partner in a small architect's office, Will's company's lawyers were claiming that he had lost a quarter of his mental and creative ability as a result of his injuries. He was now engaged in a particularly hazardous adventure: he was suing the Paris police. On extended sick leave from work, Will sat around bars waiting for the pay-off. One of the reasons for this might originally have been the necessity of demonstrating an inability to function professionally, but cause and effect had become blurred. It was difficult at this stage to know whether his fecklessness was a result of his injuries, or the undermining effects of waiting around in bars for the law to pay up; or whether indeed shiftlessness was a temperamental preference. (Years later he was found dead in a doss-house in New York.)

So it was into the hands of this damaged Southern gentleman that I was putting my salvation.

My predicament provided Will with a fresh topic and also gave him the role he enjoyed of philosophical man. He suggested that I be his guest for dinner at the Pergola. Nervous about the waste of precious borrowing time I would have preferred that he gave me the price of the meal, but I had to go along with his magnanimous gesture. I was surprised he chose this louche restaurant by Métro

Mabillon. It was noted for pimps and young prostitutes and vicious knife fights in the early hours.

We ate at a balcony table overlooking the bar below. I had my first steak *au poivre*; indeed it was my first meal in an elaborate Parisian late-night restaurant, with all linen napkins (I was used to paper) and waiters who performed like *sommeliers*. They were rather gangster-like *sommeliers*.

As we began the second course Will cut my appetite by telling me that not only did he not have money to lend me, he did not have money to pay for the meal we were eating.

Was the man crazy? Was this a lunatic way of making me accomplice to a con trick? I was suddenly aware of how little I knew him.

Will assured me he always worked on the principle that it was easier to borrow on a full stomach. I felt we were now prisoners of the kind of people who were likely to slit our full stomachs to retrieve their goods. Will told me to enjoy the meal first and insisted that he had ways of getting the money in time. I assumed he was expecting someone to meet him. I was wrong. His plan was to leave me as hostage while he, replete, sauntered around the Quarter looking for a loan.

I was now completely trapped by this lunacy. I couldn't get up and leave since I had eaten half of the meal and did not have enough to pay for the hors d'oeuvres don't mind the steak. I nibbled at the food. Scenes of violence ran through my mind: I had visions of scrapper-faced Gallic waiters, their lukewarm, garlicky breath hot on our faces as they hauled us out to duff us up at the back.

Now Will was babbling about the best way of dealing with my landlady. Shout at her, he said. Tell her to bugger off. Scare her. She's the one to scare. The French understand that sort of thing, he assured me, ordering a cigar from the waiter which I nearly plucked out of his hand and gave back.

Shout at them! If there was one thing I remembered about landladies at home it was that if you ever 'raised your voice' to a landlady you were out. And how could I shout at them when it was I who was in the wrong? I reminded him. I couldn't even claim that they charged me an exorbitant rent. It's beside the point who is in the wrong, Will said. It's who shouts loudest, the Parisians understand that.

Completely disheartened I realized Will was one of those Americans who had a cliché relationship with France. He saw the French as fictitious characters, extras from a Hollywood musical. Waiters could be chided for demanding money; landladies breezily told by the tenant to get lost because, to Will, they were only bit players. He could keep this illusion going because, after four years in France, he still could only manage a smattering of French.

When he got up to begin his hunt he advised me to order another *quart* of *vin rouge* if the waiter tried to give me the bill.

I felt like something left in a pawn shop. Without the shield of Will I slumped into craven self-consciousness which I tried to conceal by leisurely gestures: nibbling the cheese; taking dainty, insouciant sips from the wine-glass. Fearing the carafe would never see me through the night I did no more than let the purple tide tickle my upper lip each time.

If only I had a newspaper to hide behind. I was at a table horribly centred and miserably isolated (the regular clients liked to hug the walls). It seemed to me that I was progressively becoming enlarged, an inflating target for the entire restaurant and its malevolent staff. At one point the waiter bore down on me and, with a decidedly belligerent air, demanded if I wanted a coffee. Ordering a coffee meant the bill would come too so I asked for another *quart* of red wine. He gave it reluctantly and then spent most of his time fiddling with tables nearby, keeping me under close surveillance.

I decided to go down drunk. I went deep into the red wine, soon woozy philosophical thoughts my only companion. I thought about survival and extinction; of lonely defeat; of how flimsy our aspirations are, forever rent by the cold-hearted beast of life.

Suddenly there was Will coming up the stairs. He exuded good-natured triumph, and had another cigar going. He had returned to liberate me from my cell on the balcony. He only had money for the meal, not yet for the rent, but getting out of this hell's kitchen was momentarily my only concern. He told me not to worry; to trust him, go home and shout at the landlady. He would have most, if not all, of the money the next day.

Drained even of my capacity for apprehension I went home indifferent to the encounter to come.

I had hardly shut my door behind me when there was the sound of a key turning in the lock and in came the landlady. This unmannerly entry allowed me to feel genuine outrage (the conventions of the shabby genteel are occasionally helpful).

I demanded in fragments of French *quoi* she *penséd* she was *faiting* in my *chambre*? Did she not comprehend *politesse*? It was *minuit* and *plus*. I flung my fist out to show her my watch with the threadbare strap; she backed away in alarm. I plunged on shouting that I was *fatiguéd* and had *travaille* to do *importante*. How dare she be *dans* my *chambre*? 'SORTIE!' I shouted recalling the signs in the Métro. *SORTIE! SORTIE!* My sense of indignation became genuine anger as I roared.

She scurried from the room. I expected her to call her husband and we would start all over again. He might even try to wrestle me from the room. But they only came back to shout through the door that I was a thief. I put a chair under the handle and went to sleep. The next morning I got up at seven and shoved a note under their door: '*L'argent ce soir.*' I went off to hang about the Monaco all day. Around 9 p.m. Will turned up with the money. (I never discovered where he got it.)

I hurried back to rue Beaubourg, knocked peremptorily and when they opened the door thrust the money at the pair of them. Stony-faced I demanded a receipt. I steamed with genuine moral indignation which I realized at the same time was bogus. They, on the other hand, were silent and contrite.

When I came back that night, nicely oiled on the residue of Will's cash, I discovered that the landlady had been in again. This time she had left a mess of burnt custard sitting thigh high in a bowl of some sort of black fluid. There was also a small packet of biscuits. They had become a harmless little couple again. I punished them by being reticent about their gift – which I had wrapped in *Paris-Presse* and dumped self-righteously in the bin.

I was no nearer solving my problem of surviving in Paris, only more manacled by debt, so God apparently decided to intervene. (This was in the days when God and I still had a relationship.) Like something out of a Frank Capra film He sent an emissary to point the way. Our Saviour got me a job which should not have existed; or if it did, should not have been filled by someone as unqualified as myself, nor by someone from my country. I was chosen to inaugurate an experiment by the French government to teach English to children from the age of seven, rather than the usual starting age of eleven or twelve.

One day I was hanging around the Alliance Française on a routine trawl for pupils or company when I met a fellow from Kilkenny. A skinny, urgent creature, he seemed to have a busy schedule (seeing he was Our Lord's Emissary that was not surprising). He dealt with me in a few moments and I never saw him again.

He told me about this scheme by which foreign university students got jobs as assistants in French lycées, £60 a month for twelve hours a week. It wasn't really work since you were not allowed to teach, the staff, French teacher of English, took care of that. You just talked with the classes.

Sixty pounds a month – eight times my rent – for waffling before a class for only twelve hours a week! It was a breath-stealing glimpse of plenty. The problem was that all the assistants had been hired already. While some, notably Americans and Australians, didn't turn up to take posts in the provinces, hardly anyone turned down a chance of a subsidized year in Paris. So my chances of a post for that year were almost zero. (To prosper as a journalist I had to stay in Paris.) My guide suggested I put my name down for the following year. But by that time, I thought, I would be on the coffin ship back to Dublin.

My benefactor insisted on getting me a form from the office in the Alliance. The conditions of employment made it even more hopeless: you had to be a university student, and the exchange agreement was with Grande Bretagne, of which we in the South of Ireland had definitely ceased to be a part some years before. 'Don't mind that part,' said my guide.

But I wasn't a university student. 'Have you nobody at home who would forge a student card for you?' he said, his incredulity implying serious disapproval of this lack of social resource.

I remembered that Dublin abounded with chancers of one kind or another and supposed I could find someone.

'For God's sake,' he said (with perhaps more pertinence than I recognized at the time), 'can't you chance it?'

Then he vanished for ever.

I filled in the form on the spot, giving fictitious qualifications from University College, Dublin, not daring to involve the 'Protestant' university Trinity, which was full of sophisticated people who would, I felt, have academic spies in places like Paris.

The language experiment had been given a late start. It was to begin in two infant schools in Vincennes the following January rather than October; my fresh application fell into their tray at the right moment. I was chosen to be interviewed by the Inspector General of Schools, Monsieur Assenat.

I got a student card back from Dublin within ten days. A lot of gleeful research in the pubs had obviously gone into this. Some friends who worked in the Bank of Ireland had come up with a genuine card in a name close to my own. Lenihan (I smeared the top off the inky H and scooped out the A).

In those days nobody except immigration officers ever looked properly at identity cards. And anyway the sunken-cheeked creature on it sufficiently resembled me. It is not only the Chinese whom it is hard to tell apart; foreigners have great difficulty distinguishing one skinny, callow Irishman from another. A friend of mine, Joe McCauley, wrote a reference. It purported to come from my professor: he extolled his pupil's virtues in an ironic style while being sarcastic about certain scholastic deficiencies. There was a final masterly touch: it was written in green ink. Here was the authentic eccentric *professeur britannique* grudgingly introducing a brilliant student.

French haziness about Anglo-Saxon geography was a help: assuming no doubt that Dublin was in the North of Ireland – thus *britannique* – the processing clerks passed the application.

Monsieur Assenat was, for all his stiff formality, a plain man and an unsure academic. He spoke impeccable, strait-jacket English and tried to dress like an Englishman. But his pinstripe was hopelessly Continental. He demonstrated his capability for controlled lapses into informality by using carefully husbanded English slang. It was like watching a deacon making a guarded stab at ice skating. I went easy on my stout Dublin Rs so as not to shock him and was considerate of his gravity.

Two weeks later I was recalled to the Office of Schools and Universities of France at Mabillon and was informed personally by Monsieur Assenat that I had the job for a year.

I felt as if I had got a knighthood. This wonderful city was now at my disposal. As I went out it was especially satisfying to note that Monsieur Assenat's office was at Mabillon, just around the corner from the Pergola where I had so lately been left as a hostage.

I made a point of showing my appointment letter to my landlord to get the heat off any future arrears. I discovered with surprise that he seemed to be more delighted for me than for himself. He and his wife shooed me into their dim den and made me drink sweet wine and eat pulpy home-made cake. They told me about their son who had gone to live in Morocco and was rarely able to get home. They showed me his picture: a closed-faced, grievanced-looking creature with, I suspected, little inclination to come back to his worshipping parents.

Now they began to dote on me. There was no trace of the villainous cupidity with which I had associated them – indeed if I had accepted all their invitations to dinner they would have had little profit left from the rent. I no longer noticed the squint in Madame Lapineau's eye; I thought of it now as a rakish glance which went with her humorous asides. She was quite a jolly thing. And neither were deformed any more; physically they were a compact, nimble pair still full of thwarted enthusiasm.

They had run a shop, they told me, but had taken early retirement. Monsieur Lapineau was only about fifty-five. At first they had enjoyed their freedom from drudgery and routine, but already their enthusiasm had become directionless. They were a little ashamed of their discontent, as if they had come to believe they were not resourceful enough to enjoy retirement. Now, their son grown and gone away, and with no occupation, they clutched at a substitute. But I held back from intimacy with landlords and after a while they were content to be good neighbours, helpful in small ways and genuinely concerned about my future.

There was no problem with the teaching job at Vincennes. I liked children and had no difficulty winning over the good little seven-year-olds and gagging the evil ones. They did not speak a word of my language and I spoke little of theirs but we communicated effortlessly. Soon they were playing shop in English and even mastered the daft English pounds, shillings and pence.

Non-verbal communication was even more evident in the two other classes, in a teenage girls' school, that I had been given to make up the statutory twelve hours. I was in charge of about fifty edible creatures between sixteen and eighteen, the only man in the building. In my head I was constantly overwhelmed by plans for moral turpitude (particularly during a scandal when some of the girls sunbathed nude on the school roof) but cowardice and a craven enslavement to my salary kept me in check.

Five

At home the police always represented the opposite of action. Encounters with them would normally centre around the absence of a light on a bicycle. The Law, in the form of a hefty countryman, would signal you from afar to stop. You would fall into a state of passivity, already imprisoned by the long-distance gesture. The Dublin policeman was invariably a colchie – a country dunce – and you did well to pay attention to his country rhythms if you wanted to get home in time for tea. He, too, would have a bicycle, but generally did not mount it, preferring to trundle it alongside as if it were an object already under arrest. Very low tones were advisable for these encounters. Thus did the Law peacefully have its way with you in the Ireland of the fifties.

So inexperienced was I in lawlessness that I always thought of policemen singly. A relative of ours was supposed to have witnessed a baton charge in College Green one time; but my own sight of policemen in squads or mobs was on St Patrick's Day, flinging their arms forward in foolish pride as they marched across O'Connell's Bridge. So to sit one sunny afternoon on the terrace of the Monaco at Place de l'Odéon and see dozens of police skittering down the rue Monsieur le Prince at high speed, dark blue cloaks rising as they darted in amongst the traffic like crazy, low-flying blue birds, lashing out with batons at anyone under twenty-five, was extraordinary. I thought I was hallucinating.

The *agents* backed a couple of youths against the flank of a 63 bus as it attempted to shift diagonally across the small *place* and into the narrow rue Quatre Vents; one student leapt on to the open platform of the disappearing bus and kicked out at a policeman who rattled at his legs with a baton.

Trapped students crouched in doorways, arms crossed over their foreheads to ward off these demented bats. But most of the middle-aged people moving about gave all this no more than a cursory glance and continued on their business.

As an *agent* approached me along the pavement, baton drawn, I sat transfixed with a peculiar sense of incompetence. Should I run away? Or wish him a servile good afternoon? It may have been recognition of my genuine amazement which marked me as a blameless foreigner, or perhaps the impressive pile of saucers in front of me served as an alibi. Each represented a consummation, and the height of my trophies suggested I had been too busy to have taken part in the recent turbulence, whatever it was.

This *agent* suddenly darted across the *place* to assist two others hammering a group of students, then they all skipped off up the boulevard St-Germain, running recklessly through the hesitating traffic.

This was the *monôme*; the student rag at the breaking up of the Sorbonne for the summer vacation. The students celebrated by roaming around the Latin Quarter flinging paper bag flour bombs at passers-by. I could not make out why this benign disorder should excite such ferocity in the police; the students I questioned were not much help, accepting the brutality of the police as traditional.

The scene left me in that state of agitated excitement aroused when one discovers those in authority exposed in a disgraceful act. I was convinced that retribution for those who had gone berserk in full view of honest citizens could only be awful. Next day I scanned the morning and evening papers for reports of an outcry, but there were only some scanty accounts of students being dispersed by the police when the *monôme* became a nuisance to the traffic.

The police I had seen at work were not the CRS (Compagnie Républicaine de Sécurité), the legendary riot police who camped in long navy blue vans parked along boulevards, staring out at the world through wire-meshed windows until the time came to be disgorged on to the mobs. These were the ordinary Paris *agents*, the blue-cloaked flat-*kepi*ed extras who featured in everyone's sentimental snaps of the Eiffel Tower or Montmartre.

There were an awful lot of police of all shades and tendencies in Paris in those days. There were domesticated bucolic police and hard-bitten urban police; there were oppressive police and scheming, colluding and conniving police; there were semi-clandestine and quasi-seditious police.

As well as the Paris *agents*, there were the national Gendarmerie, the Brigade Mondaine and the Brigade Criminelle; the Sûreté Nationale, the Police Économique and the Police Judiciaire. There were also the more murky Direction Surveillance du Territoire (DST), the Renseignements Généraux, and the counter-espionage SDEC. Then came the street-cleaning CRS.

When you are a young exile, your life not fully fastened to the country in which you are staying, political problems have no real meaning for you. Public figures, even those of the towering, albeit rather comic, presence of General de Gaulle, have no more reality than a local monument. Politics at first did not impinge on our layabout lives Chez Maurice, a café-créperie on rue de Tournon, at the Monaco or Tournon. As a journalist at the beginning I had only a market for 'human interest' stories. The Irish papers were not interested in the details of French politics and since I was still tapping with my white cane through the intricacies of the language I would not have been yet of great help to them.

But it was the police who eventually led me into covering politics.

By 1960 the Algerian war was in its sixth year. The human consequences had begun to be felt on the mainland even by myself who had only marginal access to French life.

A protracted colonial war is best maintained by a professional army; it takes longer for its brutalizing effects to touch other classes and professions; longer for its malignant nature to become apparent at home. But the war in Algeria depended on a conscript army; the young bourgeoisie – the sons of doctors, lawyers, merchants,

51

academics – were beginning to receive their share of the wounds along with the ignorant and unemployed, whose terminal discomfort would have been of minor consequence.

Small cameos of human suffering began to be enacted even within my circles. There would be farewell assemblies for young Vincennes teachers leaving for deferred military service. We would hear of the mutilation of those who had been sent to Algeria earlier. Then came news of the death in Algeria of a former student who, only the year before I came, had been larking around the schoolyard. The son of one of the women teachers, he had impetuously joined up the moment he left school.

Vincennes was a prosperous middle-class quarter in the east of Paris. It was the merchant class's more modest version of the insouciant and elegant 16th *arrondissement* in the west. Vincennes with its wood was a confident haven for prosperous businessmen and shopkeepers. It had a hefty *mairie* planted in manicured grounds. Its boulevards were wide, its schools spacious and well appointed. It was a town of its own, looking in no need of the outside world.

But it also had in its woods a concentration camp for Algerians to which the locals never made reference. This camp was originally intended as a temporary centre to which the police brought large numbers of them picked up in routine sweeps for interrogation. The 'interrogation' had a way of turning into months of confinement in fairly barbaric conditions. Gradually stories of torture began to leak out.

I never went to verify the existence of the concentration camp during that year in Vincennes, although it must have been within less than ten minutes' walk. Embarrassment at meeting pupils out of doors, and having to play the English teacher on the street in faltering French, was at that early stage more prohibitive than my news instincts and sent me back to the Latin Quarter the moment my classes were done. There were also considerations of sloth and not wanting to become entangled in controversy by rooting, perhaps incompetently, for scandal in the area which provided my only settled income.

I was guilty, of course, of some of the same sins of self-interest that allow abuses to exist within knowledge of the most respectable communities. Like most prosperous enclaves, Vincennes was quite a defensive community and not at all ready to accept criticism of police activity.

I went back to the school one Saturday morning for the funeral of a colleague's son. Uncertain of my position, not having known the boy personally and being only a part-time, foreign teacher I did not know what was expected of me. But I felt an appearance would be a proper courtesy.

In the crowd in the churchyard the mother was like a disorientated housewife shopping for unfamiliar items – for consolation, for meaningless reassurance, for explanations of some kind; looking for scraps which would somehow give sense to the incredible fact that her son had been obliterated far from Vincennes in Algeria, a country as remote and unreal to her as it was to me. What she said to me in her naïve gratitude suggested in some sort of muddled way that my presence represented to her a kind of international recognition for her son.

He never was a soldier. Before he could be said to have achieved that status, he was dismembered by a terrorist bomb a few days after his arrival in Algiers.

The sordidness of the Algerian conflict was becoming apparent even in Vincennes. Around the teachers' tables in the canteen there was facile anger at the *métèques* (Algerians), but a corrosive uneasiness about the whole involvement was building up. One young teacher, a Communist poet, Claude Meline, doggedly engaged his colleagues in debate on the dubious merits of the war. Whose interests were being protected? A bunch of *pieds noirs*? Powerful industrialists and bankers? Anti-Gaullist, and passionately hostile to the war, Meline was the only one in Vincennes with whom I developed a real friendship, one that has lasted.

Clandestine networks had been set up to provide an escape route for young soldiers prepared to desert rather than serve in Algeria. Both Communists and Catholics were involved in this treasonable activity; they seemed to be past caring that they would inevitably be seen as giving support to FLN terrorists. One of the leading figures was Henri Alleg whose book, *La Question*, describing his own experience, exposed publicly the issue of institutionalized torture in the French army. It was published by Beckett's publisher Jerome Lindon and banned, of course. There was also Francis Jeanson's *La Gangrène*, which described how the plague of torture had already reached the Metropole. Its publisher, Maspero, was prosecuted for 'insult to the army'. Deserting had achieved an honourable status and its anthem was a banned record of Mouloudji, 'Le Déserteur'. Our Maurice in the café at Odéon left it in his juke-box, out of indifference to authority rather than any political intention.

In response to this underground protest the Government approved an unpardonable decision. With the enthusiastic support of the Prefect of Police, Maurice Papon, fifteen years after the Liberation France re-created a new Gestapo. This was a force of Muslim police, the Harkis, given 'complete liberty of action in dismantling the FLN networks in Paris'.

The Harkis moved into the Algerian quarters, requisitioning hotel rooms and cafés. Within a short time Paris had two notorious torture centres: the Goutte-d'Or, near St-Denis and another out at the Porte d'Orléans. The Harkis were mostly peasant North Africans, some recruited from jails it was said, with their own reasons for fighting the FLN.

No elaborate effort was made to conceal their activities. They were only torturing Algerians, so the rest of France did not have to disturb itself. In May of that year four policemen were shot dead on the streets of Paris by the FLN. It was not officially admitted that they and those named on death lists found on FLN prisoners were all Harkis. Public indignation against the FLN would be greater if it were believed that the terrorists were shooting down ordinary Paris *agents*.

The more radical newspapers did not go along with government discretion and there were some protests about the Harkis from officials. Claude Bourdet, a councillor at the Porte d'Orléans, was one of the few to condemn the torture chambers in his quarter. Protests from the French residents at Porte d'Orléans were generally more on the level of neighbours complaining that they couldn't get a proper night's sleep because of the screams of the tortured in the Harkis station next door.

A French girl who looked into Maurice's café from time to time was rumoured to be a courier for the FLN. Being French she could move around the country with more freedom than an Algerian. One night she asked me if I was interested in meeting the FLN. I responded to her offer with some reserve, not knowing how genuine was her involvement with the terrorists. There was a way of checking: an Algerian journalist, a scarred-faced character named Hafiz, often came to another bar we frequented on the rue Quatre-Vents – Eliane's. He was a mixture of good-humoured exuberance and ferocity. He also had that gentleness you find in Arabs, at least in their dealings with men. His credentials as a journalist sympathetic to the FLN were unquestionable. He often bore them on his face after another night of being battered by the police who regularly picked him up for questioning.

Without naming her, I asked him if a French girl in the Quarter who claimed to have contact with the FLN was genuine. He knew who I was talking about and made it fairly plain that she was.

A few nights later she arrived in Maurice's with a young Algerian we had not seen before. He was dressed very correctly for a formal outing with Europeans. The girl said if I wanted to go ahead with the meeting this friend of hers would arrange to take me. The young man insisted on buying me a drink and having ordered it presented my beer to me with great formality. Standing at the bar he then launched into a discussion on general topics in excellent French as if to demonstrate that an Algerian could be the equal of any European in café society (not that Maurice's little *crêperie* was exactly fashionable). Mostly the Algerians had dank cafés of their own across the river. He enquired courteously about the state of health of my country; hoped I enjoyed French cooking and gave a few tourist guide hints on the places of cultural interest in Paris. He never mentioned the war.

He left after about twenty minutes. This ceremonious youth played no part in the actual meeting when he eventually brought me to the rendezvous. He left immediately the introductions were made.

I had visualized being led through fetid back-streets and into a shady hotel around Barbès Rochechouart, partly because that succulent name from the north of Paris suggested to me Arab bazaars, clandestinity, the odour of dates. In fact my young guide led me down the rue Danton to the Place St-Michel, not five minutes from our café. Three respectably dressed Algerians were sitting at a terrace table almost at the pavement's edge. The guide left us. Facing us across the boulevard were the packed cafés of the boulevard St-Michel and the entrance to the rue de la Huchette, an area of bookshops, Greek restaurants and art cinemas. We were over on the quieter, west side of the place St-Michel by the fountain. Across the river we could see the towers of the Palais de Justice. I did not at first understand why they had chosen such an exposed position. I had the feeling of being on display.

When I spoke about it later to them the logic became clear. Far from being easily trapped there were any number of streets around us to fade into. Behind us, an arch led into the rue Gît-le-Coeur and the Beat hotel, where Gregory Corso, Allen Ginsberg and William Burroughs stayed. If the police came we could disappear up the narrow rue St-André-des-Arts; down into the Métro or across the traffic into the boulevard. It was the Algerian hotels, constantly under surveillance, which were not safe. It was not too unusual to see foreigners and students talking to North Africans around St-Michel. In any event only the Paris *agents* patrolled here, not the professional North African spotters – the Harkis.

It was impossible to verify with what level of FLN local leadership I was dealing nor indeed how authentically 'terrorist' these men were. I had to make up my own mind on external evidence – as journalists have to in such circumstances. But Hafiz was a reliable contact if the girl was not; it was unlikely that these three were jokers or mythomaniacs. Two of them were in their early thirties, the third middle-aged. They spoke with restraint and made no dramatic claims that would suggest the self-advertisement of bogus 'freedom fighters'.

The eldest, who appeared to be the senior man, was a 'small businessman' who had just come over from Algeria. The other two admitted guardedly to being 'chemists of a sort'. One of them was 'just a friend' not an active member of the FLN, he claimed. He had left Algeria nearly six years previously, just before the first wave of violence and now, for reasons not very clear to him, could not get back. Apart from the mechanical distrust of the police he was not especially a suspect person.

But I sensed something clandestine about the eldest man, and while his two companions did not indulge in elaborate bodyguard techniques there was a kind of practised alertness in the way they watched the boulevard while he talked. The name FLN was not especially excluded from the conversation; it had become part of the vocabulary of everyday café conversation and we were reasonably out of earshot of the nearest table.

Since I was not looking for an official statement from the FLN leadership these three were fine for my purpose. People would want to know, at a time when terrorists were a rare, inexplicable breed, what sort of individuals shot down policemen on the streets of Paris and put bombs in cafés in Algiers. What kind of people were conducting this war against France in France? Were they crazed youngsters, souped-up on pot and sent out to gun down the innocent? In one notorious forty-eight-hour period in June, the FLN had shot seven policemen, five of whom died; four assassinations a month had become the average. Had they a legitimate grievance?

When I asked outright if they worked for the FLN the leader said: 'All Algerians in France with the exception of the MNA [a rival group] work, one way or another, for the FLN according to their situation. They are asked to do things and they do them.'

Did the ordinary Algerian workers make contributions out of their salaries to the organization?

'The very least they can do,' he responded, 'and if there is someone who needs to be hidden almost any Algerian will hide him.'

'And if he gives the FLN fugitive up to the police?'

'He is suppressed.'

'What about a man who has got out of Algeria with his family to escape conflict, expressly to live in peace and avoid political involvement? Is he forced to take part?'

'There are such cases,' the leader said. But then he added, 'No, he is not forced.'

This was not quite true; terrorist organizations in enemy country cannot afford to tolerate neutrals and he gave a truer picture in his next remark. 'There is a kind of scale. We ask the younger people, the bachelors, to perform the more dangerous work. In any case, if anything happened to a father we would be responsible for the family.'

I turned to the one who had come to France to escape trouble with the police. 'How does it happen that you had some trouble in Algeria and now you are working peacefully in France?'

'Everyone has had trouble in Algiers. I was arrested, held in detention for some time and then released. I managed to come here and work.'

'Why do so many Algerians still want to come here to work?'

'In Algeria it is difficult to find work,' he replied. 'Pay is poor and the family allowance is half what it is here. A man with three or four children comes here and immediately he gets a full family allowance and often a good enough job.'

I did not have enough time to go into this curious contradiction that Frantz Fanon's 'wretched of the earth' were partly escaping total exploitation in their plundered country by coming to the country that exploited them.

'But now very often we cannot get back,' the man continued. 'I have a friend working here. For two years he has applied to go home to see his wife and children. But there is no chance. Algeria is like a big prison. You need visas to get out or to get in.'

The older man volunteered that he too had been in jail more than once in Algeria.

'Why were you arrested?'

'Oh, why!' He shrugged. 'At that time, two years ago, everybody was "questioned" more than once. The first time I was put in a camp for forty days. For no reason.'

In June that year the Government had brought in an emergency measure by which any person arrested on suspicion of having taken part in a terrorist act need not appear before a court for a month. In other words Algerians could disappear into a concentration camp and be interrogated for a month before being allowed due process of law.

'There are camps like that now in France,' I said. 'In Vincennes. Is that the kind you mean?'

'Yes,' the leader agreed. 'Concentration camps, if you like. The second time I was arrested was just before the referendum. The police came and told me to come to the station. They locked me and a friend in the cave of the *gendarmerie* for fifteen days. On the fifteenth day they just came and said, "You can go." They had absolutely nothing against me . . . But my friend was tortured. I saw it.'

'Did your friend talk?'

'I don't know. He died.'

'In his book *The Question*, Henri Alleg described an electric torture.'

'Yes, that is common. They put the wires between the fingers, under the tongue, in the ears, up the nostrils.'

He did not mention the testicles, though I knew they were also wired up. The whole tone of the interview was one of discretion and tact. I sensed that they did not wish to go into the more unimaginable barbarities in case a respectable 'English' journalist began to doubt their credibility. My own uncle had had his fingernails torn out by the Black and Tans, so I would have had no problem believing governments could misbehave.

The loss of the obscene detail did not matter; I wouldn't have been able to use the word testicles in an Irish paper. In such ways decency becomes the protector of barbarity.

'But who does this torture?'

'They all do it.'

'I understood it was only the paratroopers, not so much the regular army or police.'

'They all do it.'

'Do you know the case of Djamila Boupacha the young girl imprisoned and tortured in Algeria?' (This was a *cause célèbre* of the time.)

'Djamila Boupacha.' He pronounced the name with a certain scorn as one would a reference to an excessively publicized film star. 'There are a hundred Djamila Boupachas. It is true,' he continued, 'that in the past year, since there is a hope that de Gaulle will be able to bring about a just peace, things are not so bad. By that I mean that there is less torturing. Before, almost everyone was tortured. The police would stop you on the street for no reason, provoke you. Then you were taken and beaten up or tortured, just on the chance you knew something.

'But there are other ways of bringing pressure,' he said. 'I wanted to start a little business and bought all the equipment. But then I was told it would be impossible to get permission. On the other hand, the police said, if I were willing to supply them with a little information from time to time . . .'

'Then everyone is forced to take sides one way or the other?'

'Exactly.'

'A French municipal councillor recently protested against the establishment of the Harkis. What kind of people are they?'

'They are mostly out for vengeance for one reason or another. They are informers in some cases who found things getting too hot for them in Algeria.' (They were also young peasants seduced by the glamour of power.)

'Do you think terrorism is a good way of gaining your ends?'

'Good? It is the only way. It is only because of this pressure that de Gaulle – the French Government – have taken any steps towards conciliation.'

'What do you think will be the outcome?'

'There is no doubt,' he said. 'We will get our independence. All Africa is moving in that direction. We already have the whole structure of government set up. There are Muslims who resist independence but they are a very small minority and the tide of nationalism is against them. That will be a domestic problem.

'There is one thing we would like to make clear,' he said finally. 'Because of these last five and a half years we have the reputation of being French-haters. That is not true. We respect the French people. But we want our independence and we will get it.'

The day I posted this piece to the *Irish Times* I decided to send a copy to the *Guardian*. I was completely thrown by a cheery response from someone named Brian Redhead at the *Guardian* (still based in Manchester), saying he would very much like to have run my FLN piece but since it was probably going to appear in the *Irish Times*, and there was cross-readership, he could not use it.

I periodically tossed bottles into the ocean of newspapers and magazines worldwide, in the hope of breaking into international journalism. I aimed mostly in the direction of American magazines honeyladen with dollars. I knew already that the *New Yorker* did not want me, nor did the *Jerusalem Post*. So I was not expecting much.

Now Redhead's yes/no left me groggy. The *Manchester Guardian* was actually willing to print a piece of mine. I had made it! But also it wasn't and I hadn't.

I flung myself at Jack White by the only speedy method that occurred to me, a telegram. (We were not a telephoning nation.) I asked him not to run the piece since it was going into the *Manchester Guardian*. Offended, he replied without haste that since the piece had been offered to the *Irish Times* (the impersonal invocation of the title revealed the strength of his disapproval) there was no question of relinquishing it. Indeed, it would be appearing in the paper the following day.

It was like someone refusing to give you back your winning ticket. I sulked. I felt it was extraordinary that Jack White, who purported to be my benefactor, should not understand the immense significance for my future: how, when the portals of a great newspaper were being flung hospitably wide for me, could he deliberately block me? How could he put the *Irish Times* before me? (That he was its features editor could have suggested an answer, were I in a mood to be reasonable.) I was doubly sickened by the thought of the handsome sums a great English paper disbursed to its privileged contributors. (I need not have felt deprived; I was to discover that the *Guardian* was almost as parsimonious as the *Irish Times*. If you claimed taxi expenses they wondered aloud why you didn't use a bicycle.)

I sent a letter full of mourning to Mr Redhead and in December got a Dear Mr Lennon letter back suggesting that 'It might be worth your while to consider writing for us rather more general pieces', which it was understood would not conflict with those of Darsie Gillie, the Paris correspondent. Would I let him know what I thought?

By the following month it was Dear Peter, and already Redhead, who was one of the most supportive editors I ever worked to, was writing about distinctly unmanagement concerns such as his anxiety that I might be pinning too much financial faith on an association with the *Guardian*. 'I am always aware of the trouble of earning enough to eat regularly and if you find yourself in any way out of pocket for things you do for us please yelp immediately.'

Redhead had a natural ability to understand the insecurities of freelances abroad and recognized that because you wanted to write for a good paper you might be investing time in the *Guardian* that could be more lucratively rewarded by flashier journals. There were others on the *Guardian* who had *The Times*' attitude that they were doing you a favour in publishing your stuff. Neither did Redhead exhibit any of the snobbery that many display towards the freelance. He had an effortless ability to imagine what practical difficulties you might be facing, operating abroad with meagre resources; equally important, he understood the psychological vulnerability of people sending in copy to a mute head office. It was no accident that his lieutenants, Phil Tucker and John Course, temperamentally totally different from each other, all had this supportive approach. And then there was, of course, the classic good-hearted secretary, Wendy Barnes.

Redhead, Tucker, Course and later Ian Wright were more straightforward colleagues than some of my own at home, with the notable exception of Jack White – whom I always thought of as a kind of Englishman anyway, since he was a refined Protestant. (The first year I went back I was astounded to notice he had a strong Dublin accent.) My relationship with them was remarkably plain and open. It did not consist of a continuous initiation rite which was an aspect of my dealings with senior journalists in my own country. Never having lived in England it took me a while to grasp that these Englishmen did not hold my nationality against me, in the way that the *Irish Press* would hold my flawed patriotism or, when it came to promotion, the *Irish Times* my lack of academic background and my increasingly threadbare Catholicism. (That Catholics could be discriminated against in Dublin seems odd, but that's the way it was.) I never had to pretend to be British with the *Guardian*. But I would have had to pretend to become a faintly Protestantized academic with the *Irish Times* in the days when R. M. Smyllie, eccentric and alcoholic, was running it.

Phil Tucker, Brian Redhead's deputy and later the *Guardian*'s multi award-winning science correspondent, had nursed ambitions to be a painter, but Brian recruited him when he took on the odd job of painting the office canteen. What motivated Brian to make this unorthodox appointment? A hatred of snobbery and the need to do the *Guardian* establishment in the eye would have been factors: Redhead was permanently firing flaming arrows into the *Guardian*'s huffily encircled wagons.

John Course, aided by Phil, was largely responsible for the elegant feature layouts reclining luxuriously in spendthrift white spaces. The champions of grimly packed type considered it a scandalous waste of space but it gave great value to photographs and made the pages enticing to the reader. It also made your pieces look like tastefully hung paintings in a posh gallery. I was all for it.

John was a steady, reassuring voice on the phone. Not that the *Guardian* used the phone much either; they preferred the slow but economic technology of the Royal Mail. Occasionally I resorted to telex, very rarely to the expense of phoning in copy. One often had the impression that the *Guardian* was disciplining news, discouraging its unseemly haste.

One of the occasions which demanded an instant response was the first arrival of a newly famous British pop group at the Olympia music hall in Paris: the Beatles. The French were at first pretty lethargic in their reaction to them. I shared their indifference to the extent that when it came to the moment to read over the copy I realized I did not know any of their surnames. No matter I called them John Beatle, Paul Beatle, Ringo and George Beatle. *Guardian* readers, God bless them, took this to be a fine piece of drollery.

Still hanging on to teaching, and keeping the Irish papers nourished with innocuous gossip masquerading as news, I coasted along in the unturbulent slipstream of the *Guardian*, tossing them a minnow now and again. After some months they decided we should meet and perhaps formalize the relationship – if I were prepared to pay the fare to Manchester. So one bleak winter's day I set out to meet the crew who were teleguiding so sensitively my new international career. I knew the route between Paris and Dublin all right, but I must have conveyed in advance something of the intimidation in my mind about the trip up to the dank marshlands of Manchester. Wendy Barnes, fully alert to the implications of a freelance having to penetrate so deep into England, was detailed to guide me up.

'The fare by train is, I think, thirty-four shillings single,' Wendy wrote. 'Apparently there are motorway buses which are fairly cheap but they only travel through the night. Still, I hope you make it – even if you have to walk the whole way!'

I arrived in Manchester and for the first time could put faces to the authors of all those cheery letters. We all went off to the pub, Brian and Phil and John and Wendy and I, and marinated the friendship in tepid English beer. Brian brought me to his home in Didsbury and after a lot of talk and fireside drink sent me off up to a pretty little bedroom.

Temporarily immunized to the temperature of the room by drink, I jumped pyjamaless into bed and leapt out with a yelp. The sheets were like steel; the bugger had no central heating in his bedrooms. In winter even the most dilapidated hotels in Paris had central heating twenty-four hours a day. I thought he was cracked.

But Redhead was a most companionable man with a natural informality and an easy loquacity that eventually led to his star status in BBC radio current affairs. Even then he was already taking time off to chat on Radio Chilly Didsbury, or whatever the local station was called. You felt total loyalty towards him, not only because of his sympathetic understanding of your situation, but also because of his easy assumption from the start that you were one of his lot. That was no incidental factor: with generous loyalty to his gang went an effervescent prejudice against those who were not of it. My first alarmed impression was that this seemed to include about three-quarters of the *Guardian* senior staff.

Whatever could be said about Redhead's prejudices there was nothing furtive about them. His attitude to the editor, Alastair Hetherington, caused me acute alarm. One of the people who had to go, he told his new recruit, was Hetherington, and he said this in a loud voice in the corridor just as Hetherington walked past us. Naturally, the man to take over would be Brian.

Breathtaking tactics, and suicidal. It was not surprising that many were determined Brian would never be editor.

My own meeting with Hetherington was, I felt, catastrophic. He had clearly been talked into the encounter by Redhead and sat, wordless, behind his desk, a tall chill very Anglicized Scotsman, who, to my eye, regarded me utterly without favour. They had told me that at parties for the staff in his home he offered cocoa. The story went that one of the *Guardian*'s comic columnists, Stanley Reynolds, challenged this genteel abstinence when he arrived at Hetherington's home well tanked up one evening. He went to the bathroom and then appeared bollock-naked at the top of the stairs.

I chattered like an over wound-up toy. Hetherington stared, a slight smearing of his expression suggesting he was wondering what this creature was doing in his office. Brian and John swore it was just that he had no idea what to say; not my fault at all, they assured me.

Redhead could be harsh about people whose work he did not appreciate. He was very scornful of Darsie Gillie, the Paris correspondent who had served his time in pre-war Poland. Brian characterized Darsie as just one of the old school brought up 'in the chancelleries of Europe'. This dismissive attitude, I believe, was more an expression of a restless will to create his own kind of paper than any personal malice. In fact, Darsie was a most honourable man; gentle, transparently sensitive behind his rather patrician delivery, which was partly an attempt to master a speech impediment. I did not share his politics, which were more conservative than he imagined. The liberal English have a way of taking their bearings too closely from the status quo; they are only truly liberal in transparently humane issues, the simpler the better. Their respect for established institutions extends to misplaced trust of official bodies in foreign countries in which they work, which is a mistake for a journalist.

While our politics did not entirely harmonize I never felt uneasy in his company. He was too obviously decent a human being. He wrote sturdily in the old style and tried to get to the bottom of things, shying instinctively from notions of conspiracy or truly evil ways among high authority.

Brian got a modest retainer out of Alastair Hetherington for me and promised to lever up the fees whenever possible. We identified pockets of potential stories which would keep me active while not crossing Darsie's territory. One was the Théâtre de Nations, a two-month festival of international theatre which drew celebrity companies from around the world; the next year we added the Cannes Film Festival. We also worked out an idea for a monthly miscellaneous column, La Vie Parisienne.

To this kernel I added ideas and supplemented my income with freelance work, occasionally with American magazines. I began to amass a comfortable wage. I had also begun to dabble in short stories and sold my first one to the new *Texas Quarterly* for $400, then a munificent sum.

The momentous communications between a great national newspaper and one of its foreign correspondents continued.

Brian: Do you live in a brothel? Bill Weatherby was in Paris for three days last week and phoned you at hourly intervals but the line was always engaged.

Brian: What's all this nonsense about a tape-recorder? I want literature not electronics.

Wendy: I have spoken to accounts about your cheque and although they seem slightly confused I think there'll be a spot of cash awaiting you.

Brian: As soon as we begin printing in London [10 September 1961] you should have no difficulty in getting the *Guardian* in Paris [this proved not to be true, of course] but I see no reason why you shouldn't put the cost of it on your expenses.

Brian: I don't think I could talk the editor into using a piece about Gerodias [the Paris pornographic publisher, who published Lolita].

Phil commissioned pieces in code with a ribald touch: 'Planchon – yes. Ionesco – yes. Tours – yes. See you before Christmas – yes? . . . Wendy – yes?'

And, periodically, a special request: What hopes of an interview with Beckett?

I was settling in fine now. I had met a young Finnish political science student, Eeva Karikoski, at the 'Greasy Greek' restaurant in rue Grégoire-de-Tours. Eeva was doing a summer course at the Science Po. and that Christmas we had a rendezvous in Copenhagen. The freemasonry of the Quarter meant that you could find a free pad, short term, in almost any city in the world. Eeva planned to come and live with me in Paris.

As for work, I went my way and Darsie Gillie went his, operating totally separately in an arrangement probably only possible with the *Guardian* – he from his apartment in the highly bourgeois 7th *arrondissement*, me from my (centrally heated) hotel room.

Six

One day in January 1961 I decided to drop Samuel Beckett a line and ask if he'd like to meet a young Dubliner come to live as a freelance journalist in Paris. At home everyone at the Pearl Bar, known as the branch office of the *Irish Times*, had said, 'Oh, you must look up Sam when you're over there.' Everyone called him Sam, then and since.

I asked in the note if he would like to give an interview; it would be a great coup for my new paper, the *Guardian*. But I said it would be all right with me if we just had a drink. Very promptly I received one of his plain cards in an envelope. The trouble was I couldn't make out what he was saying: the dark writing flowed across the white rectangle as if it had been dipped in a stream.

But Beckett had put his telephone number on the card and, a little embarrassed, I rang him up from a noisy café to know whether his response was 'yes' or 'no'. It was yes and I scribbled across the card he had sent me the name of the place we were to meet, the Closerie des Lilas, a bar-restaurant at the junction of boulevard St-Michel and boulevard Montparnasse.

We met at 6 p.m. the following Friday. He had said that he did not give interviews but would be prepared to meet a Dublinman, friend of whoever it was had given me his address, I forget now who. The understanding was that while I was free as a journalist to write about his professional activities I would not reveal anything of our private encounters, an agreement I kept throughout his lifetime.

By then Beckett was a literary figure of substantial, but not yet cosmic fame – the Nobel Prize was eight years away. I was used to literary figures in pubs in Dublin: Brendan Behan, Paddy Kavanagh, Ben Kiely and great schools of lesser verbal contortionists following the loquacious currents around Grafton Street and Burgh Quay, so I was not surprised that the rendezvous he had chosen was a fashionable literary one. When I sat waiting at the bar my elbow touched a plaque marking the spot where Hemingway used to drink. I moved away in scorn to a corner table.

Ignorance prevented me from being overawed by Beckett; I had seen *Waiting for Godot*, been intrigued; sniggered over Girodias's Olympia Press edition of *Watt*:

> 'Walks she out yet with Byrne?
> Moves Hyde his hand amid her skirts
> As erst? I ask, and Echo answers – Certes.'

That was about all.

When Beckett came in the door of the Closerie, a lean, alert man, upright carriage, graceful in a very masculine way, I knew instantly that this was no McDaid's Irish pub scribbler. The lined face was that of a frontiersman and his piercingly clear blue-green eyes had given me the appraising stare with which the priest makes an instant judgement of a boy's 'manliness' (i.e. Christian stalwartness).

Citizens of politically and spiritually repressive societies, such as Ireland was in the fifties, have to be chameleons, adept at shedding unsuitable demeanours in the presence of authority. Clearly in the company of a respectable man, I put on my Sunday morning behaviour. It was the right approach. He told me how Brendan Behan had called at his flat in the early hours of the morning, thumping on the door and shouting: 'Ah, Jaysus, Beckett, are ye comin' out for a drink?' – and they hadn't even met. Although not socially a fastidious man Beckett was repelled by bad manners which he saw as a fundamental lack of consideration for others.

For me not only was Beckett a representative of literary history – Joyce's Paris of the thirties – more to the point he was a Protestant. He also had an intimidating academic background – Trinity (Dublin) and the École Normale Supérieure. I was Catholic, of a class that might be described as aspiring shabby genteel, my unsophistication no doubt as pinkly apparent as a baby's bare bottom, and, of course, I had no university background.

At home the internal mental landscapes of unliberated Catholics and those of Protestants do not naturally mesh; we are also always prepared to take offence in the company of exiles who display a too ready aptitude in adopting the ways of foreigners. Beckett had chosen to write in French and that could have been a slight of some kind. So there was an exploratory tentativeness in our first conversation, mostly on my part.

Sitting in that corner of the Closerie we chatted for an hour, nothing more than a casual litany of names of people and places. What first surprised me was that this scholarly man had a recognizable Dublin accent. (He told me later that one reason he didn't like London was that taxi drivers called him 'Paddy'.) Not a Brendan Behan flat roar but the suburban, middle-class version. There was also to my finicky ear a trace of commonness in his vocabulary. This disconcerted me. My understanding of successful higher education was that it ironed out such things, particularly your Irish accent. (We tormented ourselves with this kind of thing at home; but I gave it up after a while in Paris.) What also surprised me was his preference for idiomatic Dublinese. I thought he was acting a little out of character to put me at my ease, but I was only partly right.

'You know Liam?' I'd ask.

The head would shake in humorous dismissal: 'A terrible chancer!'

'Mark?'

'A decent man. We'll have to organize a jar with him.'

It was clear that recalling places in Ireland especially around the Dublin and Wicklow mountains gave him genuine pleasure. The Featherbed? 'Lovely spot.' Luggala? 'Glorious.' And Killiney, of course, where the remnants of his family still lived within strolling distance of the Bay.

We drank Irish whiskey, no more than three glasses. Shortly after seven he went home. My strongest impression was that I had been with a nice man, an experience which leaves you with a reassured feeling, and one which is very underrated. He was working on *Happy Days* at the time.

These meetings became a ritual at protracted intervals. I'd drop him a line so he would not feel cornered by a telephone call, or come across him on the boulevard Montparnasse and we'd fix another meeting; always the same place, around the same time; sometimes we'd get to the fourth whiskey. Although Beckett was not one for drinking with literary cliques I understood the point of the Closerie now. It was not just that it was convenient enough to his home – he had just moved to a new flat in a nondescript modern block at 38 boulevard St-Jacques – but also that there are few places more comfortable and private than a fashionable bar at an unfashionable hour. He would usually be gone before 7.30 p.m. He told me of one method for protecting his privacy: he only answered the phone between 11 a.m. and midday, so even if someone got hold of his telephone number they would have to be lucky to catch him as I had been.

Despite popular legend Beckett was never a recluse. He may have been a hermit in his head but he had a very active, sporadically controlled social life, his friends a world-wide network of sentinels of his privacy. My early insights into Beckett's way of life convinced me that Greta Garbo must never genuinely have wanted to be alone, so plagued was her privacy. Beckett did genuinely want to be let alone. That is, he did not relish the familiarities of strangers and had no business with the media.

It soon became clear that his taste for idiomatic Dublin speech and playful way with a cliché was not put on. It was part of his preference for informality. Using the cliché and satirizing it at the same time is a very Dublin way of dealing at a tangent with relationships. It is partly a way of displaying your Dublin credentials, sending reassuring signals that you are of the same tribe – relaxed about drink, mocking, at least privately, of religious attitudes, and privy to all the mortifications of a puritanical society dying to be pagan.

This is the twentieth-century Dublin style of humour founded on the wit and chat of saloon bar characters and shared even by the most

71

educated only after, I suspect, it was given literary status by Joyce and then Flann O'Brien. There are plenty of examples of it in Beckett's early writing. Mr Spiro in *Watt*: 'I personally am a neo-John-Thomist, I make no bones about that. But I do not allow it to stand in the way of my promiscuities.' Many Dublin writers would be babbling this kind of stuff all night, self-consciously on stage. Beckett would just indulge in the occasional wry aside. His delivery of Dublin idiom was significantly different from garrulous Dublin hardchaws: it was said casually, like a light salute to the homeland.

He had a very matter-of-fact attitude to his status. One night we went to eat at Aux Îles Marquises, a celebrated oyster restaurant in the rue de la Gaîeté. As we came abreast, the oyster man whose stall stretched the length of the façade, greeted Beckett. Beckett told me he had won the title of Champion Oyster Opener of France.

'How's the work?' Sam asked.

'All right,' the man said. 'How's your work?'

'All right,' Sam said.

'It wasn't going too well at one time,' the oyster opener suggested.

'It wasn't,' Sam agreed. 'But I'm getting stuff put on now so it's all right.' (Jean-Louis Barrault had plans to put on *Waiting for Godot* at the Théâtre de l'Odéon, a mark of official recognition. Although already aged fifty-five, financial success had really only come to Beckett six or seven years before, after *Godot* in 1953. He earned virtually nothing from his novels, *Watt*, *Molloy*, *Malone Dies*, *The Unnameable*.)

I was astonished at the way he was quite unaffectedly able to equate the work of an oyster opener, however skilled, with his creative work, and said so. 'It's just another craft,' he told me.

He was a frightening driver. The first time I got into a car with him we were coming back from the Sarah Bernhardt Theatre. It was July 1961, so it must have been Mihalovici's operatic version of *Krapp's Last Tape*, sung by a twenty-seven-year-old American, Michael Dooley.

I have a memory of Beckett folding himself into his little Deux Chevaux and beating the car into obedience with his elbows and knees. He appeared to be using the flank of the vehicle to sweep the streets ahead of him. We were going up to that oyster bar on the rue de la Gaîeté to meet a quiet man named Donal Hurley, who was first secretary at the Irish embassy and married to a Frenchwoman. I liked Hurley and found him helpful and unpompous in our few official dealings, particularly after an incident in which staff at the embassy wanted to throw me out on St Patrick's Day for 'writing on the walls'. I was, in fact, only drunkenly taking down a lady's telephone number on the back of an envelope placed at a crooked angle on the wall. Donal Hurley and I discussed the facts and semantics of this incident at some length before I felt in honour able to leave the premises. Sam also had a liking for Hurley's gentle ways.

When *Godot* reached the Odéon, I wrote a short piece for the *Guardian* and with Beckett's agreement told that he had taken over direction when Roger Blin, the first director of *Godot* and creator of Pozzo, had to leave the production to meet another commitment in Switzerland. This was the first time Beckett officially directed; previously he had only been a tense supervising presence for Blin or Donald McWhinnie in England.

Beckett had also just been awarded, jointly with Borges, the Formentor literary prize of $10,000. The *Guardian* heading on the piece was FINAL ACCOLADES FOR BECKETT, which seemed a bit premature considering it was only 1961.

Beckett would discuss technical aspects of his work and give facts about productions but as to the work itself he couldn't explain it. Not perversely or arrogantly wouldn't but 'couldn't' and he used that simple word to me to describe how he was unable to explain. The explanation he arrived at was the work itself, painfully mined from his own psyche, to an extent on our behalf.

My faith in his steely integrity was shaken once when Kenneth Tynan's bare bum happening, *Oh, Calcutta*, opened on Broadway and Beckett (with John Lennon and Tynan) contributed a 120-word skit, *Breath*. I assumed, disappointed, that Sam had succumbed to the general hysteria of wanting to be part of the swinging sixties. I asked him about it one day.

Tynan, he told me, had been pestering him for a piece and finally, 'So as not to be consistently unhelpful,' he had innocently given him

Breath, on the understanding it would be used anonymously and his stage directions honoured. To the direction 'Faint light, a stage littered with miscellaneous rubbish', Tynan had added, 'including naked bodies'. Beckett was appalled; in vainly trying to put some contractural veto on the use of his material he came as close as he ever did to a public row. But he could not bear public squabbles and let it go, considering Tynan to be a detestable opportunist.

Beckett's relationship to his Irishness was complex. We can identify the unnamed suburb in *Watt*; the anonymous landscapes of *Molloy* have a familiar feel, and to my mind Winnie of *Happy Days* was at her most authentic when spoken by the Dublin actress Marie Kean in a slightly anglicized, that is, Killiney, accent. But Beckett would never accept that these were 'Irish' novels and plays. To do so would be to cheapen the work, deny its universality. He must have been warned, too, by Irish writers' narcissism, which in so many cases adulterated ambition and settled for exhibitionist language. He was the man who deliberately changed to French as an exercise in discipline.

The sense of Ireland was nevertheless strong in him; there was a subterranean emotional involvement and he had a weakness for those with a particular Irish desperation and vulnerability. But he despised the ethos of the place.

Many years previously he had, uncharacteristically, appeared as a character witness in a Dublin libel action.

'So you are the author of an essay on Prowst?' the defence counsel said.

'Proust,' Beckett corrected.

'Proost?' counsel said. 'Proost!' he repeated mockingly to the jury, inviting them to have a dekko at the man from Paris with pretensions.

That Beckett had pronounced 'Proust' in the proper, immoral, French way made him suspect in the eyes of the Dublin Catholic jury. People who hobnobbed intellectually with atheistic writers (all French writers were presumed in Dublin to be atheists) were not to be trusted or indulged. The barrister was able to discredit him as a witness, thanks to this little lapse.

Beckett felt humiliated by this experience of triumphant Irish obscurantism. Later, the monthly decisions of the Irish Censorship of Publications Board, whose banned list was supported by a misguided community, could only have nourished his contempt. At times, this list of banned books seemed to aspire to be a definitive directory of all writers, living or dead, Irish or foreign.

Seven

Sylvia Beach was in a state. A stumpy little lady she stretched up in her high-backed chair and thumped the armrests vigorously. 'I won't get out!' she said. 'I will not!' Her eyes – blue, I remember – as alert and quick as a teenager's, darted round the cluttered room looking for someone to glare at. 'What does a man want with five hundred houses?' she asked. 'He can't live in them all.'

'Well, what does he want with them?'

'Speculation! It's happening all over Paris now. They buy up all these old houses where the rents of the apartments are still very low, you are not allowed to increase them, and then they give the tenant a chance to buy his apartment. But at a huge sum! If you haven't the money you get out. I haven't. So it looks as if he will get me out.'

Sylvia Beach's landlord was preparing to sever an unbroken link with Joyce's Paris by ousting her from the building where she and Adrienne Monnier started Shakespeare and Company – the bookshop which turned publisher to produce *Ulysses*. We were in the apartment in the rue de l'Odéon above the old shop, which was now a supplier of medical appliances.

'I have been here since the First World War,' Sylvia Beach said. 'When they interned me during the Second World War, I closed Shakespeare and Company down below and moved up here. I have lived now either in the old bookshop or up here for forty-two years.'

The chilly old apartment was swamped with books. Everywhere you turned there were books: on shelves, under your feet, scattered across the tables, strewn on the floor. There were pictures of Joyce with his eye-patch, a handsome young Hemingway, Eliot, frowning, thin-lipped (he didn't approve of *Ulysses*), Ezra Pound reclining languidly in a chair, Scott Fitzgerald sitting on the doorstep of the bookshop smirking like a self-conscious boy at a stout, stolid Adrienne.

'Is there nothing you can do?'

'What can I do? I never had any money. You don't make money off books – unless you write a best-seller. And how can I make money at my age?'

I gave her a tactfully questioning look.

'You needn't be cautious about asking my age. I'm seventy-four. I think when you have managed to last that long you should be proud of it. I am! There is nothing wrong with me either, except that I am a bit deaf.

'Joyce always said I had great energy,' she said. '"Let's hope Sylvia's energy will never diminish," he would say. And it hasn't.'

It is sometimes hard to know how to react to these celebrated survivors of great times long gone; difficult to know what to think as you struggle to get some kind of an imaginative grip on their once glorious past. But this literary nurse had an animation which gave her territorial rights to the present, even when dwelling so much on the past.

'Joyce was going to take this very flat at one time,' she told me. 'He sent his son to have a look at it. But it wasn't modern enough for him. There is no bathroom, you know.'

Where did she wash? She must have had to go to the public baths on rue Racine, which I used myself sometimes. How little literary associations meant in material terms. An old stove took the April chill out of the room, but the heat faded already at my back; it never reached her draughty hallway.

'He had very high-falutin' ideas, Joyce,' she said.

'I thought he never had any money?'

'He hadn't – not until towards the end when Miss Weaver took care of him. She never wanted it to be known how much she gave him, but I can tell you it was a perfect fortune.'

The absent Joyce infiltrated the conversation and took over, as he would have in life.

'When he came here from Trieste,' she said, 'he had nothing. I helped him a lot. But he was very demanding and spent money like water if he had it. He would come to me and say, "Sylvia, it's my birthday and I have nothing for my guests, would you advance me something?" And, of course, I had to. But he wouldn't just give his guests sandwiches like anyone else. Oh, no, he had to have the caterers in. Every time he travelled with his wife and family he always put up at palaces. He liked the grand style.'

'He was supposed to have a great singing voice?'

'He thought so, anyway,' she said with some asperity. 'You know anyone who took up with Joyce had to take care of all his problems. He was very demanding. He thought that people had nothing else to do but read his books. If you did anything for him, you did everything. I was just like a nurse with a child.' She laughed.

'Sometimes,' she went on, 'I would want to get away for a few days to a little cottage I had in the country, but Joyce would want me to stay and take care of his business. When I would go he would pursue me, bombard me with letters and telegrams. I never saw such a man! He was a perfect octopus!'

'His demands must have alienated people?'

'Ah no! We liked him too much. And he was perfectly charming. Mind you, he was not liked at dinners and things because he had no small talk, but with people he knew he was a delightful man. And, then, he was a great worker. Nothing could put him off, even failing eyesight. He still worked on when he was practically blind.

'I helped him,' Sylvia said, 'because he helped himself. He was never a slacker. If he was,' she put on the air of a severe schoolmistress, 'I would never have helped him. He gave himself to his work and expected you to do the same. *Finnegans Wake!* You could swim around in that! I thought Yeats was pale beside him.'

'Did you not publish anyone else?'

'How could I? I was too busy with Joyce. D. H. Lawrence wanted me to publish *Lady Chatterley's Lover*, but I didn't want to.' One of her reasons was that Lawrence already had people taking care of him; Joyce, she said, had no one.

'In any case,' she confessed. 'I didn't like his work. It was all preaching, preaching. It's nobody's duty to go in for sex if he doesn't want to, is it?'

'I suppose not,' I agreed dubiously, never having thought of sex as a duty.

'They always said,' she went on, 'that Joyce was very nice, the way he would never say a bad word about anyone else's writing. But the truth is they never existed for him. He only read his own work. Of course he had reading he loved, and when, for example, his daughter Lucia was illustrating Chaucer he would read Chaucer. But he never read the new stuff.'

'Didn't you get tired of the demands on you?'

'Towards the thirties I did get a bit tired. He was having all this trouble with pirated editions of *Ulysses* in America and he wanted me to go over, open a bookshop in America and take care of his affairs, try to get *Ulysses* past the Supreme Court. He did not like it when I would not go, but how could I? I was busy with my own work and it costs money to travel.'

'And you never went to Ireland?'

'I never had time when Joyce was alive. But when I had an exhibition of the Twenties in London a couple of years ago I rushed over to have a look. For me Ireland was so much Joyce and Joyce so much Ireland.'

They were about to turn the Martello tower in Sandycove, Dublin, into a Joyce Museum to be opened on Bloomsday – 16 June.

'I was the one who called it Bloomsday,' Sylvia said with pride. 'I didn't invent much but I invented that.

'I think we all should go over,' she said. 'Beckett and Stuart Gilbert and all. But how can I, with this trouble with the apartment?'

Brian Redhead had a way of working himself into a state of scorn about people, particularly practitioners of his own trade. This was an exercise in which relish for combat was more apparent than malice. On one occasion a piece by the literary critic of *The Times* got up his nose because of Brian's conviction (not unjustified) that the entire paper was a superciliously elevated proboscis. The critic had been dismissive of the alleged 'new novelist' Nathalie Sarraute. He reproached her, curiously, for the self-absorption of her characters, the jerkiness of her style, and the fact that she used too many dots (ellipses). He also asserted authoritatively that her writing was heavily influenced by Ivy Compton-Burnett and Henry Green.

Redhead wanted me to get to the bottom of this. Of course, if I had looked closer I would have realized that this was nothing more than sniping between a couple of Oxbridge men. But I never thought of Brian as Oxbridge, which does him credit. In any event, I was to be his sniper, carrying out a skirmish into 'new novelist' territory.

Following the readiness with which a couple of years previously public and critics had accepted the label 'new wave' for any film distributed after 1959, all French novelists, especially those the English had only just heard of, were labelled 'new' novelists. Instead of being used to identify new independent film-makers or writers in the usual muddled way, the term became synonymous with a particular style of writing or film-making. If there was manifestly no resemblance between the work of Alain Resnais and François Truffaut (of the very first Cannes 'wave') and less with Godard (of the second 'wave'), the grouping of novelists was even more absurd.

With the translation in 1962 of *The Planetarium*, Sarraute, then aged sixty, was universally presented as the leading 'new novelist'. But she had been writing since 1933. She was corralled with Alain Robbe-Grillet (forty) and Michel Butor (thirty-six). Sometimes Marguerite Duras (forty-eight) was also tossed into this grouping. But the French also could have daft expectations: Robbe-Grillet, one of the more suave exponents of the *nouveau roman*, was once involved in a aeroplane accident. Still shaken by his narrow escape, he described his experience to reporters in a banal narrative. 'Mais c'est du Balzac!' protested his scandalized admirers when they read the reports in the papers and his stock fell.

Such stereotyping appeals to lazy critics. It can also be a selling device of the publisher, although it happened not to be in this instance: most of the 'new novelists' were published by Jerome Lindon, Beckett's publisher, a man of almost comic fastidiousness in marketing.

Lindon had told me that he would be hard put to know what a 'new novel' was supposed to be; and he added with some irritation that more articles had been written about Robbe-Grillet because of this label than copies of his books sold. Labelling, therefore, does not necessarily bring commercial advantage to a publisher; it is more a handy peg for newspaper writers.

Sarraute did not favour the Left Bank; she lived in an apartment on the boulevard Malesherbes in the ponderously bourgeois 17th *arrondissement*. She glided into the shadowy salon, plump, vigilant but with a suggestion of mischief in her eyes when she responded to questions. I had the feeling that she attempted to establish an impression of both physical and emotional distance, as if she had decided this was the proper artist/intellectual stance – initially at least. Her friends said she was full of fun.

I thought I detected in her expression, as she listened to me, a curious quality of beseeching. There was no immediate context for it, but every now and then the expression would be there, so much so that at times I felt like asking, 'What is it? What do you want?'

Was she beseeching me to be kind to her in print? Was she appealing to me in advance not to reveal some intimacy, some weakness I did not know about in the first place? Or was this an indecipherable example of what she described in her writing as 'the inward action, the inward drama'?

I got down to business with Nathalie Sarraute. What about the English critics? Were they wrong in claiming she was influenced by Ivy Compton-Burnett and Henry Green?

'The critics who speak of an influence have certainly not read my books,' she said. 'They have seen that I wrote about Ivy Compton-Burnett in an essay "L'Ere du soupçon", published in 1955, the time when I first read her books. I admire her greatly, but her work has nothing to do with mine. Her method is exactly the opposite of mine.'

'And what about the comparisons with Henry Green?'

'That is even more astonishing,' she said. 'I mentioned Henry Green in a *couple of lines* in the same essay. He had said that the reason why there was a lot more dialogue in novels was that people use the telephone a lot nowadays. I found that amusing, but I don't really think the telephone is the reason. I wrote those few lines about him and now the critics say I was influenced by him.'

Was it true she was only interested in the texture of objects – curtains, carpets, interior decoration?

'Not at all,' she said. 'I am concerned only with the inner life which is going on every moment in each one of us. That is what I try to show: the inward action, the inward drama.'

I could well believe that. She was a chamber-music writer, and indeed, she spoke as if people's reactions to each other were a kind of musical duet: 'I try to record', she said, 'those extremely quick movements which pass through our minds or are on the border of our consciousness. At the time we don't actually think them, but we feel them. I try to capture the inner movements which form the texture of our real, authentic life.'

'Is it fair to say your style is "jerky"?'

By this stage Madame Sarraute must have begun to wonder just what kind of a story I was after. She gave me a rather prolonged appraising glance and then apparently decided she might as well continue to submit.

'When the inner action is fast and dramatic the style can be jerky, at other times it is not,' she responded. 'It depends which is appropriate. The style has the task of making the reader feel the movements. It is slow when they are slow, jerky when they are jerky. In any case I do not care for what is called *le joli style*.

'Of course we cannot write completely free of influence,' she continued. 'One does not develop out of nothing. The novel was revolutionized at the beginning of this century by Proust, Joyce, Virginia Woolf, Kafka. Then the ways opened by these writers were abandoned. I am interested – as are some other modern writers – in taking the development up again. We are trying to go if only a few steps further *each in his own direction*.

'I am working on a book which I hope to finish soon. I am trying to go a little further than before – so it will certainly meet with even less understanding than *The Planetarium*. But the important thing is to feel that one does what best one can with the utmost sincerity to express what one feels is real. As for the rest – I have been used for twenty years and more to find the same opposition and the same lack of comprehension.'

'Practically all the critics complained about your dots. But then in English printing the dots are placed further apart, which makes them more obvious, and perhaps more irritating?'

'That could be it. I use those *points de suspension* to give the impression of constantly bubbling, boiling, half-conscious inner activity. I think it works. In any case, the reader could quite easily become used to dots if he happened to have a little more experience of them.'

I had a feeling we might have just resolved the literary dispute of the year.

I never saw Nathalie Sarraute again: she was just another literary ghost who made a single apparition.

Few cities lend themselves so effortlessly to popular expectations as Paris; Paris can deliver what the tourists want without taking on the character of a theme park, and with its dignity unimpaired. But the Parisians are a bloody-minded lot, most of them only tangentially acquainted with the cultural tradition of which they are so boastfully possessive. Still, it was possible to survive with ease, thanks to the accommodating social system which permitted foreigners to live entirely separate and unmolested lives (unless they were North African).

I had by now moved from Beaubourg to a hotel on the rue Dauphine. My room was on the fourth floor, at the back looking across the roofs to the spire of St-Chapelle. The contact with Monsieur and Madame Lapineau disintegrated for ever.

My room had a bed, wardrobe and wash (or peeing) basin – and that was it. But it was far superior in terms of privacy and comfort to the maudlin little bedsitters with gas fires to be found at home. The room got a quick clean every day; sheets changed once a week and that was the limit to intrusion on your privacy. In Dublin you would have been looked on as peculiar if you stayed in your room in the afternoon; in Paris your hotel room was your salon; every cheap restaurant your dining room. On the Left Bank there were scores of restaurants where you could get a three-course meal with wine for about eight shillings, which was cheaper than you could cook.

Our kind of hotel did not provide meals, and cooking was banned in the rooms because of fire hazard. The residents all ignored the ban and had little alcohol burners on tiny stands like a Sacred Heart lamp with bandy legs. On this precarious perch I made meals – fried eggs, or sausages, or sometimes just potatoes with butter and salt of a deliciousness that only the famished palate can know.

At the sound of the concierge's step I'd fling the contraption into the wardrobe, wrench open the high windows and flap a towel madly around the room to get rid of the cloying sweetish smell of cooking-alcohol.

There was also a makeshift take-away nearby. In a niche just about where the tip of rue Dauphine converged on rue Mazarine a consumptive old man had planted a huge metal vat. Here he boiled potatoes and frankfurters. I had only to step out of my hotel and have a hot meal in two minutes.

The alcohol had another use. The French turn off their central heating in May and refuse to put it back on until October. We had snow one May. Ready for bed I would pour some alcohol on to the stone slab under the sink, set a match to it and, as the heat whooshed through the icy room, leap into bed. I was surprised there were so many hotels still standing after that unseasonable month, since the entire Left Bank was up to the same trick.

I was now within a few steps of the Monaco and three or four minutes of Chez Maurice, Eliane's and the Tournon, our habitual meeting places. This was very handy for a life of inoffensive dissipation. I remember being very understanding of a trait in myself which others might have described as idleness. I told myself that after an adolescence in the cauldron of an Irish-Catholic environment I was entitled to a period of recuperation.

I alternated between semi-destitution and not uncomfortable penury. I lived on a system of relocation of debt which should have earned me the admiration of bankers. It was useless to have anything to do with banks in Paris. There was no such thing as overdrawing in France. Sign a cheque *sans* provision and next day the men from the Château d'If would be calling on you. I never even heard of a bridging loan until 1970 when I came to London. (I then immediately rushed to a bank in Islington and asked for one. 'What', demanded the astute actuary, 'is on the other side of the bridge?' – showing me the door.)

Eight

I wrote short stories with faltering regularity, giving full super-stitious observance to Sundays as days of rest and to Saturdays as days of active preparation for idle Sundays. From time to time the *New Yorker* or *Atlantic Monthly* bailed me out with colossal cheques. In the case of the *New Yorker* I hit the mythical jackpot of $1,000. But this was rare.

I had a counterpart in penury: Dave Seccombe, a painter, who like most of the Americans in the Quarter was living on a GI Bill. This was for veterans of the Korean War. Dave was a gentle man from New Haven, Connecticut, who came to Paris to paint. Like most of the ex-GIs I met, he had never been near Korea and deferred taking up the bourse until he was ready to come to France. They were all obliged to do the Cours de Civilisation Française at the Sorbonne, to justify this educational bourse.

Every month they went down to the St Paul region to change their $110 cheques on the black market and then proceeded with loan distribution.

Dave's problem was the cost of canvas and paint (and possibly me borrowing from him). Fortunately he was at ease with frugality. His father had been a sculptor of tombstones which somehow suggested an unworldly home atmosphere. He had chosen a grimy hotel on the rue Guirsade, on the other side of the boulevard St-Germain. His room was even cheaper than mine and it looked as if it had been transferred from the Bowery. The building was a collapsing hulk with the top floor pulled down like a cap over its forehead. The front door lay open to a sweaty, dark hall; at the bottom of the staircase was a glass-panelled door with a tattered lace curtain, behind which a hound would yelp viciously every time you entered the building, and the concierge would peer through a rent in the curtain. He was even more belligerent than the dog; begrimed as the building, his expression was one of vaudeville villainy. He responded to the most civil enquiry with growing surliness.

Dave claimed the concierge spent his time going over the floor of his apartment with a Geiger counter, prospecting for treasure. I thought this a bit far-fetched until one day I had to peep into the concierge's apartment when leaving a note for Dave. I opened the door a fraction and there found this singular porter at work with his strange device.

Dave's was a back room, low-ceilinged with tainted walls and, like all the buildings in that clutter of streets around the rue des Canettes, offered only a view of the tops and sharp shoulder-blades of the other hotels and *ateliers*. If you expected to meet anyone out there on those roofs it would have to be the Hunchback of Notre Dame.

I often chided Dave for staying in a place so inappropriate for a painter, especially for someone of his brand of sunny abstractions. He argued that it was one of the few hotels which allowed a painter to ply his messy trade in his own bedroom. He could not afford a studio. Dave was living proof that painting, like sex, is all in the head.

I had already got one of the greatest perks that journalism had ever provided – and probably will ever provide. I had a film critic's green card. This meant that I could get into any cinema, art or Champs-Élysées, free at any time – even just to shelter from the rain. I did not even have to queue. Respect for the cinema was axiomatic in Paris; even the most ill-tempered cashiers on the Champs-Élysées honoured the card, although they would occasionally baulk at giving a second free ticket if you were with a male friend and not a wife or *amourette*. You got the card simply by sending half a dozen cuttings on cinema matters every year to Monsieur Pravard at the Quai Voltaire. (Even *film* press cards were issued by the police.)

My youthful taste for 'the pictures' developed another gratifying aspect. Mostly when one turns reluctantly to improving one's mind it is accepted that one is embarking on a doleful, effortful exercise. But a study of *Cahiers de Cinéma* revealed that the essential requirement of a film scholar in the sixties was that he knew all American gangster films, westerns and musicals. My childhood had been spent watching these; indeed, our censorship meant that virtually nothing else was available in Dublin. Without knowing it I had been a child scholar.

I gingerly moved up the social scale, half a rung at a time. My Finnish girlfriend began to come back during university holidays, Easter and long summer, so we had to find a slightly roomier abode. I moved to the Hôtel Princesse off the rue du Four. Although it backed into Dave's Stygian street, it was classier by a perceptible margin of comfort than the one in the rue Dauphine. All the cafés and conveniences central to my life lay within two or three minutes' walk: the Mabillon market was almost alongside, and behind it our favourite eating place Au Petit Vatel. We called it The Kitchen. On the rue Lobineau, it consisted of a long kitchen table seating no more than ten, chest-close to the ovens and gas rings where Monsieur Vatel, as we called him, whipped up ungristly *hachis parmentier*, golden *pommes dauphine*, honest skinny *entrecôtes* and creamy Mont Blanc desserts for sums the Salvation Army would have found hard to match. He, of course, had few overheads and his family – a stout wife, much shouted at but diplomatically deaf, and two daughters – provided the service for regulars who had to queue on the pavement for a place. It is no sentimental myth but attested to by dozens of friends over the years that Monsieur Vatel was not only not presumptuous in borrowing the name of Fouquet's celebrated seventeenth-century chef, he may have been paying him a retrospective compliment. I once brought *Time* magazine's Working Royalty in Europe correspondent, George Abel, to Au Petit Vatel and even a palate jaded with monarchical freebies was astounded by the delights of Monsieur Vatel II.

I made the honest miscalculation of once taking out Monsieur Vatel's daughter. Off-duty, she was a serious, rather determined young Catholic girl studying her way to a good bourgeois future who made an unfavourable but touchingly candid assessment of my chances of fitting into her correct and stable future as we walked out in the sun by Notre Dame – another hint – one Sunday afternoon.

After that most of the family conspired to ease the discomfort of a rejected swain when I went back to being an ordinary customer. It says much for the cooking that I was willing to go back and face the compassionate mother, intrigued sister and amused father rather than miss my *pommes dauphine*.

For a while an area of hardly more than one square mile supplied all the emotional, intellectual and erotic needs of my life – with a bit of scampering out of the safety zone on journalistic expeditions.

In Maurice's café I was taken through *Howard's End* paragraph by paragraph by a Texan of formidable scholarly capacity and decidedly unTexan physique, John Balph. Others might have thought him weird, and it was true that being a friend of the Beats, Gregory Corso and Allen Ginsberg, when they were in town he was quite frequently stoned not so much out of his mind as embedded in a catatonic appreciation of the artistic and intellectual splendours which, for that moment, preoccupied him. If our private tutorials were interrupted, say, by the eruption of a bunch of sybarites – Doug Light, a GI Bill student, and Stig Claesson (later one of Sweden's leading illustrators) on a drinking gallop, clamouring to play 'Le Déserteur', Balph would withdraw into a tolerant silence. Four hours later, peace restored, he would take up *Howard's End* at precisely the line at which we had left off.

I owe to him another introduction which marked my thinking. Thrusting a copy of the *Partisan Review* into my hands one day at Chez Maurice he ordered me to read Baldwin's *Sonny's Blues*. This snapped me out of my lingering *Uncle Tom's Cabin* perspective of 'Negroes'.

(I met Baldwin a few years later and tried to interview him. He had agreed to see me but obviously changed his mind when I arrived. He paced around the bar of his hotel by St-Michel restless and reluctant, curiously resentful, even. I had the impression he was trying to make me feel too much of a White Man. With a logic which is clear to me still, but difficult to explain, I could not go along with that. I always managed to enlighten people who tried to label me an

Englishman, but to try to convince someone I was not really a White Man was a more difficult trick, which I flunked. I left early knowing the bugger just didn't like me.)

Howard Kanovitz had earlier drifted into our group one day when John and Dave and I got a house in Deya, Mallorca, one summer. In the first year Spain was eminently accessible on my half-pay holiday money from Vincennes so we followed the Quarter's escape route, which was to Mallorca or Ibiza in the summer. There we did the usual things: swam and drank and tried Spanish girls, who didn't, and English girls, who did. Howie had not yet made up his mind to be a painter (shortly after he became a founder member of the new photo-realist New York school). He had been to art school with Dave and by accident came across him sitting on the step of our house in Deya. (We would bid Robert Graves good morning but never fitted in with his set.)

Back in Paris Howie featured more as a jazz trumpeter than a painter, sitting in on sessions at the Chaméleon and blowing smoke with John Balph in mutual admiration pot sessions. They hospitably tried to teach me, but I couldn't inhale; being a loyal whiskey man (when I could afford it) I mistrusted drugs. That was one reason I didn't hang around with the Beats. Burroughs made me think of dry rot and I had no wish to fathom him; Ginsberg, with considerable urgings from Balph, was civil but distant. Corso was the only one I could respond to naturally. He reminded me of a Dublin street kid.

By another tide, new characters would appear who would then form part of the pattern of life-long international friendships which is the great bonus of living in a foreign city for a time. They may all go their separate ways after a while, but a network of friends is created and endures, making yet more countries accessible by their hospitality.

Nine

It was coming up to Christmas and I had to bestir myself and produce some decent features. I now had real headquarters. I had found a two-roomed, bathroomless apartment over a shop on the rue d'Odessa by the old Gare Montparnasse. The station has been moved back to the avenue de Maine now, and a mighty tower planted in its place, but then it was a modest old provincial building like a railway station transplanted from the sticks by mistake. It faced down rue de Rennes; diagonally across was Rougeot's where the waiters, all middle-aged men, were dressed in black waistcoats and long white aprons, as they must have been at the *fin de siècle*.

I spent the first hour in my new home feeling wonderfully free and private; it had been a long time since I could step out of my bedroom and still be in my own home. There was an ingrained fatigue in living in hotel rooms, I realized, as there is in living in someone else's house. I did not mind that the hole-in-the-ground lavatory was out on the landing, although in winter the saw-toothed winds pinched your bum. I had my tiny kitchen, a draughty minuscule foyer, my sitting-room-office and a connecting bedroom with an immense, it seemed to me, double bed. For years I had had to do my erotic wrestling on single beds; a double bed seemed almost a perversity. There was no shower, of course, but the public baths did weekly service for that, while on ordinary days you washed, as the man said, down as far as possible and up as far as possible and then dealt with possible as best you could.

I lolled in the great bed, the flat illuminated by the street lamps, and listened with tolerance to the hubbub outside. I was now a proper resident of Paris, indeed a Montparnassian. This was the backside of Montparnasse, the glamorous boulevard was on the other side of my block. At the top of the street the prostitutes loitered or strolled down the rue Delambre to hang around the flank of the Dôme.

I liked the genuineness of my street: no tourists; no St-Germain Jean-Claudes or Marie-Yvonnes; no ritzy shops, just the mix of small hotels, family apartments and little stores you would find in any modest Parisian quarter.

One winter's morning I was jolted out of my sleep by a thumping on my door. The flat was freezing. I pulled on my trousers over my pyjamas and dragged on a rollneck sweater.

It was a salesman peddling cheap jewellery. His breath blew frostily over his wares reminding me of why they were known as 'ice'. I shuddered and shut the door. I stood in a stupor wondering what to do. A quick infusion of hot coffee in my local café seemed like the only solution now that, after a fashion, I was dressed. I put on a raincoat and went out.

Sitting in the café's glassed terrace I realized I had better organize some work. I remembered reading in Carmen Tessier's gushing column in *France-Soir* that Salvador Dali was in town, at the Hôtel Meurice on the rue de Rivoli. I could try to start in motion the laborious machinery for setting up an interview with this elusive creature and then go back to bed with a spurious sense of achievement. I had had a beery night and was not really in a state to be functioning in society.

I went down to the public phone by the lavatories – I didn't have a phone in my new flat. Other journalists would have considered this a drawback and I didn't mention it to my British colleagues in case it was too much for them to cope with. (The *Guardian* didn't catch on for months.)

I braced myself to shout my way past the snooty receptionist at the Meurice and then come up against resistance from Dali's probably supercilious secretary, but the hotel put me straight through. Dali himself answered the phone. It was a sorrowful, hoarse voice, which suggested that he might be having the same trouble in coming to terms with a frosty morning as I was.

'Come over now,' he said in a cobwebby tone and hung up.

In my pyjamas? I didn't even have a notebook. But my raincoat pocket was stuffed with a handout from Unifrance Film. They obligingly sent me copious bumph printed on lovely glossy paper, white on the back. I used it for writing short stories or for the first version of my *Guardian* pieces. I had little time for companies whose publicity material was printed on both sides. I also had a pen and a couple of Métro tickets. It seemed like adequate equipment. I felt that if I went back to my flat to do something unessential (like change out of my pyjamas) some subtle alteration would take place and destiny would sabotage this opportunity. With the delay Dali might have time to mull over his impulsive willingness to see a complete stranger. Or his secretary might come to work and erase me from his dancing card. I went straight down into the Métro at Montparnasse and headed for Châtelet, changed, and three stops to the west I was at Tuileries, on the steps of the Meurice.

Sitting in the clattering Métro I had worked myself into an agitated state. After all, Dali was not one of your usual bland, ingratiating celebrities; he was a nut, and probably a desperate one. He smashed the plate-glass windows of galleries. Photographs depicted him as suave as Basil Rathbone, flamboyant as a popinjay, a man of imperturbable vanity. His horned moustaches were an outward manifestation of irredeemable arrogance; he had been going around town telling people he was a genius; and he was as rich as a Rothschild, which would make him untameable. He took liberties with people and almost certainly had a hatred of bourgeois journalist scavengers. I grew hot at the liberties he might attempt to take with me. I would smack him in the mouth if he did. Or maybe it would be more effective to flash my pyjamas at him like a police badge? Maybe he would be in a really wild mood, souped-up on Spanish cognac, swinging from the chandeliers and slashing at me with swordstick.

When I came through the swing doors of the Meurice a workman in blue overalls was standing by the reception desk holding a long ladder against his ear; to my left a pale young priest was sitting on a divan, head bent, penitentially stroking his soutane. They were not more peculiarly attired than I, I thought, comforted and at least my fancy dress was invisible. Indeed, the foyer was filling up with characters out of a musical comedy: bankers in frock coats and elderly ladies who had, by all appearances, stripped the wallpaper off their bedrooms and wrapped themselves in it. I mounted the broad staircase expecting the music to strike up an operetta overture.

I tapped on Dali's door. Would his secretary only speak Spanish? I shaped my lips for basic Spanish phrases.

Dali opened the door and backed timidly into a huge, faded salon overlooking the Tuileries gardens.

He had shrunk since the latest picture I had seen of him. His face was drawn down in deep lines and his complexion was sleep-encrusted grey; his unwaxed moustache ends drooped pathetically like two threads. His black hair was bunched up and sticking out at the back and his dark blue suit was crumpled as if he had been sleeping in it.

We faced each other like a pair of amateurs not knowing how to begin the interview.

He placed himself on the edge of a dainty chair; his eyes were damp and seemed to plead for tolerance.

The moment I sat down on a *chaise-longue* he hopped up as if I had sat on a release button. He stepped a couple of paces back and then hastened towards a large overmantel mirror. Peering at himself he began to flatten down the tuft at the back of his head.

'I am sorry,' he said in a voice without energy. 'I have been slipping. No, no,' he protested at my apologetic gesture. 'You wake me at the ride mo-ment.'

'You were signing your book *Dali de Gala* at a St-Germain bookshop,' I began. (Gala was his wife.) Quite unintentionally, my tone was that of an interrogating policeman.

He admitted it, apparently anxious to be forgiven. 'I am going to New York where I will have an exhibition of fidee? – fifdeen? Feeftee? – new paintings,' he said.

His English was halting and made him miserable. I felt very masterful having him there, unprotected by secretaries, wrestling with a foreign language. But I began also to feel compassion for him. How awful to have continually to perform like an actor for the press, when you have no real talent for acting, as seemed to be the case with him. The press must set it all up, I guessed. They would photograph him making violent, bombastic gestures but report nothing of his droopy indecision. There was no force in this rumpled man; he looked like the kind who is easily bullied, his only escape to go to the nursery and play with his paints. But he was very good at that.

'I thought you would be a violent man,' I said.

'No, no! I am gentle.'

I wanted to make things easier for him so I let him change to French which he spoke fluently with a kind of self-conscious Catalan *élan*. But now he had trouble understanding my accent: 'Comment?' he'd say. And: 'Vous dîtes?'

That irritated me. It seemed like cheek from a man who had just been kneading the English language out of shape. I frowned at him and he made a better attempt to pay attention.

'Do the English papers say I am violent?' he asked wistfully.

'Well, some of the more sensational ones may,' I said tactfully.

'Many years ago I did violent things. I smashed the window of a gallery because they had interfered with my work. But not lately. The press always speaks of these things.'

'You had a row with Béjart. You wanted a real quarter of bleeding beef hanging on the set of his ballet.'

'His beef was cardboard,' Dali pointed out reasonably.

There was a silence.

'I am a genius,' he suddenly told me, and watched me for a response.

What does it feel like? I wanted to ask. But instead I said: 'What are you a genius at? Painting?'

He considered this, in a perplexed way for a moment, and then said, 'That is part of it but it is more my creative intuition.'

'You have a superior insight? A greater understanding?'

'I am very receptive,' he said. He took a crumpled magazine featuring his work from the table. He pointed to a reproduction of one of his works with, in the corner, something spiralling off into the air.

'There,' he said. 'I painted the molecular structure of deoxyribo-nucleic acid years ago and now four scientists have won the Nobel Prize for discovering it.'

I had heard about the double helix. We both looked at the picture without much excitement. I didn't know what to look for and he didn't seem very convinced of the truth of his own statement. After a few moments he put away the magazine.

There was another aimless silence. I wondered if it would bring us closer if I told him I was still wearing my pyjamas. He might be intrigued, ask to see them, on impulse do some doodles (of a double helix?) on the arms and legs and then insouciantly let me wear these sketches home. What would they be worth? At least $250,000.

That was the kind of impulse that could change your whole life.

'You'd be surprised,' I began cautiously, 'the strange things people do . . .'

He agreed listlessly. His indifference cooled me down.

I reverted to a formal manner. 'Do you feel you have anything in common with other painters?' I demanded. I was feeling a bit miffed, as if he had actually turned down a request to draw on my pyjamas.

'Only with old masters,' he said. 'Raphael, Vermeer, Velazquez.'

'Personally do you feel you have more in common with people in your own profession or people in other professions? Actors, perhaps?' There was a small note of reproach in my voice.

'No. Not painters, not actors. I feel closer to mystics, philosophers, theologians.'

'Not with the Beat Generation mystics?'

'No. I live a very classical life. I don't take drugs. I don't smoke or drink.'

He became anxious at the realization that he had not been a good host. 'Would you like a drink?' He stretched back to put his finger on a wall bell. 'It would be very easy.'

'No thank you,' I said piously.

He stood and took up his walking stick.

From a seated position I said reproachfully, 'You want me to go?'

'No, no,' Dali said and, putting away his stick, sat down in a posture of close attention.

'How old are you?' I asked.

'Fifty-seven? Fifty-eight? I am not sure. My papers disappeared in the revolution.'

'Before I was born,' he volunteered, 'my brother died. So when I was born my parents gave me the name of my dead brother, Salvador. All my childhood I lived with the terror that I was my own brother and had really died. I began to do all kinds of extravagant things to draw attention to myself, to prove I was myself. To prove I was not my dead brother.'

I had heard weirder things in the Monaco café at Odéon many a night.

'Do you think the exaggerated publicity you invite is good for you as an artist?' I was being censorious again.

'I do,' Dali confessed. 'When I was young, to reassure myself I played at being a genius. I cultivated a legend. Then the press took it up and after a time I began to be convinced I *was* a genius. Now I am convinced.' He put on an air of great simplicity. 'The press has turned a legend into reality.'

'Do you not feel that telling people you are a genius intimidates them and makes it difficult to have genuine contact?'

'Perhaps with some,' he said. 'There are always handicaps.'

The interview seemed to have run its course. We stood up and said goodbye. I wondered what was the point of this encounter; perhaps he was wondering why he had agreed to see me.

Out in the corridor I thought of scribbling a note, 'Monsieur Dali, during this interview I was wearing my woollen pyjamas', and slipping it under the door. But I didn't. I decided it was better not to try to compete with surrealists.

I met the playwright Eugene Ionesco and drank champagne with him in my first month in Paris without knowing who he was. I was wandering down the rue St-André-des-Arts when I saw people standing in that narrow street outside an art gallery, sipping from champagne glasses. Through the plate glass window I could see young women merrily urging champagne on the small mob inside. I noted no coin was changing hands.

This was more like the Paris I had dreamed of so I sidled in. As a defensive strategy I put on an expression of happy curiosity ready to go into a foreigner-with-no-French routine at any unmannerly challenge. I edged through the spaces between the groups until I found myself deep in the gallery but up against a cul-de-sac of backs. This was not too good. No one had offered me a glass, which would have given me temporary membership of this modish tribe, and I could think of nothing to say that would win me an introduction to the inhospitable shoulders on either side of me. The only opening that occurred to me was, 'Where's the lavatory?' but that did not seem very promising, since they might become uncomfortable if I still loitered without satisfying my apparent need. Even if I did hang around, the obligatory subject of conversation would be the work on display. I had no notion what I could say about the work only glimpsed in fragments over the assembled heads – although I could have given a dissertation on French hairstyles, of which I was making an uncomfortable study.

While I was wondering how to get out of this situation with honour I noticed a little balding man with a wrinkly face staring at me. Obviously the store manager about to demand my credentials, I thought. But as he approached through the crowd his expression was one of hospitable interest and his first words were reassuring.

'You do not have a drink!' he said, with compassion, in French. I instantly recognized a man who treasured his drink. Encouraged by his amiable mien I decided that truth would serve me as well as anything.

'What is this?' I asked in primitive French. 'Why are they giving out free drinks?'

'You don't know what this is!' Ionesco, for it was he, said. His eyes slowly opened very wide, like a man receiving unexpectedly excellent news. 'You don't know the painter?'

'No,' I confessed.

'It is a *vernissage*,' he told me gently.

I had never heard the expression, but it sounded nice. A private feast for the varnishing, in theory, of paintings before a public exhibition, Ionesco explained.

'Private! I must go then,' I exclaimed insincerely.

'Above all not!' he cried. It was clear he had found a rare specimen at a Paris opening: someone who had never heard of a *vernissage*.

'Come, young lady!' he called, in an old-fashioned manner to a physically gifted creature going past with a tray. 'This young man requires nourishment.'

I noticed the group Ionesco had been with eyeing us with a touch of cynicism. For them, Eugene had just discovered a new drinking partner.

But now that I had my drink and a legitimate companion I paid no attention to them and set about getting acquainted. At least he got acquainted with me. He learned with pleasure that I was from Ireland; it would have been less satisfying if I were only English or American. I tried to be helpful by supplying as many exotic touches as possible, such as that I was educated by the Christian Brothers and my parents had been revolutionaries (only true on one side of my family). I played if not the crude stage Irishman, the stage Irishman who had gone to finishing school. I amazed him with the information that on St Patrick's Day all the pubs closed; you could only get a drink at the sedate dog show or at Amiens Street station platform (the line serving Northern Ireland). He guessed immediately that the platform was crowded all day, while empty trains came and went. (I wondered later if I might have supplied him with a plot for another absurd play.)

He offered a sketchy account of his own national past and occupation. Although he told me he wrote plays, the fact that he was a foreigner, Romanian, and looked too crumpled to be prosperous, made me assume he was just another Parisian layabout who had squandered his youth (he was then forty-seven). This idea was reinforced by the amused tolerance with which his prosperous friends treated him. He was already happily squiffy. I forget what else we babbled about. But at the third glass of champagne I had the onset of one of those tiresome atavistic attacks of decency which descends on one like a shroud. I decided I must not carry the free-loading too far. I left him, disappointed, I like to think, with nods and wreathed smiles.

Months later a French friend pointed out a minute figure scrambling across the traffic on the boulevard St-Michel and told me with amusement that he was chief of the avant-garde in Paris; his plays, *La Cantatrice Chauve* and *La Leçon* had been running for years in the Théâtre de la Huchette round the corner.

'But it's the little man who got me the free champagne!' I told him. I felt deceived: the Romanian piss-artist was famous and not a layabout at all.

When much later I heard he was having a shot at film-making I decided he might be worth a piece. I went out to the Joinville studios and found him in a shabby overcoat hanging about the set of a dining room. He had contributed a sketch for an omnibus film entitled *The Seven Deadly Sins*. His sketch, illustrating Anger, told of a domestic row that begins at dinner over a fly in the soup (Ionesco borrowing from hoary old material again), spreads from household to household and proceeds to the explosion of the planet.

He did not recognize me and somehow I did not feel inclined to remind him of our first merry encounter. He had been expecting me but he was at first restless and reluctant to talk. I had to circle round him for a while to get him to sit down and pay attention.

Ionesco's initial wariness might have had something to do with the fact that on his first film venture he was up against impressive competition. Jean-Luc Godard was doing Sloth; Claude Chabrol, Covetousness. Chabrol was a princeling of the 'new wave' cinema; Godard a kind of tyrant king already. It was not that Ionesco was intimidated by their talent – he described Godard's and Chabrol's work to me as a bad mixture of Italian neo-realism and Hitchcock. Only Resnais, whose Marienbad marionettes in a sculptured garden had just been released to the public, met with his approval. One could imagine the characters of *Last Year at Marienbad* as upper-crust Ionesco characters, just as wackily uncommunicative.

We finally settled at a rather exposed table in the unreality of a half-dismantled film set. There is something melancholic about a film set when work is in abeyance; the threadbareness of the make-believe is all too evident.

I asked Ionesco if he spoke English, hoping to give myself an advantage – I did not remember speaking any with him at the gallery.

'Not really,' he replied in French. 'I read it. But when I am in England I can manage. I can say: "A Scotch whisky."' He thought for a moment. 'A double Scotch,' he corrected himself.

Ionesco already looked like a humorous gnome; his wrinkled rubbery face continually creased into mischievous expressions. He articulated like a little boy sucking wine gums, rounding his lips and savouring every syllable. Conversation was like a duel to him; a matter of cajoling, scoring points, entrapping his opponent. After a particularly ingenious riposte he would fall silent, smiling, as if awaiting applause. But behind all the waggishness I sensed a subterranean gloom.

Did working for the cimema require a completely new approach for him? I began formally.

'Oh no,' he replied. 'My theatre is visual, rhythmic. The cinema is a good medium for it. It all depends on whether I can get across what I want without interference.'

There was little danger he would not get his way. For one thing he had chosen his own director, a theatre producer Sylvain Dhomme, the man who had first produced *The Chairs*. But also the traditional obstacles to film-making had been demolished by the *nouvelle vague*. The mystique of expertise gone, the inexperienced were no longer excluded. Art films were no longer supplicants for space in commercial exhibitors' strategies; they now had access to at least modest distribution, on the growing art cinemas network.

(*The Seven Deadly Sins* omnibus film turned out to be mediocre and Ionesco's contribution a naïve exercise in apocalyptic cinema. It was the kind of conceit – essentially a skimpy sketch – which you could probably get away with in a Left Bank theatre; a playful morsel with a fill-it-in-yourself resonance. But the camera looks coldly on intellectual metaphors; they come across hollowly on the screen. Rhythmic and visual Ionesco's work might have been on stage, presented in piquant tableaux, but it was not effective in the cinema.)

Ionesco had complained of theatre directors who '"enrich" the text in weighing it down with fake jewellery, with cheap rubbish without value because useless'. He now chose to direct his fire at a specific individual, Roger Planchon. Planchon was a young stage producer who had recently won national status for the Lyon Villeurbanne company with imaginative productions of Brecht, Hasek (*Schweik*), Molière and a particularly effervescent *Three Musketeers*. The periodic visits of his company to Paris packed the enormous Palais de Chaillot, home of Jean Vilar's Théâtre National Populaire. Compared to the torpid affectations of the boulevard theatres or the products of that catacomb of French theatre the Comédie Française, it was exhilarating.

But Planchon took liberties with Ionesco's text. In his attack on Planchon, Ionesco was firing shots across the bows of any producer who might consider meddling with his work. 'Planchon', he began in a gentle voice, 'is an upstart. A joker. To suit his purpose he thinks he can deform the work of dramatists, people with much more talent than himself. He has been given too much praise and now takes too many liberties. In fact, he represents the new conformity of the Left.'

Ionesco was one of the few creative talents in France who was right-wing, partly a reaction against the environment of his native Romania, I imagine.

'Planchon is the worst,' he told me. 'He has a sense of fantasy, but his sense of self-criticism is non-existent. The critics have made a great mistake in giving a preponderant place to Planchon.'

'Who would you consider to be a reliable critic in France?' I asked.

'Myself,' he said. 'When I write criticism.'

He looked highly amused.

But he spoke warmly of Roger Blin, the original producer of *Waiting for Godot*. 'I consider him the best stage director in France today,' he said.

That was a widely shared opinion but his admiration must have been fortified by Blin's championship of his own work. When *The Chairs* had been first staged, eight years previously, Blin and the avant-garde playwright Arthur Adamov physically obliged the critic

102

of *Le Monde*, Robert Kemp, to applaud. Kemp had been snoozing during the play, waking up from time to time to ask his wife, 'Is there still nothing happening?'

Ionesco's arrival in the theatre had a bad beginning. For weeks, he related, they played to an audience of one, his wife. 'Then one night,' he said, 'my wife had toothache and we played to no one.' Eventually Raymond Queneau came to his rescue defending *La Cantatrice Chauve* publicly; later Jean Paulhan and Jean Anouilh joined in.

Ionesco willingly named a producer he considered more talented than Planchon: it was Nicolas Bataille, the man who had first put on *La Cantatrice Chauve*. But he did not want to discuss any other French dramatists – except later Beckett. He had two notable rivals in the avant-garde, Adamov and Arrabal. Arrabal I never met, but Adamov, then fifty-three, lived round the corner from me in a hotel room on the rue de Seine. He was always to be found in the early evening at the Old Navy. We went to this café on the boulevard St-Germain occasionally when the Monaco and Tournon took on too much of the aspect of Salvation Army refuges for international *clochards*. The Old Navy, a *tabac*, was a few francs more expensive than the Monaco and a kind of staging post towards St-Germain-des-Prés.

Adamov was Russian. Perpetually dark-chinned with eyes all a-hunting he had a bizarre, not recognizably Russian, accent in French. He mostly emitted sounds that go with a grimace or a groan, his grinding voice rising almost to falsetto when expressing amazement. He never looked at the person he was talking to: his eyes were too busy seeking demons in the distance. He finally committed suicide.

Ionesco, Adamov and Arrabal were all regularly producing fresh wares.

I got the impression that Ionesco did not have a high opinion of Adamov's work, but since Adamov had supported him in the early days he did not want to hurt his feelings and would not comment.

'Do you like Beckett's work?' I asked.

'Very much,' Ionesco said promptly. 'Beckett has a true sense of the tragic destiny of man. He has no false messages. And his work is not the work of despair – it is beyond despair. If we have the courage to see our condition truly we can surmount despair.'

It was thrilling never to be disappointed in people's reaction to Beckett. In the rancorous world of the theatre, at the mention of Beckett's name all ungenerous or vindictive considerations evaporated. Everyone spoke with unforced respect and without a trace of envy of a man whose reputation had, in the previous ten years only, assumed unassailable proportions.

'He is certainly one of the two great living playwrights,' Ionesco said.

'Who is the other?'

'Myself.'

Ionesco again refused to pass judgement on other French dramatists. 'I don't want to say evil things about a colleague,' he explained sweetly. 'It's a question of politeness.'

'You were evil enough about Planchon,' I pointed out.

'Planchon is a producer,' Ionesco said, which apparently put him beyond sanctuary.

But Ionesco was not inhibited in talking about English playwrights or critics. He confessed contempt for Kenneth Tynan, the *Observer*'s drama critic, and *Look Back in Anger* with its 'petty preoccupations', was, he said, 'infinitely boring. Brendan Behan's *Quare Fella* [George Wilson had just put it on at the TNP] treated a theme of much greater importance – death,' he said.

We got on to the protocol of reviewing. He said it would be awkward for him to praise a certain critic (Harold Hobson of the *Sunday Times*) because that critic had praised his work; it would look like 'an exchange of courtesies'. On the other hand, people might misunderstand if he were to attack a critic who had attacked him. It now became apparent that Ionesco wanted to use me to settle a score with Tynan.

Living my own life in Paris, and only reporting on France, I had no great compulsion to follow closely what was going on in another foreign country, England. I seldom read English papers, so I did not know that two and a half years previously Ionesco and Tynan had been engaged in a celebrated slanging match in the pages of the *Observer*. It turned into a public debate on whether or not the playwright had a political and social duty. Lindsay Anderson, Philip Toynbee, George Divine and, most notably, Orson Welles joined in.

Tynan, reproaching Ionesco for a lack of social commitment, had written: 'As with shaggy dog stories, few of M. Ionesco's plays survive a second hearing.'

Ionesco had responded: 'A playwright simply writes plays in which he can offer only a testimony, a personal effective testimony of his anguish – not a didactic message.'

Orson Welles wrote: 'It is not "politics" which is the arch-enemy of art, it is neutrality – which robs us of the sense of tragedy.'

'Tynan is intelligent enough,' Ionesco said. 'He has the necessary kind of brilliance. But he is essentially a critic *à la mode*. A follower of fashion. He could be a Marxist one moment and an anti-Marxist the next.

'We are all either the Watched or the Watcher,' he said, looking solemn and giving the subs an easy headline for the piece I would write. 'The only escape from our jailers is death.' Ionesco had a sometimes disabling obsession with death; it was soon to become a central obsession of his work, the *Rio se meurt* its most naked expression.

He revived now to attack one of his favourite hates, Brecht. 'Someone like Brecht, with his political messages,' he said, 'only leads us out of the old [theatrical] confinement into new prisons. You know Nabokov?'

'Yes.' I nodded gloomily. 'I know Nabokov's work.'

In my first weeks in Paris I had gone to Maurice Girodias with the idea of doing a piece on his Olympia Press, although how I intended to report on its mucky output for Irish readers I don't know. The Olympia Press was Henry Miller's original publisher and special-ized in items such as *The Sexual Life of Robinson Crusoe*. Broke Americans needing their passage money home used it as a kind of welfare office. Girodias paid $100 for two opening chapters of a pornographic novel. Since most of the authors decamped when they got their first payment and since the books had to be finished, much

of his output had multiple parentage. When I met him Girodias gave me two books he suggested I might find interesting. They were first editions of *Lolita* and *The Ginger Man*. I immediately went down to George's bookshop, the Mistral by Notre Dame, and sold them without as much as reading the first page of Lolita. Later I was suitably mortified by this hastiness. When I said I knew Nabokov's work I meant I had handled the currency that had provided me with a couple of meals in a Greek restaurant. Ionesco probably took my sudden gloom for profound appreciation of Nabokov.

'I once asked Nabokov', Ionesco continued, 'if his books delivered a message. He said, "No, I am not a postman."' Ionesco giggled. 'Brecht', he said, 'is a postman.'

I wondered aloud if I wanted to be Ionesco's postman, delivering insults to Tynan.

'Why not?' he demanded.

'It's a question of politeness,' I said, borrowing his formula.

'But it is I who am saying it and not you,' he objected. 'In any case you asked me the question about critics. If you don't want answers put away your pen and your bits of paper.'

I had a long-distance personal link with Ionesco. When *The Chairs* was put on in Helsinki the lead was played by Elina Salo, a close friend of my Finnish girlfriend. At rehearsals Ionesco made what could be construed as an ambitious pass. Earlier in the conversation I had, off the record, asked about this. Now I reverted to it. 'But sometimes I ask a question for personal interest not for publication,' I said.

'You can't do that,' he protested.

'Yes, I can,' I said. 'The question about the Finnish actress, that was personal curiosity.'

Ionesco dropped his reproaches. 'She seemed to think I was an ogre,' he confided.

'Are you?'

'No. I think I'm more of a *chien loup*,' he said, and he made a sound between a giggle and a laugh.

But then he joined his hands on the table and began again to work on me to turn me into a postman.

'You know you are entitled to ask me any questions, but when I answer them you have a moral obligation to publish what I say,' he said.

'Have another beer,' I said as a full stop to this nonsense.

'No, thank you,' he replied primly.

'Well, have some of mine,' I said and gave him what was left in my bottle.

We parted amicably, as always with Ionesco; he was rather good-natured. I did my moral duty and reported his attack on Tynan.

It must have been in 1962 that a new pattern entered into my relationship with Beckett. An old friend of his from Dublin, A. J. 'Con' Leventhal, retired and came to live on the boulevard Montparnasse. Leventhal, although ten years Beckett's senior, was the man who in 1931 had taken over his post as lecturer in French at Trinity College after Sam abandoned it. Abraham Jacob Leventhal got the name Con from the business plate on his father's hall door in Dublin.

LEVENTHAL CON-
TINENTAL EXPORTER

It was my credentials as an *Irish Times* occasional stringer rather than my connection with the *Guardian* which prompted this retired scholar to present his card to me. A nimble, highly convivial Dublin Jew, a lady fancier, he was in the process of selling off his library to help subsidize his stay in Paris. From our first meeting it became clear that here was a man determined to get even more pleasure out of the proceeds of the sale of his books than he had had in the possession of them. Helped by Beckett he rented a small apartment across from the Closerie and later took up with a good-hearted Canadian lady named Marion.

Some time previously I had discovered at the back of my flat, in the rue Montparnasse, a late-night bar called the Falstaff. Despite the name it was more on the American style than British, softly lit and panelled, with a central pillar; small, about nine tables, and a short bar. It had the accoutrements of discretion that a pavement café lacks. Completely peaceful up to about nine o'clock it was a perfect retreat from the more public Coupole or Sélect and you could hang on until three in the morning. If you needed to soak up the booze it did a limited line in dinners, mostly steak *au poivre*. I decided the Falstaff would make an ideal additional drawing room, an extension to my tiny flat. It was there I entertained friends.

I soon discovered I had a rival tenant. Jean-Paul Sartre, normally associated with the Deux Magots or the Coupole, used it to entertain the young Algerian girl who was later to become his adopted daughter. At least once a week they would appear there sitting shoulder to shoulder eating steak *au poivre*, Sartre talking in an unstoppable stream, she carefully watching his lips move.

Only American tourists believed that French celebrities sitting in cafés were a sort of tourist attraction, waiting to perform in the interests of foreign exchange. In Paris bars and cafés, the proximity of a celebrity gave no right of contact, one of the factors which helped Beckett preserve his privacy. When we gave up the Falstaff, eight years and about five hundred steaks *au poivre* later, I still hadn't exchanged a word with Sartre.

Though he lived at the other end of the boulevard, Con Leventhal found the Falstaff to his taste, and now Beckett, who probably knew the place already, began to make frequent appearances. He'd come with Con or bring along Abigdor Arikha, an Israeli painter, an intellectually energetic young man with a curious persistent stare. The painter Hayden, to whom fame came in his seventies, he having been overwhelmed by the competition of the Parisian art set of the twenties, would often be there with his wife Josette, old friends of Beckett.

The Falstaff became the centre of our social life. Beckett introduced his nephew, Edward, who had come to study the flute at the Conservatoire. A very cheery lad, a great favourite of Sam's who would also bring him along to the Rosebud, in the rue Delambre, another of our late-night bars. Beckett was willing to go there sometimes because Gilles, the discreet (he gave us extra measure) barman of the Closerie, had moved there.

There was also, when he was in town, John Kobler, a Saturday *Evening Post* journalist who had written a life of Al Capone. For some reason the *Post* thought this equipped him to write a profile of

Beckett, but the paper folded before he could get it finished. Occasionally Gerald Kemmet would look in, an Irishman who was eagerly anticipating his status as an about-to-be-ex-correspondent of the *Sunday Express*. Only he was capable of deconstructing the invisible partitions which separated the tables at the Falstaff. He would snatch off his glasses and perform an eerily exact imitation of de Gaulle addressing the clients as if they were riot police. 'Vous êtes jeunes!' he told them. 'Vous êtes nombreux!'

The Beckett of the Falstaff was not the young man in a permanent alcoholic dream described, not without bias, by Peggy Guggenheim twenty-five years previously. He kept level with us, but drink never made him boisterous. If anything it made him more remote. A recent myth about him, bearing all the marks of juvenile fabrication, described him hiding under a table from a bore and crawling out to ask a girl for a kiss. This strikes me as wholly unlikely and totally at variance with his style, boozed or sober. I suspect it was part of an Irish need to recruit Beckett to the back bar of Irish literature. He would certainly drink, and he did have an extramarital relationship, the agony of which is expressed in *Play* (*Comédie*), in which two women and a man trapped in urns up to the neck frantically regurgitate their desperation. He was a physically reticent man and mentally always under some constraint or control. But he was not morose. It was he who used to detach his nephew Edward from his studies, bring him for an oyster meal and then around the corner to the Trois Mousquetaires in the Avenue de Maine for a few games of billiards at which he was deadly.

In the early hours of the morning we would come out of the Falstaff into the silent boulevard Montparnasse. Con would be revving up his right leg for the swing up the boulevard. Beckett would say goodnight with a stretched handshake, leaning shyly back, his head at a slant, a grimace of regret. Across the road the church skulked in the shadows, and the empty boulevard had that curious leaden taint which great deserted avenues have in the dead of night. Standing there in the cold, the drink already dying in us, we felt like Krapp – 'Past midnight. Never knew such silence. The earth might be uninhabited.'

Ten

In 1958, General de Gaulle was recalled from the political wilderness by President Coty to become prime minister in an attempt to restore stability to a country destabilized by economic problems and riven by tensions over the future of its Algerian colony. De Gaulle quickly promulgated the subordination of the legislature to the presidency and in 1959 took office as constitutionally the most powerful French president in history. He was granted by Parliament the use of referenda and presidential rule in periods of emergency. He worked consistently in his aloof and guileful way to disarm the power of the political parties, appealing in moments of difficulty directly to the people whom he courted through television, which he controlled virtually absolutely, or in elaborate national tours. Throughout his reign there was uneasiness, and not just among the Left, about just how he might, under pressure, use these powers. But his reign was bedevilled by the freelance 'adventures' of some of his police, military and ministers. Increasingly he had also to deal with the terrorist activities of the right-wing Secret Army Organization, the OAS.

Maurice Duverger, a professor of law at the Sorbonne and a political journalist of European reputation was a prime target of the OAS because of his column in *Le Monde*, where he deflated with scholarly irony the febrile ambitions of these renegade soldiers. He also tackled, with acerbic wit, de Gaulle's constitutional meddling. Duverger's home had been attacked twice. In one instance when he was lecturing in the Sorbonne nearby a bomb went off and he joked that perhaps it was his apartment. A few moments later a student came running into the lecture hall with the news that it was.

It was now early 1962 and the OAS, led by outlawed French generals and colonels of the failed 1958 putsch in Algeria, were making their final rash attempts to sabotage possible peace initiatives in Algeria. At that stage no one could decipher what de Gaulle's exact intentions were but the legitimate army also suspected that he was capable of sloughing off the North African colony. The honour of the French army was involved: just a few years previously the army had been humiliated in Indo-China (Vietnam). But it persisted with the classic delusion of believing, or feigning to believe, that it could hold on to a colonized country by force. One consideration was that without Algeria its occupation was virtually gone.

There was also the problem of what to do with the North African French, the *pieds noirs* who controlled the commerce of the country. The only solution there was the apparently outlandish one of re-patriating more than a million settlers (which in fact was done). Inevitably these landowners and businessmen had powerful support from bankers and industrialists in Metropolitan France. Add the sauce of racism, very marked towards Arabs at this time, and it was not at all certain that de Gaulle would be capable of preventing insurrection and anarchy.

What was unusual about the OAS plastic bombing campaign, and revelatory about French culture, were the victims. Certainly some of the intended victims were politicians, and there was the usual bid to create general terror in the streets – one night twenty-one plastic bombs went off in Paris. But the OAS were trying feverishly to intimidate intellectuals. Indeed, they persistently indulged in that most drastic form of literary censorship, bombing publishers and journalists. The most notable of these, apart from Duverger, was the founder of *Le Monde*, Hubert Beuve-Méry, and Beckett's publisher, Jerome Lindon.

The victims were further disadvantaged in that the police were largely sympathetic to the OAS, out of racism and muddled patriot-ism. The police had refused to give Duverger protection, offering the excuse that there were 3000 potential OAS targets and they did not have sufficient manpower. Duverger pointed out that the police came out in thousands in Paris when there were demonstrations against OAS bombings, and had sufficient manpower repeatedly to cordon off entire sections of the city. There was a feeling that the police were being used more to stop anti-OAS demonstrations than to prevent the bombing.

It was later discovered that the first bomb directed against Duverger was planted by Barbance, one of the men involved in an attempted machine-gun assassination of President de Gaulle as he drove home to Colombey-les-Deux-Églises with his wife. The elimination of the General was thought to be the speediest way to right-wing control.

The OAS aggression had seriously disruptive effects on the lives of the targeted journalists. Duverger had to send his family to the country to stay in safety with friends and increasing tension developed between middle-class intellectuals and their neighbours. The plastic bombs often pulverized the wooden staircases of the old apartment blocks, resulting in the evacuation of the whole building. Bitter feeling was created between 'blameless' tenants equally exposed to danger and the 'guilty' writers. In the early period of the campaign, there was no compensation for terrorist bomb damage, and landlords began to avail themselves of a law covering 'troublesome' occupants to evict their unwelcome tenants.

'Since many of the other tenants in my building are connected with the university,' Duverger said, 'they have been very understanding, fortunately for me.'

Duverger was a scrawny man with an American crew-cut. He was full of nervy movements: when you asked him a question his head came up like an impatient pointer. In his apartment by the Pantheon he worked with a pistol in his desk. When I arrived there were a couple of deck-chairs in the corridor in which students took turns to spend the night as unofficial bodyguards.

What precisely did the OAS hope to gain by this campaign?

'I think it is quite clear,' Duverger said. 'They want to stir up public opinion; to create a climate of uneasiness and insecurity. They can then blame any protests and demonstrations by democratic groups on the Communists alone.

'The OAS feel', he continued, 'that they will be able to put themselves forward as the only hope against an apparent rise of Communism. In that way they believe they will be able to force de Gaulle to go. So far they are succeeding quite well – at least as far as the first part of their programme, stirring up public opinion, is concerned.'

Beckett's publisher, Jerome Lindon, was not only bombed by the OAS he was continually harassed by the police. His offence was specifically that he published books revealing the existence of institutionalized torture in the French army operating in Algeria. The OAS had sent flaming Molotov cocktails through the windows of his publishing house and set off powerful plastic charges at the door of the apartment where he lived with his wife and three children.

His publishing house, Les Éditions du Minuit, was founded by Vercors (author of *Le Silence de la mer*) as a clandestine Resistance press during the Occupation, so it had noble origins. Lindon had turned it into the most successful avant-garde publishing house in France. He had already been charged with 'offences against the security of the state', with 'publicly inciting soldiers to disobedience' and with 'insulting the police'. If he had to answer to all the warrants he would have been liable to sentences totalling more than a hundred years. Although he was frequently fined, the authorities realized that it would have created a world outcry to jail the publisher of Beckett, Nathalie Sarraute and Marguerite Duras, among others.

Lindon was then thirty-six, a tall, gangling creature, speaking in explosive jets. He had Dickensian offices at the back of the present Drug Store in St-Germain-des-Prés. The narrow staircases were as steep as ladders and his office, overlooking a skimpy yard, was always in twilight. Hundreds of books sandbagged the walls.

The son of an Appeal Court judge, Lindon had been brought up to respect the law. An inconveniently gifted pupil, he made no distinction between common and officially sanctioned lawbreaking. A short time before he had written directly to André Malraux, famed novelist and champion of liberty, then de Gaulle's shifty Minister for Culture, to protest against abusive censorship. (He was wasting his time with that adventurer.)

Although his natural rectitude made it inevitable that Lindon would take political stands his preference was not for politics: 'I am only interested in literature,' he said. 'I am not a politician. When I entered this business in 1947 my only interest was literature. But circumstances have forced me to take issue in these questions and the more I go into it the more appalled I become.' He went on, 'The army is exasperated by people like me. They call us *"exhibitioniste du coeur"*. But I am not a romantic. I am simply reacting like any ordinary decent person would. Things have gone this far in France because there is so much cowardice.

'What most people do not realize', Lindon said, 'is that torture is no longer a question of politics but of morals. What are being used now are precisely the methods used by the SS during the last war. We fought against that. It is difficult for us to accept the fact that torture is now entering into the *moeurs* of our country.'

What was not evident to outsiders, nor easily sensed by local expatriates, was just how emotionally close the Occupation still was to any French person over thirty. It was as if there was, subterraneously, an uninterrupted memory of Paris run by the Nazis. The moral dilemmas of the time, the (not terribly abundant) acts of heroism, the habits of submission, cowardice and collaboration were all too easily recalled and the deepening Algerian crisis seemed to prefigure a resumption of Fascist control. Stale animosities, unresolved grievances were constantly resurfacing. When the Left took to the streets chanting 'Le fascisme ne passera pas', it was more than a pious declaration: it was giving notice of bloody battle if necessary.

The visitor registered almost nothing of this. A little explanation was needed for the plastic bombs, but since they were not massive they could be dismissed as a domestic argument quite untypical of Paris. In fact, the Algerian problem barely impinged on most visitors' consciousness; torture was a subject one might associate with a South American republic, certainly not with Paree. To the tourist every blemish was obliterated in the white light of Parisian romance, cuisine, elegant architecture or quaint intellectuality typified by the Sorbonne. Yet institutionalized torture was an everyday fact of French life.

Jerome Lindon was now producing a collection called *Documents* devoted to the issue of torture in the army. Official harassment, if not as deadly as plastic bombs, was financially deadly. At that time in France a book judged undesirable could be banned by a simple administrative decree. Once banned it could no longer be put on display, advertised or even figure on the publisher's list. It ceased to exist so far as the public was concerned. The Ministry of the Interior was applying a law designed to stop the circulation of 'obscene' American comics. There was no effective appeal against these administrative decisions; once a book was listed in the *Journal Officiel* a judge had no power to consider whether the content warranted banning; he could only deal with legal technicalities.

The censors refused to inspect manuscripts. Clearly with the intention of creating maximum financial loss, they waited until a full edition was printed and then seized the lot. They did this repeatedly with Lindon. When he asked the raiding police once what they hoped to achieve by these seizures (Lindon always kept back a few copies for the press), one officer said frankly: 'We are trying to ruin you.'

One of Lindon's banned books was *Le Déserteur*. Written under the pseudonym 'Marianne' (France), it was a fictional account of the experiences of a young conscript forced to witness torture by French officers in Algeria. This was so accurate that the army, in a move which suggested admission of guilt, decided it was fact and hauled Lindon before a tribunal on the charge of 'insulting the army', a curiously antiquated-sounding accusation for the sixties.

Another banned book, *St Michel and the Dragon*, a sober account of the harrowing experience of serving with the army in Algeria, was compared favourably by a Swiss critic to the Culture Minister's *La Condition humaine*.

During the prosecution of *Le Déserteur*, Lindon deliberately did not call intellectuals as witnesses for the defence; he produced young

Frenchmen who had served in Algeria. They told of their desperation when they handed over Algerian prisoners for questioning knowing that they would be tortured as a matter of routine.

When one of the young men giving evidence told of his mental state after having buried alive four Algerians, the judge told him he should not have done it. 'You see the terrible confusion in the country,' Lindon said, 'when a judge is obliged to tell a soldier that he should have, in effect, mutinied. I have two young boys. If they reach military age before the Algerian problem is solved they would have the choice of either being a party to torture or deserting. I would prefer a hundred times that they deserted.

'Time after time,' Lindon continued, 'during the course of these trials, judges were given information about cases of murder and torture – both crimes punishable in France by death. We even offered names. But the judges did nothing about it. In most countries an enquiry would immediately be opened.'

Lindon was apprehensive about the future of France. 'France is now like a house eaten by termites, ready to fall at any moment,' he said. 'If de Gaulle dies you will find that behind him there is nothing – no law, no institutions. Not even during the time of Pétain has the situation been so precarious.'

De Gaulle's quelling of the generals' attempted putsch in Algeria when he had come to power, four years previously, temporarily calmed fears about the deteriorating situation and the threat of civil war. The continual amassing by the President of exceptional powers by means of direct appeal to the populace in referenda, bypassing the democratic process, was disturbing enough. But what was truly alarming was the evidence that de Gaulle really did not have, or perhaps did not choose to have, command of his increasingly lawless security services. Uncontrollable forces were clearly at work in France. Many of de Gaulle's ministers, notably Prime Minister Michel Debré and Interior Minister Roger Frey, had obvious sympathy with the aim of the OAS: to keep Algeria French.

This officially sanctioned lawlessness was periodically demonstrated dramatically. There was the occasion when, clearly operating with the endorsement of some Gaullist ministers, unidentified freelances brought an end to the nuisance that one of the rebels, Colonel Argoud, had been creating for the Government from his place of exile in Germany. As he could not be extradited he was kidnapped and delivered, bound hand and foot, to the *pavé* of Notre Dame – which faces the Prefecture of Police. With brazen insouciance de Gaulle accepted this convenient gift of a troublemaker, without concerning himself as to whom he might be indebted – 'patriotic' gangsters and rogue cops, it turned out.

Two notable literary figures lent respectability to the regime of ancient combatants, political gangsters and unrepentant Fascists over which de Gaulle presided. Malraux was one, of course; the other was François Mauriac.

Mauriac, christened 'the Praying Mantis' by Jean Cocteau, had a column, first in the weekly *L'Express* and later, more appropriately, in the right-wing *Le Figaro*, where he made weekly obeisance to President de Gaulle. There is something disgusting in a writer who unloads his talent unconditionally at the feet of a political leader. There was a particularly off-putting tone in the manner of Mauriac's veneration of de Gaulle; a sweaty element of redemption-seeking at the shrine of a Holy One. Mauriac prayed aloud in his column, legitimizing everything de Gaulle did or which was done in his name.

In the late afternoon of 4 October 1961, the Métro at the Opéra began to disgorge Algerians in hundreds, men, veiled women and children. These dark figures poured down the avenue de l'Opéra joined by thousands of others coming in from the *grands boulevards*, filtering through the frightened pedestrians, mobbing the traffic, the women giving off their ululating cry, which sounds like a cross between the call of a bird and a wild beast. It was actually a peaceful demonstration in protest against a new police curfew on Algerians. But these gloomy, forbidding figures, wielding their culturally alien cry as if it were a weapon, terrified the shoppers coming from the Galeries Lafayette and drove the traffic police to panic.

It was not until darkness fell and word began to circulate to us over in Odéon of bridges across the Seine being blocked by police that we began to understand that something was seriously amiss. Opéra to the Left Bank of the Seine, and Concorde to the Hôtel de

Ville began to take on an aspect of a no man's land; there was no one in view but batches of cloaked police in distant groups, standing sentry over great deserted expanses of the Louvre and Tuileries gardens. They stood in tense lines, masters of long stretches of the roads running by the river. When we went down to the Seine to watch they kept us at a distance as much by their indefinably dangerous aspect as by their metal crowd barriers.

Back at Eliane's bar on the rue du Quatre-vents Hafiz, the Algerian journalist who had introduced me to the FLN, told us that Algerians were being tossed into the Seine and clubbed by police when they tried to crawl out. This was hard to believe; we were reluctant to accept that such savagery could be unleashed right in the centre of Paris. But it was also hard to discredit what Hafiz told us, partly because of his matter-of-fact way of not insisting that we must believe him. 'Wait,' he said.

So we waited in elegant Paris, by the untroubled Luxembourg gardens, in St-Germain and St-Michel where there was no apparent break in the stride of nocturnal feasting. Only a central segment of Paris was in limbo. But this interdiction soon spread west towards the Palais des Sports.

As the hours went by news began to trickle in, by radio and early-morning papers, that first wave of untreated news in which the statements of police and officials pollute or overpower the few independent eye-witness accounts. The official version was that the Algerians had been called out to riot by the FLN in protest against the curfew banning any Algerian from the streets of Paris after 8.30 p.m. The FLN had let their men loose on the streets by the thousands, it was said, and the police had to defend themselves; hundreds of arrests had been made and many had been brought to the Palais des Sports for verification of papers.

Initially public sentiment was strong against the Algerians; people felt it was an outrageous, not to say ominous, development, that the Algerians had dared to invade the Opéra area, a heartland of ostentatious culture and prosperity. Even the students stuck to their own territory when demonstrating.

The origin of this affair was an aggressive attempt by the Prefect of Police, Maurice Papon, to curb the activities of FLN terrorists operating in Paris. But to forbid Algerians the freedom of the streets at night was as absurd as it was provocative; many of them provided cheap labour as factory shift workers and would have to be allowed to circulate after dark anyway. As a strategy for curtailing terrorism it was, at best, hit and miss; many of the night workers would be active in the FLN in one way or another. But it soon became clear that the object of the curfew was mainly intimidatory and calculated to indulge a racist mentality in the police.

Papon sent in the ordinary Paris *agents* to deal with the demonstration rather than the disciplined CRS, who would have been less inclined to panic. Without doubt the Prefect calculated on a bloody confrontation which might swing public sympathy, the little there was, against the Algerians. The *agents* were genuinely frightened by the scenes they confronted. Then when rumours began to circulate of comrades being murdered in other parts of the city (deliberate misinformation, it was later established) they responded savagely.

Papon made a point of going out on to the streets in the early hours of the morning and congratulating his men on 'defeating the FLN in Paris', in case anyone had doubts about what it was all about.

More than 11,000 Algerians were rounded up that night and packed into the Palais des Sports, which could only seat 5000. As they were marched in many had to run a gauntlet of blows. They were interrogated brutally, many suffering broken limbs and, as often happened during Parisian clashes, the police deliberately delayed medical attention.

But it was before the Algerians got to the Palais des Sports that the worst excesses were committed. In the days that followed eye-witnesses told of Algerians stopped in the night, ordered to produce their papers and shot dead 'in self-defence' when they reached towards their pockets. Over the weeks solid evidence indicated that the police had bound the hands of some of their prisoners and thrown them in the Seine. More eye-witnesses described police stationed at intervals along the banks of the river to prevent those thrown from bridges climbing out. All night Algerian families defied the curfew, scouring the riverbanks (still associated with romance) in attempts to rescue

119

their menfolk. It was never established how many hundreds were murdered by the police that night. (It is believed that it was a condition of the Évian agreement the following year that the new Algerian government should not pursue the matter.)

Although some Algerian families attempted to bring prosecutions against individual policemen, none was ever charged. One of the few prosecutions was of a Frenchwoman who, seeing what was happening, leaned out of her window and shouted 'Assassins!' She was prosecuted for insulting the police.

What happened in Paris that October night was a grisly echo of the infamous Vélodrome d'Hiver affair when, during the Occupation, Jewish families, including small children, were rounded up by the French police and handed over to the Nazis for transportation. It was not until 1980 that it was officially established that Maurice Papon, when Secretary General of the Prefecture of the Gironde (1942–4) had also participated in the Final Solution by delivering French Jews, adults and children, to the Nazis. In 1961 Papon had reintroduced elements characteristic of the Occupation: the curfew and a hunt after people based on their appearance. (Needless to say, French people experienced none of the discomforts of the curfew.)

Worse was to come.

One evening a month later Claude Meline, my friend the poet-teacher from Vincennes, turned up late for an appointment. It was untypical of him, particularly since we were going to the TNP (Théâtre National Populaire), which refused entry after curtain up. When he did arrive he was in that state of exaltation and agitation I had already begun to associate with those who had expected clashes with the police. Claude had just taken part in an impromptu demonstration at Vincennes following an incident the night before. When they were taking Algerians in their *paniers à salade* (Black Marias) to the interrogation camp at Vincennes, the police had stopped to lynch a few of their prisoners. They strung them up in the trees and left them there.

This was difficult to take in, even after the events in October. The brazenness of such barbarous acts indicated that either the police were out of control or the French authorities had become incapable of restraining killers in uniform. Torture centres already existed in the city; now ordinary French *agents*, on routine round-up duty, were turning into lynch vigilantes.

There is a habitually biased process of selection in all news reporting to which journalists adhere automatically. The rule is that when dealing with a friendly nation a damagingly discreditable event is only reported fully if it fits in with the current image of the country. Nothing could be too bad, of course, to report on the Soviet Union, and it had become acceptable to report on lynching in the southern states of the USA. But no one had got round to acknowledging the existence of lynch law in France.

The British papers reported the October slaughter mechanically in terms of an Algerian demonstration that had turned into a riot, put down, perhaps a bit too brutally, by the police. It was, in fact, a peaceful parade of unarmed demonstrators of which the police had been fully advised in advance. It was the police who had rioted. Since for days there was no official confirmation of deaths the foreign press was unable to deal adequately with the story. It appeared, if at all, trussed up in a context of allegation and rumour. Later, when the facts were available, it was evidently deemed too stale an issue, and was not fully reported for a couple of decades.

Still a new boy at the *Guardian*, I had my gentlemen's agreement not to invade Darsie Gillie's political territory. But Claude's story was too much for me. I decided I would have to write something. I did not warn Darsie, less out of fear that he might try to stop me than from uneasiness that if I discussed with him what I was going to do I might lose my nerve, or begin to believe I was behaving in a peculiar way. I found a way of evading our understanding. I wrote a theatre piece into which, in recounting the reasons for missing the perform-ance, I packed many of the details of the October slaughter and the lynching.

I sent the piece without forewarning or comment to Brian Redhead and Phil Tucker in Manchester. They ran it as a page lead in one of their beautiful panels, across five columns 'La Vie Parisienne: STRANGE FRUIT IN THE TREES'.

I thought it terrific that I did not even get as much as a phone call demanding to know if I was sure of my facts. I took this to mean they had complete faith in me. (Of course, they could just have been saving money on phone calls.) No doubt they did check with someone. But I never mentioned the piece to Darsie and he never reproached me. From that moment I felt completely at ease with the *Guardian*.

On 9 February 1962, seven years into the Algerian war, Parisians had their first experience of the kind of terror tactics to which the North Africans had been subjected for years. The previous day eight OAS plastic bombs had gone off in Paris. One was at the home of Professor Georges Vedel. He had written a denunciation of violence, torture and maladministration of justice which had been read out at protest meetings in all the university towns of France the day before.

Another bomb had exploded outside the home of André Malraux on the avenue Victor Hugo, just by the Étoile. The public outrage was immense when it was discovered that the bomb had blinded a four-year-old girl, Delphine Renard, daughter of Malraux's *concierge*. The name Delphine Renard, like that of Djamila Boupacha, the young Algerian woman tortured by French paratroopers, became, briefly, a national reproach to the almost daily outbreak of disorder and barbarism in the capital. The bomb at Malraux's building had gone off in daylight, despite a police guard on the minister. Some Secret Army Organization (OAS) activists had been arrested that week, but some still doubted the enthusiasm with which the police hunted these French terrorists.

The problem was that the battle was partly between former comrades in arms, those who considered it a dishonour, and a fatal diminishing of the army's status, to have to relinquish a colony, while others were obedient to the will of the constitutionally elected powers. The trouble was that even among the members of Parliament, and certainly among leading industrialists, there was a powerful determination to hang on to Algeria. Although the OAS was composed mostly of a ragbag of disaffected officers it was impossible to tell what support they might get at a showdown.

However, most of the targets of the *plastiquers* were Communist:

the Tass agency; the newspaper *L'Humanité*, which was another attempt, no doubt, to create the impression that this was a fight against Communism.

The day following the spate of bombing the Communist CGT and the Catholic-led CFTC trade unions organized a demonstration to march from the place de la Nation along the wide boulevard Voltaire to République. This was the way, still quite novel to me, that the French made their demands: whenever they really wanted the Government to do something they came out on to the streets. At home we would have been writing to the newspapers. The industrial unions were joined by students and teachers with a seasoning of celebrities. While this was being set up more bombs exploded, twelve in the course of the evening.

That night I checked on the build-up at the point of departure, place de la Nation. The massing on the boulevards, the purposeful air of the organizers, the mixture of grave excitement and heady antici- pation was familiar to me, as was the initial absence of police. Everywhere I could feel that attractive, energizing sense of youthful seriousness and adult dedication to a cause.

To begin with, the show-business celebrities hung around the front lines, lending their candle power to the austere gathering, but they soon took up positions scattered in the body of the crowd. At a stage door, they would have been mobbed, but on these occasions they were off-duty as stars, blending with the crowd as concerned citizens. No one was going to turn this into an autograph-hunting session.

But this gathering was unusually tense already. The demonstration had been banned; sooner or later the riot police would intervene.

I waited until the procession had begun to move off and then went into a café for frankfurters and chips. I decided I would have a couple of beers, too. Tradition would allow the march, although banned, to get under way; I calculated there would be no confronta- tion until it approached République. I could easily catch up with them at a destination they might not reach for nearly an hour. The demonstrators were not aware, neither was I, that Maurice Papon had decided to move in his new *force d'intervention* early in the game – and brutally.

Half an hour later I took the Métro two stops towards République. I got out at Charonne, the exit being just off the marchers' route. Surprisingly, the main body which should, by my calculations, have been still shuffling past was nowhere to be seen. It was seven o'clock.

I came up the short flights of steps of this Métro, which was not deep underground, and came out on to the rue de Charonne which cuts across the boulevard Voltaire. I was about to set off across the road with that elated feeling that anticipation of action brings when I suddenly sensed that something was truly wrong. The street was unnaturally silent, abnormally dark: the street lights were out – a common trick of the police. Instead of some relaxed stragglers from the main demonstration small groups stood in doorways, looking into the distance. Disconcertingly they whispered when they should have been at the garrulous, noisy stage. To my left, a café alongside was locked and barred, lights out.

In the darkness, far down the street, a mass stirred. Within seconds it had turned into a crowd of men and women, some children, a loose-running bunch with little of the character of demonstrators about them, dashing towards the Métro entrance. Behind them I caught a flash of police helmets and riot shields.

I was well used to calculating the speed of arrival of riot police and practised in discovering sure routes for escape. But as I stepped a few paces towards the fleeing demonstrators they were on and past me at such speed and with such a quality of high-pitched fear about them that I stopped dead. Something told me that this was real danger, not just the risk of a cracked skull.

The fleeing people stumbled and tottered down the Métro steps.

In an instant I had caught the panic and leaped back down into the Métro. I remember my head was empty of anything but a windy fear as I crashed down the steps with them and raced along the crowding platform. It was a very short platform; all too soon I was up against the end wall. Back down the length of the platform the mouth of the exit was like the lower drooping lip of a gargoyle, spewing out fear-infected people. If the train did not come in within seconds I was trapped. It came as I formed the thought. I got on, foolishly out of breath. One station later I reasserted my professional poise and got out again, ashamed of myself. I still did not know what I was running from.

Some hours later I found out. The police had caught up with the demonstrators at the mouth of the Métro a few seconds after I got down to the platform. Many tripped and fell down the steps, others tumbling after them. The police wrenched the chained marble-topped tables from outside the café and threw them from a height on the human bundle; then they went down and beat them with their long truncheons.

Seven people were killed. Some were Communists, some were not. Among the dead were a man of seventy, three women and a young boy. Several hundred others were injured that night including about a hundred police.

Next day the city was stunned. This time the victims were not Algerian but Parisian.

Five days later 250,000 Parisians took to the streets in a silent, defiant march along the same route. There were no police to be seen this time. It was a demonstration against – the French sometimes have a curiously impersonal, almost abstract way of expressing their emotions – 'Hate and Torture'. The ordinary people of Paris had lost patience after seven years of intermittent brutality, corruption, violence, mutiny, sabotage and living with the rather baroque threat of invasion by the Foreign Legion from Algeria.

The Paris *agents* unlike the riot police (the CRS) were regarded as relatively blameless. They were involved in some riot dispersal but traditionally they were associated with traffic duty and chasing *voyous*. But now the CRS were claiming that they had not been out that February night at Charonne nor had they been involved in the October slaughter.

So who was at fault: the notorious CRS or the cuddly, blue-cloaked *agents* beloved of tourists?

I decided, not without some trepidation, to go and talk to some riot police. A *Life* photographer I knew had told me once of his experience. He was covering a turn-out of left-wing trade unionists massing on the *place* by the Bastille. The workers had come to a halt, about twenty abreast, squads of CRS blocking their progress.

'What are you going to do now?' the photographer, with wholesome American innocence, asked a CRS captain.

'I am going to blow my whist-le,' he replied, 'and then we will start 'itting peoples on the 'ead.'

He did blow his whistle, and hit the photographer on the head.

The first CRS I met was a countryman, a private from the Auvergne. We were waiting for his captain. Two years previously, he said, he had the prospect of slow starvation on his father's small farm shared with two brothers. Now he had a steady salary and free meals when on duty. The current unrest meant he was getting a lot of free meals. But he complained morosely about the reputation they were getting.

'Do you like hitting people on the head?' I asked him with as steady an air of scientific enquiry as I could muster.

He looked as though he was about to give me a demonstration but, disciplining himself, said: 'If I do hit people it is under orders. You wouldn't ask a soldier a question like that, would you? The captain will explain it better.'

The captain was another rustic; sturdy, shrewd, with the emphatic manner of one used to giving orders.

'If I agreed to talk to you,' he explained, 'it is because there has been too much wild talk about the CRS. We are getting blamed for everything.'

'Let me tell you about the CRS,' he said, already incensed. 'The CRS patrol the beaches to save people from drowning, climb mountains to rescue foolhardy alpinists, give instructions on civic spirit in schools, and performing these activities we are well liked. We are also called out in case of civil disturbance,' he conceded. 'But we are a paramilitary group and never, never in these cases do we operate individually. We always move in blocks. We wait around in formation and only move in under the direct order of our superiors. You never see a CRS careering down a side-street after a demonstrator.'

'Who will you see?' I asked.

He became glumly discreet. 'Well, you won't see a CRS, that's all.'

'But cooped up in those wagons for hours waiting, your men must get fairly well worked up. They must be glad of something to hit when they are let loose.'

'That is what people seem to believe,' he retorted. 'But in fact our men are specially trained for that. They are taught patience and strict discipline. It is the others let loose without proper training who do the damage.'

'The others?'

He refused to be specific.

'Do you mean the ordinary Paris *agents*?' I pressed him.

After some coaxing he put it this way: 'The municipal police are not used to that kind of work. Picked from here and there in the city, banded together and sent out to quell rioters they are more liable to lose their nerve or act in confusion.'

Next day I got on to one of the policemen's unions, the Syndicat Général de la Police and told their spokesman that the CRS were blaming them for the killings of October and February.

There were vital differences between the forces. If the CRS was paramilitary the *gendarmerie* was a disciplined military formation under the Minister for the Army, but put at the disposition of the Minister of the Interior. The Paris *agents*, on the other hand, were solely under the Prefect of Police of Paris.

The spokesman for the *agents* was extraordinarily frank. 'We know perfectly well that people are beginning to call us fascists,' he said. 'People are puzzled and disgusted by these recent ugly incidents. But we have repeatedly requested that the *agents* should only be used for traditional purposes: traffic duty, catching thieves.

'Now we are being formed into the Prefect's famous "companies of intervention" and armed with *bidules* [batons] at least a metre long, to break up demonstrations. We don't like that. But there are more serious objections to using us in demonstrations.'

The *agent*, he explained, had a completely different training from the CRS. He worked on his own, generally, and was used to making

127

up his mind when to take action; when to interfere in brawls, when to punish.

'Lacking the strict discipline of the CRS,' this cop said, 'when *provocateurs* spread false rumours of what is happening to his comrades in other areas he is inclined to move in, out of a sense of *esprit de corps*, and attack demonstrators.' But also, he admitted, when a couple of *agents* found themselves hemmed in by a few hundred demonstrators, they were inclined to panic. 'Then they "exaggerate".'

I wanted to point out that exaggeration, a popular French euphemism for unseemly behaviour, was hardly an adequate expression for the barbarity of October.

'The root of the problem,' the police union official admitted, 'is the policies being followed.'

Launched on a mood of frankness he told that they had not only asked not to be used for riot duty in October, but also suggested better ways of dealing with North African demonstrations.

'We knew what might happen on 17 October,' he said. 'We appealed to the authorities to let us arrest the FLN collectors and organizers – we have known most of them for years. In that way we could have neutralized the demonstration, disorganized it at its roots. But we were not allowed. Then when our men saw thirty thousand Algerians come swarming through the streets – with memories of years of terrorism behind them – they were not going to hand out any presents.'

Having gone so far this policeman decided he might as well go the whole way. 'It is the Administration which must bear the responsibility for all this,' he said. 'I don't know what game certain sections of the Administration think they are playing, but it is certainly a political one, and a dangerous one.'

The game was Papon's Occupation strategies.

A few months later there was a ceasefire in Algeria and then on 3 July the Évian agreement, giving Algeria its independence, was signed. But this was subject to a referendum about the country's future. Was there a majority in favour of Algérie Algérienne? Algerians at home and in France prepared to vote. In Paris this involved massive effort by the FLN who had the task of instructing their followers, many of whom were illiterate, in voting procedures and making sure there were no violations of the treaty.

One afternoon I went over to the notorious Goutte d'Or quarter, near Pigalle, where the Harkis had had their torture chamber. The Harkis were gone, but not back to Algeria. They had no home any longer in North Africa and no genuine welcome in France; they were consigned to life-long insecurity under the not-very-enthusiastic protection of the French.

I don't remember how I made the contact but I found myself waiting for a FLN organizer in a tiny Algerian café by Barbès Rochechouart. The Algerian customers acted as if I did not exist. It was a dour little café: a few brown wooden tables and chairs, an understocked short bar with none of the range of colourful *apéritives* and *digestives* you find in any Parisian café. The men, most of them elderly, dressed in dark suits and open-collared white striped shirts, like peasants in the Midi on Sunday, were mostly drinking coffee. With a Muslim clientele, trade in alcohol could hardly be brisk. There were no women. These North African cafés always had a special gloom about them, a combination of the sombre panelling and dark faces suggested poverty and suspicion; the silence when a stranger appeared translated into menace. For consolation I remembered scarred Hafiz, the Algerian journalist of the villainous appearance but good heart. I tried out a heart-warming smile on the corpulent barman but his dark pupils, looking into mine, promised only a sticky end in the Casbah.

Although peace had come there was no sense of exoneration on either side. The Algerians were still watchful, defensive and morosely sceptical. A short time earlier, despite the ceasefire, there had been a battle in this quarter between police and Algerians in which one North African was killed and scores injured.

When my contact came into the bar there were no further surreptitious looks in my direction; realizing I was meeting the FLN they scrupulously displayed no curiosity.

My guide turned out to be a thirty-year-old 'interior decorator', who only identified himself as Monsieur B. With him was a house-painter in his early twenties; this one was tense and jumpy and seemed to be continually trying to verify my *bona fides* by prolonged staring.

Monsieur B decided we should go to a place where there would be no fear of interruption. We cut through some back-streets and then he stopped before an *hôtel de passe* – a hotel for prostitutes. The logic was that the police could not deduce anything subversive from strange men continually going in and out of a brothel.

We walked up the shabby narrow staircase, passing women, posing in various stages of undress, like girls on a carnival float. Monsieur B gave a masterly display of pretending that the women we brushed past were not there. But the younger man could not help watching for the effect on me. I put on a deeply urbane expression.

The girls, few of them Algerian, made way without comment. They were clearly practised in recognizing when men were about a different kind of business.

We went into a musty bedroom, bidet on open display, and the older Algerian drew the curtains. I sat on the edge of the soiled blankets while the younger man, in a fussy state of alertness, barred the door like a sentry.

I asked about the recent battle with the police.

'We were arrested for nothing,' the younger man blurted out furiously. 'We were peacefully filling out forms for the referendum and they crashed in and attacked and arrested us. When we marched in protest they smashed into us with their cars. They took thirteen of us to the station. I was one of them. Brutalized us in the cellar. Then when they were obliged to release us they let us out two at a time and beat us up as we came through the door of the police station.'

Monsieur B intervened firmly. 'We are convinced that the briga-dier who led these men was drunk,' he said, determined to play down the incident. 'We refused to go with him since we had done nothing. When he took five of us we called out three hundred brothers and marched peacefully to the police station to demand their release. It was then the police drove into them, killing one of us. Seventy of us were injured. There will be no more incidents like this,' he said firmly.

This was the new party line. No reprisals.

He said that some Frenchwomen kindly invited them to shelter in their homes when they were fleeing from the police. The ordinary Parisian could be generous when faced with all too obvious police brutality.

So the war was really coming to an end; terrorists were turning into diplomats. But the younger man still stared at me belligerently, not, it seemed to me, to express hostility but to convey that he certainly was not ready to forgive.

We talked about the referendum, but I really wanted to see the infamous Goutte d'Or café where the Harkis had carried out their dangerous trade right in the heart of this Algerian quarter.

They took me there. Unlike the other shabby cafés in the same street it was sparkling fresh; the ceiling was new pink, the walls sea blue; formica table tops shone and lights peeped out from sugary decorations. Monsieur B, the interior decorator, had been at work.

'We gave it a little oriental decoration, freshened it up,' he said. 'We are tidying away painful memories.'

I asked if he would stay in France.

'No. For the past seven years we have been living on our nerves. We have experienced a little lack of respect, a little brutality and insecurity. We have had enough,' he said.

As I left the café he said: 'France is not a bad country but we have too many bad memories.'

The outcome of the referendum was no surprise. France lost its colony.

Eleven

The Algerian war over, the newspapers had only the new productions at the Folies Bergère or the Lido to get excited about. My first experience of what we then considered to be a 'dirty' show was the Lido, a press freebie with a glass of second-rate champagne to induce enthusiasm. The show consisted of a group of covered wagaons driven around in a circle by girls naked to the waist. A sexless tenor sang 'Home On The Range'.

I felt hugely embarrassed, not by the breasts on display but at the foolishness of presenting such a show to a supposedly sophisticated, or simply grown-up, audience. I had not expected Paris to have any need of *faux* eroticism; the Americanization of the show seemed particularly pathetic. This was followed by tableaux of boudoir vignettes in dumb show. Clearly the producers did not think it necessary to instil any talent into the affair. Bobbing boobs apart, this was the kind of charade that might have been thought up by a nurse to divert her infant charges.

As for the Folies Bergère, that was a series of fatuously over-dressed parades of disheartening banality. There was a strong element of fake gentility in the performance: the girls seemed to be afflicted by a crick in the neck of the kind affected by ladies over-ambitious to appear respectable.

The Mayol, around the corner from the Folies, was reputed to be 'dirtier', but I doubt it had any real invention either. It was clear that some conspiracy of tourist bureaux and the media kept the reputations of these risible places afloat. It was not until Nicholas Bataille,

132

Ionesco's director, was invited briefly to devise erotic shows that anything like energy and invention was introduced into Pigalle's nightclubs.

The French cinema also had its equivalent of the Lido; Roger Vadim was its most notorious exponent at the time.

I went out to the St-Maurice studios where Vadim was doing some commercial sex packaging. He was shooting *Le Vice et la Vertu*, a transposition to Nazi-occupied France of de Sade's *Les Malheurs de la Vertu* and *Juliette, ou La Prospérité du Vice*. Although French cinema had the reputation of being far more liberal than Anglo-Saxon, this was true only in one aspect: on screen the French were much more relaxed about showing a woman's naked body. Beyond that, official censorship was severe. French films might be naughty, but naughty was all they were. So there was no chance that Vadim's *Le Vice et la Vertu* would lead us to the core of de Sade's erotogenic volcano.

The set at St-Maurice was more elaborate than the usual patch of film fantasy. There was already a small warren of halls and boudoirs, suggesting a set-up for a tracking shot through a Naughty Housewife's sinny retreat. In a shaded, partially screened alcove stood a black bath; nearby was a low bed with a white coverlet and furred footstools. Instead of making me feel randy it set my teeth on edge.

A black staircase with a green carpet led up from the *entrée* to where a Nazi officer (O. E. Hasse) leered down and repeated for five takes: 'But it is our little *ingénue*. Come up, my child, our *soirée* lacks a little freshness.'

Then he stepped back behind the set and looked worried. Actors in costume waiting to go on are at their moment of least credibility. They look foolish dressed differently from the rest of the technicians and their expressions of self-conscious nonchalance make you suspect they might be bad actors.

Vadim, out of sight on a dolly, called for silence. Vice (Annie Girardot) standing behind me gave a blonde Virtue, dressed for the boudoir, a poke in the back and the young girl walked past me towards the lights to mount the staircase.

I was struck by the artlessness and indeed gaucherie of this young girl acting in her first film. Annie Girardot, a veteran, would be well able to take care of herself. But I saw in this young person, who looked barely nineteen, straight from the country no doubt, the beginnings of the fatal corruption of a pure young imagination. From now on she would be fed with shallow and foolish values; she would no doubt be fooled – almost certainly was already deceived – into believing that she was working with one of the great names of the cinema. How could a country girl know better? Couldn't she realize how humiliating the whole experience was? I could imagine Vadim availing himself of her and then casting her aside; used, abused.

I was working myself into quite a state. I am not sure I did not contemplate rescue of some sort. I did contemplate having an avuncular word with her, with no suggestion, naturally, of delicious reward, but decided that a film set was not the place to raise moral objections.

If I had spoken to her, I wonder what effect my advice would have had? The *ingénue* was Catherine Deneuve. She did, indeed, succumb, slept with the director and had a child by him. But she refused to marry him, dumped him, and went on to have a spectacular career, at her happiest in roles with a touch of erotic perversity. If I had spoken and persuaded her, Buñuel would have had trouble later casting *Belle de Jour*.

The morning's shooting completed, I braced myself for the encounter with the man I suspected had had his way with Virtue.

Vadim's silly films – *Et Dieu Créa la Femme*, *Les Bijoutiers du Clair de Lune*, etc. – had little erotic power. In the last, his notion of titillation was to have Brigitte Bardot, skirts flying, chased by a horseman up a tree. Vadim's eroticism was that of the lingerie salesman, discreetly prurient, aiming for that false gentility favoured by the Lido. He was a favourite of city hicks. But I always imagined French peasants returning to their farmhouses perplexed at how paltry was the erotic charge they had got from a supposedly daring film.

Brigitte was a useful calling card for Vadim's introduction to the film world. But her talent and sexual appeal were very limited: she was the businessman's sulky schoolgirl whose skirt they were permitted to lift vicariously from time to time. I thought she had almost no range as an actress and little charm; she slouched gracelessly, from one film to another, a purveyor of peevish adolescence.

After he broke with BB, Vadim attempted to introduce an element of artistic respectability to his work by adapting classics, an old trick of the pedlar in search of status. The first was *Les Liaisons Dangereuses* into which, under his insipid direction, not even Jeanne Moreau and the dying Gerard Philippe could introduce conviction.

Then he had the notion of purloining Sheridan Le Fanu's vampire novel and, by making the vampire a woman, introducing some lesbian thrills. There was an awful lot of neck-sucking of his own new bride, Annette Stroyberg, in that film.

Now Carmen Tessier, *France-Soir*'s gossip columnist, a mistress of banalities, had been expressing astonishment at his daring in tackling de Sade, although I suspected Vadim's slushy talent was about to douse the fire of the old reprobate.

Vadim's air, as he approached the table in the canteen where I sat, was already grudging. Aged thirty-three, over six feet tall, fleshy in the way of an athlete going to seed, as he came nearer he angled his body away from me giving a bizarre impression of pushing himself along with huge reluctance. His glance when he met mine was not hospitable. This was obviously a chore he did not want to perform; he was more at home with *France-Soir* than the *Guardian*. In addition, I was distracting him from an activity described by his publicist as 'caressing an old dream', preparing de Sade for the *grands boulevards* cinemas.

He sat down at the table and asked what I wanted to drink. 'Un demi.' They didn't have draught so he ordered two bottles of Tuborg in a slack voice. If I had not been in a somewhat similiar frame of mind, anticipating no interest or pleasure from the encounter, I would have felt insulted. I wondered whether if I admitted to him my own indifference would we just sit there mute? But I had a duty to look for a story. Unfortunately my mind was a blank. I had no wish to encourage this creature to give me a potted biography of his Russian origins (I could not bear it if he dragged in Eisenstein) nor did I wish to discuss Brigitte with him.

135

What was the theme of this new film? I began.

'It is the story of two sisters, Juliette and Justine, one is Vice and the other is Virtue,' Vadim said in a thick bass voice. 'One succeeds in remaining herself; she is not corrupted. The other goes too far and is destroyed.'

So he wanted to give the impression he was making a moralistic film. How embarrassing.

'So it will be a moral film?'

'Yes,' Vadim agreed. 'Juliette tries to exercise her power but she is destroyed by it. I would like people to think that this is something that can happen anywhere in the world. Especially,' he said, tapping his temple, 'when one is intelligent one can go much too far.'

I wondered if this moral line was for the benefit of the *Manchester Guardian*, which he might have confused with the *Christian Science Monitor*, or if this was the path his brain trudged when he wanted to be 'serious'. I tried to fathom Vadim but found myself in the shallows.

I wondered aloud what was moral about *Et Mourir de Plaisir*: 'The relationship between the vampire and the victim was clearly a lesbian one?' I suggested. (In the early sixties this was still a daring subject for cinema.)

'Eh?' Vadim said. He was not prepared for such frankness from the *Manchester Guardian*. He admitted reluctantly that there was an element of lesbianism in the relationship. (Entirely absent from the Le Fanu book.) 'But it is also a psychic relationship. They have a deep psychic relationship. In fact I wanted to take this film further to make it more like the Sheridan Le Fanu book. But Paramount was joint producer and they wanted the film to be suitable for world-wide release.'

Now Vadim suddenly had the inclination to give a lecture on national attitudes to sex.

'In Europe,' Vadim informed me, 'we think it is normal to show a woman's body, her legs,' he said, nonchalantly, 'her back.' He stretched his back. 'And even her . . .' Vadim put his hand under his armpit meaningfully. 'Her eh . . .'

'Her eh?' I said.

He passed over the invitation to pronounce the word 'breasts' and continued his dissertation. 'I think a woman's body is beautiful and can be exhibited in the way a Roman statue can,' he said. (In *Les Liaisons Dangereuses* Gerard Philippe, fully dressed, chats on the phone, his elbow on a naked woman's bottom.)

What would you say was the moral of *Et Dieu Créa la Femme*?

'Before,' Vadim said, 'a girl who slept around was regarded as either a prostitute or someone who was sick. I wanted to show a modern girl who likes to laugh, who is sentimental and yet who does . . . that.'

That? I tried to imagine him in Régine's night club being squeamish about using the word for sexual intercourse.

'She is not sick,' he informed me. 'But the morals of our society are so strict a woman cannot live like that without distress.'

'How does the film end?' I asked. I had not forgotten, but I wanted to hear him describe the fatuous finale.

Vadim became a shade more animated. 'Well,' he said, 'she had betrayed her husband and she is sick and desperate. She begins to dance in front of him provocatively because she wants him to kill her. So the husband takes a gun.'

'And kills her?' I enquired eagerly.

'No. His arm is pushed aside. But he goes up and *slaps* her. She was not killed by the shot. But *something* was killed. The idea that she could live like that. So she goes back to her husband.'

I verified the points aloud, gravely: 'She had a good dance and then got slapped. Not too severe a punishment! Was that what you wanted?'

'I was not making a tragedy,' Vadim retorted sharply.

I displayed enthusiastic signs of wishing to go deeper into these issues of sexual morality. But Vadim was staring at me closely.

Without a word he got up and walked away, leaving me to pay for the Tuborgs.

Lurking in the mind of the hack who is frequently permitted to dip his bowl at the feasts of the great and notorious, but rarely gets to join their sybaritic tribe permanently, is the notion of adoption; of being invited, say, on the slimmest of motives to become part of the Hollywood set. Paris should have been the wellspring of such opportunities and in the early days I had slapdash dreams of encountering a celebrity who would offer me a Ziegfeld staircase to fortune. Such dreams hung in the mind like gas jets, ready to pop into flame at any far-fetched opportunity.

The cheapest (in terms of effort) route to fortune was to be given, on some caprice, a part in a film and outshine the star. There was no serious work involved in that. Writing an Oscar-winning script was another rhapsody for journalists who knew nothing about scriptwriting except that in screenplays there are very few words to a page.

Making a film of my own was one of my more daunting fantasies, involving intimidating technology, staff control and being more self-assured than the glamorous. That was relegated to moods of more solemn ambition. (Ironically, it was this dream which would later materialize. But in the throes of doing it, anxiety replaced rhapsody and I was cheated out of day-dreaming pleasures by the frantic work pace.)

A parody of the Hollywood dream now came true. I got a part in a film and after a few days was promoted to be script-writer, but except for a few rags of muttered dialogue blowing in the wind it was a silent film: Jacques Tati's *Playtime*. As for acting I played, briefly, a mute, but dreadfully mumming, chorus-line leader of a gaggle of stateless windowshoppers.

In March that year I had gone out – with Maurice Hatton, the photographer – to the St-Maurice studios in the east of Paris to do a piece on Tati shooting *Playtime*. He had already been tinkering with the film for two years, so it was hardly a hot subject. But the *Guardian* was not in the business of impetuous scoops. Nor was I. I had worked out that if you are really late covering a story – say, a year or two – you made it news again.

It had not been a great encounter. Tati affected a certain forced brightness, dredged from a curious veiled depression. What he had to say had the unmistakable staleness of old quotes too often repeated. Hatton was continually frustrated in what he was allowed to photograph.

138

Tati had covered a field near the St-Maurice studios with tarmacadam and constructed fragments of collapsible modern skyscrapers. There were three main warehouse shapes capable of taking, at various levels, an exhibition hall, an air terminal, offices and restaurants. Planted around them on three sides were propped up skyscraper fronts in shrinking perspective, which could be shunted around to give an illusion of a vast, futuristic city. As futuristic as Manhattan fifty years earlier, Tati's idea of modernity was already pretty old-fashioned: it was a rather elegant, glass-fronted environment, not oppressive. He did not want Hatton's pictures to betray any of the illusions and his producer, M. Maurice, fussed around and imposed restrictions in that fretful, exasperated way with which Parisians prefer to begin negotiations. We both left with a sense of having got mediocre material.

Maurice was a photographer with ambition. We had already worked together on the mournful-voiced wailer, Charles Aznavour. Later, Maurice was to direct *Praise Marx* and *Pass the Ammunition* and, dogged by bad health, prise what he could out of a perpetually derelict British film industry.

A couple of weeks after our first meeting I got a phone call from Tati's production office – a wooden hut in the field – saying that Monsieur Tati would like the 'tall Englishman from the *Guardian* to play a part in the film'. Maurice Hatton was not a midget, but one would not instantly apply the word 'tall' to him. Secure in my Irish identity I was at first baffled as to who the Englishman could be. When it was established that it was me they wanted, and for a period of up to four weeks, the fantasies of hot and cold running, loot-strewn fame began to boil again. You could get in an awful lot of screen time in four weeks. (With any director other than Tati, that is.)

The fact that the producer had said, 'Bring a good suit – if you have one', did not prevent my optimistic imagination whistling like a steaming kettle.

Riding alone in the bus through the woods of Vincennes for my first day as a film star illicit thoughts of luxury and lust, Hollywood concomitants, were tolerant companions of my journey. In my reveries I was already playing the role of one ethically above tinsel ostentation but constrained by fealty to my fellow millionaires to go along with their gasconading way.

The romancing dimmed abruptly when I arrived at the bald fields where Tati, remote from the passing parade of celebrities at the studio proper a couple of miles away, plied his toilsome trade of stitching gags together.

The production staff in the bungalow office now exhibited none of the admiring curiosity they had previously displayed towards a visiting journalist. The girls who had only a couple of weeks before treated me like a *britannique* celebrity now refused me any special consideration. I was obliged to join the other doleful extras who sat on benches like patients in a doctor's waiting room: professional extras have a permanent air of convalescence. Although previously the girls had responded merrily to my banter now they refused to exchange badinage with an extra. They knew I was panhandling for fame.

My interpretation of the reason for their indifference made me cross and I flirted with ways of being severe with them as soon as Tati came in and revived my status. But when he did he gave me no more than a reluctant nod. I was now an extra to him too.

I think there was an intention that I might serve as one of the many *faux* Hulots who criss-crossed Tati's path at various points in the film (they had been muttering about using me as an 'intelligent silhouette'). But the idea was abandoned, I always believed because I was in such a state of giraffe-like alertness, scanning the horizon for the approach of fame that I must have looked more like a lightning conductor than an Hulot.

They sent me off to the wardrobe caravan to be togged out in a knee-length black overcoat, a trilby and a briefcase. The undersized hat perched on top of my head like a pie and only in an obsequious bow did the sleeves of the overcoat reach my wrists.

In contrast to Tati's fastidiousness in everything else there was little rehearsal. After just a couple of sketchy attempts to direct us, the 70 mm camera nosed in, rolled; then we were sent back out of the way to our buses to sit gaping at long hours of inexplicable inactivity.

Tati tried with obsessive meticulousness to get the camera angles right, but there was a curious indecision in this fastidiousness. Problems of reflection from the glass fronts must have been resolved long before; the angles from which a comic movement is best seen must have been worked out months, indeed years earlier. He spent five years in all making *Playtime*. Moderate familiarity with location work made it plain to me that these delays had little to do with technical hold-ups. Two years of minute preparation had already been spent on the film to no robust result. The whole enterprise seemed stricken with sterility.

Tati appeared to be the only one with authority to do anything. Monsieur Maurice would make a distracted appearance on the empty lot, a lone figure in a fragment of a metropolis watched by two score American army wives in flowered hats, and camera crews standing at ease. He would then retreat, like another Tati figurant, to his office.

Not only was Tati the only person who knew what had to be done (and didn't do it) the whole enterprise fell away from the person of his Hulot character with nothing substantial supporting him. Tati never played against well-known actors, nor minor character actors with a strong personality. He used the untutored American wives to create an off-putting babble in a background, often crudely synchronized. The few professional extras had nothing to do but move dispiritedly to instructions which rarely came.

Tati (family name Tatischeff) was the grandson of the Tsar's ambassador to Paris, but he was born in Versailles where he still lived. In 1916 the family spent their holidays at Mers-les-Bains where Jacques's father, on leave from the army joined them by the seaside. All day they hung around aimlessly, his father not having the right to be out of uniform. This melancholy holiday was the seed of *Les Vacances de M. Hulot*.

He sidled into feature-film making when René Clément abandoned a project to develop a short Tati had made about a postman, *Soigne ton Gauche*. He was given the chance of shooting *Drôle des Facteurs* which developed into *Jour de Fête*.

Tati had only made three feature films in twenty years: *Jour de Fête* (1947); *Les Vacances de Monsieur Hulot* (1952) which I had seen by accident, laughing out of control in a back-street London cinema on my way over to Paris the first time; and *Mon Oncle*, 1958. For me Tati still represented a purity of comedy not equalled by sly Chaplin, a comedian I always found a little distasteful. Tati's was the comedy of the knight errant propelled by incompetent amiability, an endearing relationship to life. I was convinced that *Jour de Fête*, the story of a demon cyclist village postman, made with the lazy aid of the inhabitants of a little Normandy village, was one of the great comedies of the cinema. Tati's style was an untroubled marriage, at that late date, between silent and sound comedy. *Les Vacances de Monsieur Hulot* had the unassailable authority of a dream: a series of murmurings in sleep-walking motion among the bungling entanglements of the well-intentioned. But already by *Mon Oncle*, Tati had begun to reveal a finicky temperament, more carping than comic.

Now he was being hustled by fame into making a *big* picture. He followed this fatal course willingly. 'Why should I at my age, with my grey hairs,' he said at our first meeting, 'content myself with a little film in black and white about a country railway station or something?' He was fifty-six.

So he harnessed himself to a 70 mm camera and the wide screen. His mistaken and curiously naïve belief was that 'a man sitting in an office bored and doing nothing or a pin dropping on a carpet is really something in 70 mm'.

Now, with *Playtime*, he no longer had the resources of a real village to draw on, so fruitfully mined in *Jour de Fête*.

The atmosphere on the set was aimless and dejected. The presence of a couple of score American army wives, bussed in from SHAPE headquarters every day as extras, did not produce the kind of chattering animation you might have expected. They had been selected by Tati when he served them incognito as a waiter at one of their army Antique Teas.

'My husband just rolled in a ball when he heard and laughed and laughed for half an hour,' said a matron from Akron, Ohio. 'He felt, you know, sorry for them – the movie-makers.'

They were soon feeling sorry for themselves. They had been at it for months, billeted in coaches alongside the fake skyscrapers, submitting to the discipline of being busbound for hours on end while nothing happened outside.

They complained of pains in their legs. 'Because you're using muscles you never used before gettin' in and out of buses all the time,' an automobile fanatic from Louisville, Kentucky, explained.

For all their protracted stay in France – some were well into their second year abroad – they still only saw the French at a distance. Normally they were, by choice, deprived of the most direct of contact with the locals: shopping. They got all their goods, from comestibles to furnishings, cut-price at the commissariat – the PX. Every purchase, cornflakes and ice cream, coffee, candies and cranberry sauce, baseball bats and runners, hollered out its Americanism.

Normally the French played bit-parts in their lives; now they were extras for the French. Again they made no contact – none spoke French. 'After a certain age the cords in your throat are too set and you never learn to speak a foreign language,' a lady from Idaho explained to me. They did not seem to be aware that they were selected to play caricatures of themselves. Tati's notion of what American women should look like was also way out of date; he re-dressed them to look like Andy Hardy's neighbours.

Initially they must have had expectations of coming across Jean Gabin or Daniel Gélin. But they were deprived of this thrill by being permanently parked in a field well short of the studios. 'I just feel wilted down,' one summed up their feelings.

I tried to get something out of them but they defeated me by their empty volubility. They established a false intimacy by addressing me immediately by my first name and then dealt in brash banter, which was a disguised form of reticence. I would go home in the evening and rattle my notebook like a prospector, hoping some usable nuggets would remain, but there was little. The McCarthy era was not long passed and maybe these military wives had a high security threshold.

Occasionally Tati would get us out of the coaches and line us up for a take. He would approach, dressed in his Hulot gear, and attempt an air of jollity like a school teacher trying to persuade children they were going to have lots of fun but, like a school teacher, not being very convincing.

The sequence was simple: we were to get down out of the coaches, bringing whatever skills we had to the business of looking in wonder at the skyscraper world about us, and then curve off towards the glass-fronted entrance. Later we were to sweep Monsieur Hulot back into the lift from which he was attempting to emerge and carry him up to an imaginary top floor.

The leading lady, Barbara Dennek, had been an au pair girl with no acting experience working with a neighbour of Tati's in Versailles. At first he would greet her on his street in the morning with comic elaboration and then one day asked if she would like to play the lead in his film. It must have seemed like the beginning of a splendid life for her, but there was nothing about her reserved, rather resentful personality which suggested the actress, and nothing in the film to act to.

She was often marooned with us in the coach and had the standoffish air of one whose prestige had been neglected. I tried to question her but she responded in the begrudging manner of someone who is out of their depth and has discovered she has nothing to say about what she was doing. It was plain she felt she had been lured into an enterprise promising adventure and glamour which only produced tedium. She must have felt cheated that this great opportunity in her young life had only produced a weird kind of imprisonment. It was to last four years. She would have been one of the few, outside the film crew, bound to a proper contract. Everyone else was cheap labour.

In conversation Tati had none of the tics of the compulsive entertainer, although every now and then he would illustrate a point with some perfunctory mime. His normal carriage was the assertive roll of the rugger forward, not Monsieur Hulot's bouncing gait, which is more reminiscent of an inquisitive ostrich. His first public performance was for the Racing Club when he gave a one-man impression of a rugby match. He had been a gifted rugby player.

Tati affected a nonchalant style in conversation, but there was something distinctly reluctant about his sociable manner. This glumness was more barren than melancholy; it was a disgruntlement that did not invite sympathy – you find this in people whose creative power or status has become drained. Tati's creative powers were never robust. I got the impression that he was overwhelmed by wide-screen expectations that he was afraid he could not fulfil.

After the droll invention of his early films and their delicious human vignettes Tati was now labouring with banal ideas about the depersonalizing effect of the modern urban environment. Whatever the truth of this theory he did not have the intellectual power to make points forcefully, nor did he seem any longer to have the ability of the great comic intuitively to produce original satirical insights. His filmed lamentations had no more force than the jeremiading of a suburban neighbour peevish about disruption of his habitual comforts.

At this point Tati, hoisting up that air of bonhomie, approached me and asked if I would be interested in working on the script. He led me behind one of the skyscraper façades and showed me a luxury trailer parked out of sight. I think it might have been his own hideaway. I noticed again that curiously watchful element in his manner.

We stooped in and, mimicking the debonair manner of a deft salesman, he indicated the amenities of this miniature office. He pointed with humorous pride to the desk, typewriter, short filing cabinet and the domestic extras – a bunk, electric stove, coffee pot and a tiny toilet. These would be my quarters; as a writer I need no longer doss down in the bus.

His emphasis on the comforts and minor prestige of the as-yet-undetailed promotion nearly – but not quite – put me off asking the essential question: what was the pay? It would only be a matter of a few days here and there, he replied evasively (a daily rate; not a contract, I guessed), and it would, of course, be more than the pay for an extra. (No bag of gold here, I realized.) Monsieur Maurice would handle the arrangements. I reckoned that if Monsieur Maurice offered me double an extra's £6 a day I would be lucky. It was with such scraps that the French produced their cinemascope epics.

Tati's immediate problem was to create dialogue in English for a sequence in which a chairman is pacing up and down in his glass-fronted, high-rise office, reading a report to his board. Distracted by the darting Monsieur Hulot down below, he does not realize that the wind periodically blows the pages, back and forth as he strides about. The board members react with astonishment to the chairman's increasingly surrealistic discourse. Tati wanted me to think up a suitably subverted report. I suggested one sprinkled with details of a new comical invention the company were about to put on the market. He was pleased and I was a little surprised that an idea came to me so promptly. Encouraged I suggested that the invention could be some kind of pump, since that would give an opportunity for references to naturally comic activities such as leaking and puffing and thrusting and steaming. My imagination stopped there.

Tati agreed that I should go and research some engineering jargon in the Bibliothêque Nationale. To express his satisfaction he decided to demonstrate the remaining amenities of the caravan. He showed the advantages of the adjustable chair and, bending down, opened a small cabinet at floor level. There, standing shyly, was a full bottle of whisky. He hesitated. I watched him, still on his knees, weighing up the insult of openly removing the bottle against the hazards of leaving booze within reach of a journalist.

'You can take it away,' I told the back of his neck, which was a challenge to leave it. Reluctantly he left the bottle where it was.

I only took an occasional sip. This was partly because my right to enter the caravan was strangely curtailed. On my next turn as an extra I went as usual to get the key of the caravan from the production office so I could hang around in comfort. I was told that the caravan was not available to extras. I said I was now a script-writer. Not today, the company's chief *concierge* told me.

A couple of days later I was a script-writer again and this same creature graciously handed over the key. I gave her my grimace normally used on Inno France check-out girls who claimed they had no change. It didn't bother her. Ladies in film production offices had that stoniness you find in civilians with law enforcement authority.

I did some research in the business pages of the *Financial Times* and *The Times*. I cobbled together phrases from the annual report of

146

Alexander Howden (Holdings) Ltd (heavy oils and lubricants) and Kango Electric Hammers Ltd. In another version I united a Courtaulds' refurbishment report with a presentation of retirement gifts to several members of the staff 'to make them hang better; to stop them stretching and sagging'. Into these I tossed a mix of pumps pounding and squelching.

The idea was to be suggestive but not, of course, in those days, obscene; obscenity could not yet be used – even in my own mind – lightheartedly. I wouldn't claim that I had come up with an inspiring comic turn. The device was too mechanical, the kind of smile-inducing joke which comic actors support with a knowing raise of the eyebrows.

Tati dropped in and took away my half-dozen versions of what was already to me a feeble joke. He exhibited the same indecision about the bits of monologue as he did about directing scenes. It was not at all clear what he could possibly want from me in the line of script-writing. After all, *Playtime* was virtually a silent film – and in French at that. He gave no indication of what other scenes might require English dialogue but wanted me to stay on. So I lolled on my couch some more and doodled. (After I gave up he hired Art Buchwald, the *Herald Tribune* humorous columnist, who seems to have had a proper contract. At least, it was good enough, and substantial enough, to sue Tati later for non-payment of fees.)

Some days there were no extras about, the American wives given shore leave. On those blank days Tati would occasionally be seen in discussions with his chief cameraman, a Japanese (already the second lighting-cameraman on the job; no senior technician could afford to hang around one picture for years).

Script-writing became infected with the same aimlessness which obtained in the rest of the lethargic production. I had to bring my own booze so that the whisky bottle would not chart too precisely my descent into sloth. I had long ago done my piece for the *Guardian*. There was nothing in this for me. Neither Tati nor Monsieur Maurice seemed to know what I was supposed to be contributing as scriptwriter, and I suspected as an extra I would not leave much of a hole. I told Monsieur Maurice I was giving up; he took it fatalistically.

Two years later the lift into which I had jostled Monsieur Hulot finally reached the top floor where I should have led my little army in, sweeping Hulot out again. Tati's office rang and asked me to come back and complete the sequence. I wasn't free and it was all too dreary to make a special effort.

I heard no more. When *Playtime* was released I went to see how the sequence was dealt with. We swept Monsieur Hulot into the lift, but a totally different crowd, a later generation of depressed extras, swept him out again.

I was hoping *Cahiers du Cinéma* would spot it and identify it as an example of hidden surrealism in Jacques Tati.

Twelve

The freelance who sets up his little independent kingdom abroad is like Alexander Selkirk – without being lord of the fowl and the brute. A foreigner, detached from the routine support of family and old friends, he is at first in a kind of limbo: no face is reassuringly familiar, the people around him have only fleeting identities as full human beings. Unlike Selkirk his rights are frequently in dispute. He must set up his shelter unaided. (Throughout the sixties the *Guardian* had no company bureau in Paris; Darsie Gillie worked from his apartment in the 7th.) With the labour and patience of a castaway the freelance must gather together those aids to survival and comfort which distinguish the gent from the dosser.

I had been very lucky with Redhead and his team. Brian helped me construct my first financial hut – a retainer, which was gradually pumped up. He and Phil Tucker and John Course saw to it that space was made in the paper for me, no doubt at someone else's expense. By mid-1962 I had the basis of something approaching a comfortable income.

I got married on the strength of incipient bourgeoisification. (I remember when driving up to the oyster restaurant one evening with Sam Beckett I told him I might marry Eeva, my Finnish girlfriend.

'So you're thinking of taking the plunge?' said he.

I was shocked. I felt a great literary genius might have offered a more stylish comment on such a hazardous undertaking.)

Once married, Eeva, who had switched from sociology to journalism, began to build up her contacts for a freelance career in

Scandinavian journalism. But almost immediately we showed signs of turning from Robinson Crusoe and Girl Friday into the Swiss Family Robinson: my wife was expecting a baby. So we moved to a more elaborate apartment (one with a bathroom this time) down the boulevard Montparnasse to rue Mayet.

At this point, meddling Fate began to cobble for me the pair of Denver boots it likes to present to those with the illusion that their time has come to fly. Brian Redhead moved on to become northern editor and was replaced by John Rosselli (whose father had been murdered by the Italian Fascists during the war). Phil Tucker, disappointed in not getting the job of features editor, was asked what other hobbies he had, apart from painting. This was the *Guardian*'s way of astute vocational identification. Daft as it was, it often worked as well as any scientific method. Tucker revealed he was interested in science. So began a prize-festooned career as the *Guardian*'s science correspondent.

Although Rosselli was a scholarly man, honourable and considerate, this simple change of regime at features demonstrated how vulnerable a freelance can be, even when the replacement is a man broadly sympathetic to your interests and politics. By simply pursuing a sensible strategy (for the paper) Rosselli almost dismantled the edifice I had only just built up. The freelance abroad needs an active champion at head office; since Rosselli had inherited me, and not discovered me, he was inevitably not as alert to my needs as Redhead had been. When a new film critic, Richard Roud, was appointed in London, Rosselli gave him the task of covering the Cannes Film Festival, without thinking of the effect this would have on me. It was a particularly logical move since not only was Roud chief film critic he was also the director of the New York Film Festival and monitoring Cannes would have been one of his duties. It was very likely that the New York festival was also paying his expenses; an attractive proposition for the *Guardian*.

But the Cannes Film Festival had provided me with not only a subsidized two weeks on the Côte d'Azur, it also guaranteed a batch of pieces in the paper. Normally a freelance has to space his foreign pieces so as not to overburden the parochial taste of readers, or, indeed, of editors. In one casual stroke I had lost one of my main story sources for the year. (The other was the three-month Paris theatre Festival of Nations.)

But worse: a fall-back position of covering the concurrent, but less juicy, Cannes Television Festival had also been snatched from me by an unknown creature (with a Cambridge background, of course) who had written in offering to send a piece. Rosselli thought it was worth a try since there would again be no expenses for the *Guardian*. (When I eventually met this interloper, Peter Graham, at Cannes, I made it plain that I did not wish to consort with such types. But he turned out to be an obstinate character who perversely refused to take my hostility seriously. The years have shown what a failure I was in trying to make an enemy of this cinema buff, gourmet-gourmand, author of, among others, an entire volume devoted to cheese recipes.)

A painful correspondence ensued with Rosselli in London. My letters throbbed with baffled reasonableness (but privately I knew it was absurd that a stringer and not the chief critic had been covering Cannes). My only case was deprivation, a glum and inelegant argument at the best of times, and I did not know what legitimacy that might have in London. (The *Guardian* having dropped 'Manchester' from the title two years before had now also moved its head office to the capital.)

Behind the jaunty reproaches, insecurely tethered to a sense of standing up for one's rights, was the fear that I had no rights. Being obliged to settle territorial or fee disputes by letter is one of the more intractable problems faced by a freelance. Like all such exchanges between a correspondent and head office the arguments were tedious in the telling. Back in London you could corner your section editor in the pub, but in handling the problem by letter all the apparent triviality of the affair was painfully emphasized. There was the danger that at some point an editor, exasperated and indifferent to the insecurity of a freelance, would simply tell you to get lost.

'This is too tiresome,' Rosselli wrote when the complaint about Roud was followed closely by a distempered objection to Peter Graham. But Rosselli was a genuinely considerate man and, in letters half scolding and half encouraging, he worked out a deal: I would go to Cannes, but as a feature writer on reduced expenses. The photographer Maurice Hatton would come over to work with me and take me down in his car. So once again Robinson Crusoe was back in business.

Maurice Hatton had a great idea. When we got to Cannes we would make Alfred Hitchcock play Prufrock for us, bottoms of his trousers rolled and all. It would make a great picture sequence.

'He's there showing his new film *The Birds*,' Maurice reminded me, as if Hitchcock's simple presence at Cannes left him at our mercy.

Maurice gave me a copy of T. S. Eliot's 'The Love Song of J. Alfred Prufrock' to study as we bucketed down to Cannes in his Morris Minor.

I could see the potential. No doubt we could get a couple of starlets to oblige with '. . . sea-girls wreathed with seaweed red and brown'. And Hitchcock wearing 'white flannel trousers and walking on the beach' could be a cinch, I supposed. 'But do you really think you can persuade Hitchcock to wear the bottoms of his trousers rolled?' I asked Hatton.

'Hitch? Of course,' he snarled. Maurice had a lashing style of irascibility for those who did not trot enthusiastically with his brainwaves.

'And where do we get a footman to hold his coat . . . and snicker? I admit the last bit might be the easiest.'

'You're so literal,' Maurice said pityingly. 'Are we scoop merchants or aren't we?'

The first part worked out fine. We did spend 'a restless night in a one-night cheap [*routiers*] hotel' and not the fog but the trucks outside rubbed their muzzles against our windowpanes, snorting and hissing all night. We resumed the journey at dawn, sleep-deprived and like Eliot's patients 'etherized upon a (moving) table'.

We called ourselves Scoop The Hack and Fumbles, the photographer. But it was I, Scoop, who fumbled: I had got the date wrong and we arrived a day too early for the festival's gala opening. The novelist Christine Rochefort, a likeable and easy-going woman, was the press officer and did not consider this confusion of any great consequence. But Maurice sulked. I decided it was a good opportunity to have the wine stains removed from the leg of my dress trousers and left them at a twenty-four-hour cleaning service.

The next night we dolled up for the formal opening. Cannes etiquette was unbending: if you didn't have a monkey suit, press pass or no press pass, you would not get past the *gros durs* at the entrance to the Festival Hall.

Maurice came into my room impeccably attired, but I was only beginning to dude up. I leaped up on the bed and flinging myself in the air sang out: 'Puttin' on my top hat, puttin' on . . . *my trousers*!' I yelped in mid-air.

They were still at the cleaners. Immaculately attired to the waist my sartorial elegance would tail away to grubby grey flannel pants.

The *gros durs* would never let us pass.

Good film buffs, we remembered how Cary Grant got Katharine Hepburn out of the nightclub when her skirt was ripped in *Bringing Up Baby*. Cary got in close formation behind her, and they stepped out in unison, he holding his top hat as a bottom shield. In the queue up to the bouncers we did a slow-shuffling version, Maurice my front shield. The bouncers only had eyes for necks and chests, so we got in.

The next day we had an attack of superstitious dread when we discovered that Fate had been on the look-out for us. The vice-president of Universal Pictures was preparing a party for Hitchcock on his yacht: Hitch would be received on board by a pair of bewigged footmen. Evading his PR men, we grabbed Hitchcock at the Carlton and brought him up to his suite where he rolled up his trouser ends for us. (Once you got to him, Hitch liked to be nice to the boys from the press.) While Maurice crawled over the furniture getting cute angles I engaged Hitchcock in conversation. He attempted to pay homage both to my nationality and to the cultural status of my paper by producing some halting banalities about Sean O'Casey whose *Juno and the Paycock* he had made a mess of in 1930.

We then hustled Hitchcock down to the yacht where the festivities were beginning, fearing he might at any moment tire of the game.

We planted him out on the deck and got a flunkey to pinch up the shoulders of his jacket with a supercilious air. Hitchcock's only defence was his sly, depraved-cherub smile.

'Hey those guys are making a fool of you, Hitch,' a coarse American voice shouted, just at my shoulder.

Deeply immersed in our task – Maurice shooting, me directing mentally – such an interruption was intolerable. I swivelled my head in the direction of the heckler and yelled, 'Fuck off!'

'Hold on, now,' the voice behind me said. The tone suggested someone who knew better than I what was going to happen next.

I glanced at this middle-aged American, who now took on some of the aura of a Chicago abattoir boss, and said coldly, 'Who are you?'

'I am the vice-president of Universal and this is my yacht,' the man said without redundant aggression, as one can when one realizes that the other fellow is in the epicentre of the frying pan.

Maurice took his camera down to his chin and I looked away into the distance, seeing only a blankness with no guidance inscribed on it.

The flunkey removed his fingers from Hitchcock's collar. Hitchcock gave his rendition of a Stan Laurel dippy smile.

'These boys are leaving,' the VP of Universal said to an assembly of wintry sentries.

We left without a word, on the principle that you never take on a battle you have lost in advance.

Hatton and I did well at Cannes. We had a session with the kids from Peter Brooke's *Lord of the Flies*; I interviewed a new Greek director, Nico Papatakis, and on the way back we picked up enough material for a piece on the *pieds noirs* at Aix. We had salvaged a potentially wrecked month.

On the way back through Avignon we thought up a stunt to shame the *Guardian* for putting us on restricted expenses (no transport money) and, in passing, take a side-swipe at its notoriously lackadaisical response to news.

I described a *Guardian* team called Scoop and Fumbles, the ace photographer, sent to respond to a five hundred-year-old newsflash that the bridge at Avignon had fallen down. On site Maurice threw himself on the ground by the bridge, placing a twig close against the lens, to represent the forest territory we had battled through to get our story. Describing the hardships of the trip, particularly in relation to expenses, I told how we cunningly christened our Morris Minor 'Grade A Hotel' and itemized every meal: 'To: Lunch in Grade A Hotel £2 15s 5d. Dinner/Grade A Hotel £3 19s 2d (no *garçon* cheating).'

Maurice's picture of the fallen bridge in a shallow river had a kind of daft urgency. DANGER BRIDGE THREATENS AVIGNON, we captioned it.

With great aplomb John Rosselli ran the picture across six columns and gave the piece a three-quarter-page spread. And he paid the expenses.

While I was brought up to accept that stately major-domos in restaurants had a dispensation to abuse you if you were gauche (such as contemptuously passing off plonk as vintage wine), I had no idea until going to Paris that overcharging and short-changing could be a normal part of a waiter's routine. More astounding, being caught in the act carried no taint of disgrace.

There was no cheating in the Monaco: no one had enough cash to finance such an activity. At the Tournon Madame Lazare was largely in the business of distributing credit. As for Maurice, the saintly patron of the crêperie café at the foot of rue de Tournon, he was more a male nurse to our hangovers than a predator. But the advent of comparative prosperity and the move to a more tourist quarter, Montparnasse, exposed me for the first time to the full blast of the shotgun, as the French put it.

The problem was that Paris waiters had no wages; they survived by being let loose on the customers to extract obligatory tribute. In those times a Parisian *garçon* was a fully qualified plunderer. While regular customers were spared, outsiders and tourists were cheated on the price of every round or every dish. Caught, and required to make an adjustment, the dacoit's addition would be faulty in his favour; frustrated in an attempt to defraud you thus, he would then abduct your change. Obliged to return the kidnapped coin, he would, as a last desperate reflex, cheat you on the refund. You had to be well hardened in Parisian ways to withstand this siege.

Later Jeanne Moreau told me that when she brought her English relations out to dinner in Paris they always said: 'Coo! Everything is one-third cheaper when you order!' For a decade I felt a special warmth towards this exquisite siren, not because of her glory or glamour, but because of the private complicity we shared in the war against *garçons*.

(I caused great offence back in the London office writing about Jeanne Moreau. I revealed that the slithering sensualist of *Les Amants*, the blasé beauty of *Les Liaisons Dangereuses*, the wicked whipping lady of Losey's *Eve* had spent her childhood in Littlehampton; her sister had a butcher's shop in London and her mother lived in Brighton. I also revealed that this sultry lady's favourite dish was roly-poly pudding with strawberry jam.

Already exasperated by some of my irreverence in other areas, one of the *Guardian*'s more punctilious sub-editors took this jaunty disrespect towards a distinguished actress as final proof of loss of standards on the paper and resigned. One of the other subs, Michael French, looked up the Brighton telephone book and, finding Mrs Moreau senior's number, got confirmation of these facts. But it was too late to placate the purist.)

When both the Paris *Herald Tribune* and the *New York Times* joined the crusade on behalf of defenceless American tourists, the French Tourist Commission took fright and launched a scheme intended to seduce waiters to honesty. They gave books of Smile Cheques to incoming tourists who were then supposed to issue them to waiters they found to be helpful and honest. The waiter who gathered the most cheques was promptly sent to Tahiti. This suggested a certain ambiguity as to whether the tourist board actually wanted honest waiters in the country.

I became zealous in my skirmishing with *garçons* and tutored *Guardian* readers in how to destroy their morale. 'Bring chaos into their lives!' I advised readers. In London they began to worry that I might be losing that treasured *Guardian* ability to reflect on everything with two hands: on the one and on the other.

We had had yet another change of features editor. John Rosselli had moved into academic life and now Christopher Prout Driver, later editor of *The Good Food Guide*, took over. At the best of times one's contact with London was insubstantial but when Christopher phoned (we had taken to using the phone) he articulated in such a dreamy way that one was left wondering if one was supposed to be part of the dream. As a gourmet, he was intrigued by waiters: 'Why don't you go and see how the buggers live!' he suggested.

I discovered that by the hip of the butte of Montmartre there was a café known as La Mère Cascade's which was a contact point for itinerant waiters looking for jobs. I decided to try my hand.

Sixteen art-nouveau Métro stations from Montparnasse I was standing like stout Cortez contemplating the foreign shores of Montmartre. This was the drab eastern flank of the butte to which few tourists strayed. The café was the only commercial premises in a short residential street at that moment deserted of all humankind.

Once, at the height of a summer onslaught on *garçons*, I had a dream – that I was in a café where everyone was a waiter. Not only were all the *garçons* waiters but also all the customers were waiters, and so were all those converging on the café from the surrounding streets. I was now in that nightmare.

Everyone in La Mère Cascade's was a waiter. (She had started life as a waitress.) They sat around at tables or loafed in the doorway, sentinels waiting for the phone on La Mère's counter to ring with offers of a few weeks' or a few days' work.

La Mère was an excessively corpulent lady with a sleepy demeanour. She was washing glasses indolently in the counter sink when I went up to her. I noticed a baby's bottle among the wine glasses. She caught my glance.

'My granddaughter,' she said. 'A beautiful child.'

'*Sans doute*,' I said.

Nothing about me, I hoped, suggested a waiter, yet neither La Mère nor any of the other professionals treated me as anything but a waiter. Why else would anyone want to come to La Mère Cascade's?

I told her I was trained in Mooney's of London. She had never heard of Mooney's, but she accepted the improvised reference. I wasn't going to risk getting a job in a restaurant and end up dropping hot ratatouille into the lap of some Montmartre gangster, so I told her I only did the bar – *salle* or *comptoir*.

The waiting waiters treated me with a kind of off-hand civility. As with men on the run, the custom seemed to be not to pry into each other's past. That suited me great. I only made one *faux pas* during that first long, lustreless day. After drinking a coffee I naturally left my empty cup and saucer on the table.

A waiter standing at the door came over, pointedly picked up my soiled crocks and carried them to the counter, giving me a reproachful glance. The waiters on either side of me also gave me cold looks. La Mère Cascade had no waiters. We were expected to be self-waiting. This meant, of course, that there was no tipping, and no cheating, so that was a refreshing change.

At one point a couple of disoriented Swedish tourists, tall, flaxen-haired and androgynous, wandered along and sat down outside at one of the single line of pavement tables. An unemployed waiter from Gascony got to them first. He stepped out nimbly and put on a classic demonstration of waiting. He flicked the table top elegantly with a dish-cloth, listened with deep courtesy to their order – *deux café crèmes* – and retreated backwards with a bow as if from royalty. The Swedes became increasingly nervous and soon got up and left.

The others had watched this display with a critical eye. For some, the time between jobs had been so long that there was an element of nostalgia in their regard. I imagined them longing for some great roaring *brasserie*; flapping swing doors; loaded trays at a jaunty angle; the skilled slalom through the massed tables. They longed for the roar of their profession like superannuated jockeys long for the track.

Among the regulars – a couple of steam-faced second-hand gents, a shifty little guy who looked like Frank Sinatra, and a tall grey-haired man in a bow-tie who appeared to be trying to establish a personal superiority but was uncertain where to park it – I admired most the Gascon. A dapper man in his late thirties, thoroughly polished from slicked hair to luminous raven shoes, the sheen of his mercilessly brushed dark suit emphasized a threadbare hairiness at cuff and turn-up. He was one of those people who could be buoyant and busy all day about nothing at all, like some kind of little mobylette its engine constantly running but not going anywhere. On the second day he began to give me advice. I should wear a tie even for the *comptoir*, he warned, and he was not too sure about my running around in sandals. They would never accept that in a *salle*.

This Gascon stood in the doorway most of the day calling out remarks to the few women who passed by this dreamy street. He told me about his mistress, a bourgeois lady in the 16th *arrondissement*. Visiting her he could not bring himself to go in by the front door, and now the neighbours were beginning to wonder why Madame's caller always used the servants' entrance.

He showed me snapshots. But they were not of the woman; they were pictures of her furniture. He was fascinated by the ponderous luxury of her home.

The system at La Mère Cascade's was first come first served for any jobs that came up, although some appeared to have a hidden prestige and went off to lucrative temporary work almost as soon as they arrived. I was down with the lowest at the bottom of the list ready to take even a day's work. At first most held out for better offers – a week perhaps or at least a few days – but as the workless days accumulated their standards dropped and they all began to compete for scraps.

It is easy to shed your identity when out of your normal environment and become possessed by the expectations of others. I found myself guiltily hoping for a juicy café crammed with American tourists reckless with their money.

But every morning I went off to La Mère Cascade's trying to be a success as a waiter and came home a failure. After days in that scullions' antechamber, cut off from friends, miles from my own quarter, I no longer felt like a journalist and I knew that to confess I was – (was I?) – would gain me no place in their hierarchy. I began to take it personally that no one offered me work. I wondered if La Mère was secretly not proposing me because, wise in her trade, she had spotted some inherent factotumarian deficiency in me.

For hours I watched the pigeons strut around the empty street outside and began to detect in them a particular indifference to us which I interpreted as a recognition of our lack of status.

The unemployed waiters mostly talked about their employers, hardly ever about the customers. Even though the boss paid them nothing he or she could make life hell for them. La Mère Picon was one of the most notorious. What she really wanted, they said, was a charlady; you never made more than 35 francs a day in her dump.

'La Mère Picon?' Frank Sinatra said. 'It wouldn't surprise me if that woman sprouted horns, your hands are in the water all day. "Why aren't you coming tomorrow?" she said. "I have my hands," I told her, "and I can't feel them."'

Then La Mère suddenly recalled a request for an urgent replacement for a couple of midday hours in a café down at place Clichy. The others gambled that it was not worth losing a place in the queue for a couple of hours' work.

'C'est pour toi,' she called to me.

I looked in a panic at my sandalled feet. I had forgotten Gascon's advice.

'Mais c'est pour le comptoir, imbécile,' La Mère said amiably.

True, I'd be behind the zinc, no feet showing.

'Mais la cravate!' fussed the Gascon.

'I'll buy one,' I shouted as I trotted off down towards place Clichy. There was no direct public transport so I had to pant down the hill to the boulevard Clichy. Would I be able to work the espresso machine? No, I told myself truthfully. Would I be good at giving rapid change or at remembering five orders flung at me in slang. Probably not. So what was I going do? Get a tie to begin with.

I went into a clothes shop and chose a sombre tie. They wanted two pounds for it. Two pounds! 'But I'm a *garçon de café*,' I said indignantly. They knocked off ten bob.

Now properly haltered I headed on towards the café: it might be a little quiet one, I comforted myself.

But it was one of those no-nonsense *tabacs*, feverishly busy. The customers, who were all knowing locals from adjacent offices, would want their *cafés*, *apéritives*, *demis*, sandwiches and *oeuf durs*, fast. They stood, three-deep at the counter, baying as if at some terrible auction.

I quailed at the prospect of having to face them, protected only by an apron. They all sounded scornful, sure and impetuous; I wondered how any waiter ever got the better of them. They were the kind who would never ask for a simple *café crème* or plain drinks: it would be a white *café 'bien noir'* or a *mars de Haute Savoie* instead of a simple Cognac. *De Haute Savoie* – they'd probably end up with a *Calvados à la pression*.

I went up, faint-hearted, to the lady at the *caisse*. 'I'm the waiter from Mère Cascade's,' I said.

She had heavy threatening shoulders, screwed up eyes like sucked olive pips, a rolling, slow, disdainful manner, and looked like the kind who would short-change you over a single stamp and dare you to complain. But now, like a pudding out of its element, she wobbled and looked guilty. 'But we expected you last night,' she said. 'Someone else came, so we took him.'

I went back to La Mère's, nursing indignation – but it was better than actually having to do the job.

'And she didn't even give you a present? Not a *rond*?' the Gascon roared. 'Oh, *la salope*!'

I left that evening and never went back. But that night I signed a a couple of bookfuls of Smile Cheques in my own favour and posted them to the Commissariat du Tourisme. There was always the chance, I thought, that that trip to Tahiti would go to Pierre, the *garçon du comptoir* of La Mère Cascade's.

I finally achieved fame in Britain, fame far transcending the normal *Guardian* catchment area. But it was not for the sort of reporting that traditionally wins foreign correspondents' acclaim, although the day the piece came out the *Guardian* was changing hands on the stock exchange at ten times its cover price.

It was a Saturday morning in July in the pixilated week leading up to the 14th. I was thumbing glumly through PR handouts looking for some celebrity I could transfix or event I could artistically inflate for the benefit of our readers when I noticed a five-line paragraph announcing the imminent publication of the life of an obscure French music hall performer. In the latter part of the nineteenth century this man, Joseph Pujol, had achieved European renown simply because of a noise he made on stage. Since then he had suffered cruel neglect.

I took one look at what that noise was, leaped from my couch, and trotted down to St-Germain where the publisher's offices were. I was too impelled by enthusiasm to be stayed by the fact that publishers were not open on Saturday. And indeed Monsieur Jean-Jacques Pauvert's office was shut. But he was inside and I could see him. I tapped like a mendicant on his window and he, with a bad grace, opened up and enquired what I wanted. A copy of the book! He gave me one and a picture and went back to his affairs.

I went home, sat at my Olivetti and spent a couple of hours spelling out the story of Joseph Pujol's life and achievement. Because of the standards of the day I had to proceed with great delicacy. I disciplined myself to recount the tale with the same consideration and sympathy I would apply to, say, the life of Madame Curie and consciously observed the style and format of traditional biographies of that nature.

It went like this:

For 14 July, the time when Parisians give voice with petard and brass-band to whatever dry store of joy is still left in them, a French publisher has very appropriately produced a handsome tribute to one of the most celebrated noise-makers the European stage has ever known: M. Joseph Pujol. At the height of his career as star of the Moulin Rouge, Marcel Pagnol in his book *Notes on Laughter* tells us, Joseph Pujol could draw matinée gates worth 20,000 francs while Sarah Bernhardt the same week only managed 8,000. Eye-witnesses claim that he was one of the greatest amusers of all time. His career spanned more than twenty years.

Why then does the name Pujol mean nothing to us today? Because to perpetuate his name it is necessary to describe what he did, and for a couple of generations this simply could not be done in print. (Perhaps it still can't.) Dear me, how styles of entertainment have changed! Pujol described himself as 'Le Pétomane'. Not to beat about the bush, Pujol's talent was that he could fart like nobody else in the world, before, then, or since.

He could fart tenderly (*le petit pet timide de la jeune fille*) or aggressively (*le pet rond du maçon*); rapidly like a machine-gun – or he could produce a deep, slow cannon-roar lasting up to ten seconds. He could give a very good account of a doh-ray-me-fah *derrière*-wise, imitate a violin, a bass or the timbre of a trombone.

Pujol was no scurvy, back-street perverted farter. He only farted in the very best places and for considerable sums of money. Eye-witnesses insist on the gravity and impassivity of his performance and the essential seriousness of this father of ten buxom children.

In 1887, the year Mallarmé published *L'Après-midi d'une Faune*, Pujol, aged 30, appeared for the first time on a public stage in Marseilles. His talent had already been the envy of his schoolmates, the admiration of his regiment and evoked the solicitous respect of his family. Within a week Marseilles was crowding to see the Pétomane. For the next twenty years, in Marseilles, Paris, Brussels, North Africa, all over Europe, Pujol presented an unchanging ritual. Dressed in a red coat and black satin knickerbockers, he would approach the ramp and announce gravely: 'Mesdames, Mesdemoiselles, Messieurs, I have the honour to present to you a performance of *pétomanie . . .*'

He would then stoop and begin his finely graded, escalating performance. In his history of the 'Caf'conc', Jacques-Charles describes the scenes at the Moulin Rouge. 'At first the audience would remain astounded. Then someone would be stricken with a crazy laugh. In a moment people would be howling and staggering with laughter. Some would stand paralysed, tears pouring down their cheeks, while others beat their heads and fell on the floor. Ladies would begin to suffocate in their tight corsets and for this reason there were always a number of white-coated nurses in attendance.'

Mlle Yvette Guilbert wrote: 'It was at the Moulin Rouge that I heard the longest spasms of laughter, the most hysterical cries of hilarity that I have ever heard in my life.'

The King of the Belgians travelled incognito to Paris for a private demonstration by Monsieur Pujol.

But it was not only an audience in search of a belly laugh who flocked to see Pujol; the Academy of Medicine in Paris was, so to speak, hot on his tail. Pujol, partly to prove the authenticity of his performances (which he could hardly do on the stage of the Moulin Rouge) submitted to a number of elaborate medical examinations which are described in *La Semaine Médical* of 1882 by a Dr Marcel Baudouin with a zest and enthusiasm for detail which unfortunately cannot be reproduced here.

Pujol finally broke with the Moulin Rouge and opened his own theatre, the Pompadour. Then, in 1898, the year Marie Curie discovered radium, Pujol discovered that the Moulin Rouge was going to present a rival female pétomane.

He brought an action for unauthorized imitation. Lawyers had to attend the theatre and note the range, quality and form of the lady's performance. But before the case actually came to court the lady was exposed as a fraud (she had whistles hidden in her skirts).

Pujol, who lived to be 88, was an outstanding example of man's ingenuity in making the best of whatever gifts nature bestows – be they ever so curious. With extraordinary courage, and by the sheer quality of his performance, he imposed the fart on a stupefied but defenceless Europe.

He was a star until 1914 when the countries of Europe decided to get together on a roaring orgy of petomania of their own which was, no doubt, distasteful to this gentle and scrupulous performer. (By the way, he claims never to have suffered from stagefright.)

How has his name come to light again? Simply because his family of honest bakers and masons in Marseilles were pained that their famous ancestor had become so neglected. Last year they appealed to a pair of well-known journalists on the *ORTF* pointing out the injustice that: 'France has done nothing for the memory of its Pétomane!'

Now justice has been done. But, alas, given the standards of our time, the tribute could be neither aural nor visual.

I thought they might just run the piece, but it was purely as a joke for the boys back in London that I included a picture of Pujol gravely bending to perform. But Christopher Prout Driver, a man of mischievous impulses, was on duty the day the piece arrived (and, the story goes, the more fastidious editor Alastair Hetherington was off). He put the piece and picture in a tasteful setting.

The publication of the book (really only a series of documents and letters) created no interest in France. But in anally conscious Britain they went wild over the article. People still ask the *Guardian* library for copies.

Five years later when I was in London working as a feature writer for the *Sunday Times* I was also briefly its television critic. After my first column appeared I went to Broadcasting House for a preview. I arrived to find a substantial queue of senior BBC executives all anxious to congratulate me on my work. I thought this was pretty decent of them, if not a little exaggerated. I pointed out that I had only written one TV column so far.

'Oh no,' they said. 'We are not thinking of your television column. We just wanted to meet the man who had written the Pétomane article.'

I began to be uneasy about being known as a journalist the highlight of whose career was writing about farting. But time went its healing and coarsening way: later you couldn't look at a screen – cinema or TV – without seeing a bum or hearing its small range of grunts, gasps and explosions cheerlessly repeated.

They made a film about Pujol, starring Leonard Rossiter. But they miscalculated: there was only one joke in the story really and repeating it over an hour and a half, without the merit of being live and authentic, made the whole thing pointless.

Thirteen

Towards the end of 1964 I was leafing through a copy of Jean-Paul Sartre's literary magazine *Les Temps Moderne* when I came across an anonymous piece by an unrepentant gangster. The St-Germain-des-Prés literary parlour had been accessible to any *truand* who could write ever since Jean Genet warmed the spot a few years previously. Judging by his piece in *Les Temps Moderne* this anonymous *voyou* was another one with a scalding contempt for bourgeois values.

Unrepentant wrongdoers intrigued me, coming from a country where it was considered normal to be perpetually on the way to confession. My mind was all too willing to give accommodation to that mental parasite guilt (although there was still a disappointing supply of reasons for being guilty). In approaching this gangster, I may have been toying with the possibility of picking up a few tips from a professional on how to invest less in useless remorse. At the very least I wanted to discover how culpable he felt privately or how genuinely aloof he could be to his own crimes. He had spent fourteen of his thirty-eight years in jail for 'armed aggression' and other felonies. He had also notched up an acquittal, a 'relax' and had had a case dismissed for lack of evidence. In real life, I suspected, gangsters were probably slouch-brained creatures living at the threadbare end of cheap melodrama. But this one might be an exception.

Les Temps Moderne gave me the name of their anonymous author, Georges Figon, but they had no telephone number or address for him. The police of Montmartre – traditionally a gangster quarter –

166

were taken aback at a request from a foreigner wanting to pay a social call on a gangster and indignantly hung up on me. Balked at every turn I used an unprofessional ploy: I looked up Georges Figon in the phone book (journalists prefer circuitous routes).

His mother answered the phone. She gave me another number. When I rang, the receiver was lifted at the other end but no one spoke. I called hopefully into the emptiness: '*Allo*. This is a journalist from the *Guardian*. Gwar-dee-anne. Le Mon-ches-teur! [The French often preferred to call it that.] I would like to interview you. Are you Georges Figon?'

'*Ouais!*' A single breathy word came out of this deep, dark hole.

'Could we meet? I'd like to do a paper on you.'

'Ring tomorrow,' the voice said and hung up.

Throughout our acquaintanceship Figon never responded on the phone until he knew who was on the other end of the line. He would just stand in his own darkness and wait. I imagined him always conscious of a threatening world lying in wait outside. In any event, to lift the phone and respond cheerily would have been to deny that his existence was clandestine; tension gave point to his day which would otherwise, as in the case of all those only intermittently employed, be aimless.

There was one peculiarity about Figon which made him an exceptional gangster; he was the son of a senior civil servant, a Commander of the Légion d'Honneur. There was not much of a drug problem among French youth in those days, so *fils de papa* ending up in jail were rare. But Figon was not just a middle-class boy who had been a bit obstreperous; he had created of himself a gangster personality based partly, I suspect, on a private fiction. And he had a philosophy to go with it. During his trial, charged with shooting it out with policemen come to arrest him for a hold-up, Figon took over his own defence. Already back in 1955 the court reporter of *Le Monde*, noted his 'refusal to adopt the conventional demeanour of criminals who invariably try to minimize their guilt'. On a capital charge, the *Le Monde* reporter wrote: 'Figon demonstrated that a criminal has a place in society as much as those who judge him.'

Figon liked to pit his wits against the law and he was furious when his defence lawyer refused to use sleight-of-hand with photographs, which would have confused a witness into swearing that one of the men involved in the hold-up was Pope Pius XII. (He had noticed his own resemblance to the Pope.)

There was talk that Figon wanted to make a film about gangsters with an all-gangster cast. That was a promising peg for me.

What I did not know then was that Figon existed at the point where the criminal and the bourgeois establishments meet and make use of each other, in his case with catastrophic consequences. A year later that association was going to put Figon at the heart of an event which at one point looked as if it would topple de Gaulle.

After some persistence I finally got him to agree to a rendezvous. He designated Harry's Bar near the Opéra, a detestable trendy joint for expatriates and anglophile French. He told me later he thought my call was a practical joke by one of his friends, putting on an English accent on the phone. So, one evening in November I sat in Harry's Bar, my eye on the glass swing doors, feeling like some shady character who flits nocturnally between bootleggers and the law in a Warner Bros film.

Figon came in; standing three feet away, he enquired at the bar for me. The barman, playing his role conscientiously, kept on polishing a glass and nodded wordlessly in my direction. Figon was a puny little man who looked more like a depressed bank clerk than a gangster. He wore a knee-length, slate-grey raincoat – along the lines of those affected by plainclothes French cops. His low voice was often directed at the table top. He sat, round-shouldered, smouldering with suspicion, his expression often one of theatrical contempt. But he warmed up a bit with the beer and my solicitous interest.

I asked him how he got his sentence. 'It was a sombre story of a suspected jewel robbery,' he said.

'Did you steal the jewels?'

'*Toujours non*,' he said, making no attempt to sound convincing.

It was in 1950 near the Porte Maillot. About a dozen armed police came to pick up a suspect. Figon claimed they started shooting first. 'They told us to put up our hands and we didn't,' he said. 'I got five years, what they call "prevention". Then I was brought to trial and served six and a half more.'

Figon had originally come in contact with gangsters when, after doing his *baccalauréat* at eighteen and a half, he got 'mixed up in a little adventure' and was sent to jail. It was there he found a confraternity worthy of his admiration.

What did his family think of his career? 'My mother is not overjoyed about the whole thing,' he said. His father remained throughout a figure in deep obscurity, silent and unforthcoming, like Figon standing by his phone.

I had heard Figon wanted a well-known Pigalle gangster, Jo Attia, to play the main role in his proposed film. Would Attia play the part of a gangster who reforms?

'Certainly not,' Figon said indignantly. 'It will be a perfectly amoral story. The character played by Jo is completely unsympathetic by your standards. Jo can just act natural.

'Of course,' he added, disgruntled, 'we have to let the police get him in the end, otherwise we couldn't make the film.'

Had Attia ever acted before? I wanted to know.

'Yes,' Figon said. 'He was playing in a film once, but one night he came into our bar in Pigalle with make-up on and the boys said: "Look at Jo! All made up like a sister!" and he never went back to film again. The producer sued him.'

Jo Attia was another unusual figure. He was under a judicial ban to keep out of the Paris area and the fiction was that he lived down south. But he was frequently seen around Paris. His immunity was put down to his having helped the Resistance during the war and a lot of people owed him dubious favours.

As we left Harry's Bar Figon started to rant about a Parisian journalist who had recently published a picture of Jo Attia in banned territory in Paris. Figon dealt with this in a thoroughly bureaucratic manner. He wrote a letter to the newspaper and had it delivered formally by a *huissier*. The letter said that the guilty journalist 'had not scorned to share a bottle of Dom Pérignon with M. Attia.'

He showed me the letter; it ended, 'This incident does not

enhance the opinion we already have of journalists, but without doubt your rules of civility are not the same as ours.'

I took this as a small warning to myself.

Figon had a swaggering loyalty to the milieu he had chosen, like a kid newly recruited into a gang. But he must have been as disconcerting to ordinary villains as he was to the law-abiding citizen. When he got worked up he would begin to vibrate and start pummelling the air with his fists. I was always afraid he was about to go off the rails. Still, we got on pretty well. I coaxed him to have another meeting and he agreed to let Louis Stettner take pictures. Though he would only allow the photographer to take the back of his head, standing at the zinc in a café along the boulevard des Capucines.

Louis is now accepted as one of the outstanding photographers of the century, superior, in my mind, to the more anecdotal Doisneau. He is back living in Paris. At that time he already had a considerable reputation amongst those not quite as ignorant as I about photography.

He had been a member of the Photo League, a New York collective founded in the thirties and destroyed by McCarthyism. It was Louis who in 1952 arranged the New York exhibition that introduced Brassai, Doisneau, Ronis and Izis to the Americans. But if I knew that at the time it passed over my head.

I only registered that he was a stringer for *Life*, and, having all the characteristics of an exuberant layabout and being, in addition, an undeflatable Marxist proselytiser, he was not likely to advance beyond that status.

We had met at George's bookshop, the Mistral across from Notre Dame, where he slapped me about amicably with declarations such as: 'He who remains aloof from the struggle of his generation cannot be said to have lived.'

We had a couple of beers to wrestle with this kind of thing properly and when this did not diminish the ardour of the debate we went to dinner in a cheap Greek restaurant, the usual path to new friendships in Paris. Like most friendships I made, the work had nothing to do with it. But it was handy that Louis was also a photographer.

I kept up contact with Figon. This became easy when I discovered he frequented the Scotch Bar in rue Delambre, Montparnasse, a couple of doors from the Rosebud. It was a chill place, usually three-quarters empty, with fussily panelled walls and coloured glass windows to preserve the privacy of the regulars. One night, Gerald Kemmet, on a night off from imitating de Gaulle in the Falstaff – and to avoid someone in the Rosebud next door – went into the Scotch Bar. The moment he walked in, a girl he knew, sitting at the bar, said: 'This man has insulted me!' and pointed to an individual alongside her.

Gerald was a man whose verbal skirmishing might well start a fight, but he would never participate in one. So this should simply have been a prelude to a mystifying dissertation from him on the nature of male/female relationships as adumbrated in the philosophy of Flann O'Brien's nephew (Gerald could do this in French with footnotes by Raymond Queneau). But, quite uncharacteristically, this night he must have felt a need to give Fate a rev.

He said to the man in his Dean-of-Discipline, Holy-Ghost-Fathers' voice (he had gone to Blackrock College in Dublin), 'Step out here, my good man!' The stranger (whom Gerald, no doubt, had registered was of puny build) went, perfectly docile, and they confronted each other in a little yard alongside. Gerald began to dance around the yard, fists up, thumbing his nose, like Ben Turpin off a hot stove.

The stranger lashed out with his foot and a revolver fell from his pocket.

Gerald instantly switched back to his role of verbal dazzler; within minutes he had transformed the relationship into one of comradeship. He led his opponent, arm solicitously around the shoulder, back into the bar and offered him a comradely Cognac.

That was how we discovered it definitely was a gangster hangout.

Figon occasionally gave me insights into the criminal world. He told me that conditions in the French penitentiary system had improved in recent years only because the jails had begun to fill with a different clientele. First there were the collaborators, businessmen who liked their comfort and had not entirely lost their influence. Then the OAS ex-army officers completely transformed prisons such as Fresnes: they had powerful political contacts and when they started to agitate for better conditions something was done.

Figon told me that the more notorious gangster bars, those of Pigalle, were really only for pimps; they were too well known to the police to be useful for serious gangsters' meetings. Around that time the real gangsters favoured the northern area of the Étoile, immense commercial cafés at Wagram, also frequented by the bourgeoisie. Another favourite was an actors' late-night bar near the Théâtre St-Martin.

Figon would hold forth on the incapacity of the type who is not a *voyou* to understand the mentality of the *voyou*. Journalists never got it right, he said. 'The men of the milieu have been so deformed by the press that it's unimaginable,' he complained. 'Everywhere you look you come across species of myths that have been honeyed up by journalists.' One reason you never got a true insight, he admitted, was that, on the rare occasions that the criminal speaks in public – when he is on trial – he is playing a part so that he can be acquitted. He is not being natural. 'In my film,' Figon said, 'the criminal will be natural – that is, odious.'

I discovered that what he really had in mind was to get me to persuade Joseph Losey to direct his film for him. I had met Losey when he was in Paris making *Eva*, an Italian co-production with Jeanne Moreau, one of his more foolish efforts. In 1962 the Cinémathèque, rendering the kind of service to Losey that they did to so many directors, gave a week-long homage to this McCarthy-blacklisted director, showing all his work from his remake of *M* up to *The Damned*. It was Losey's prison film, *The Criminal* (1960), which had impressed Figon.

I asked him why he had not approached French directors. He said he had sent word by a friend to Godard, but when Godard was told he had a good script he had retorted: 'Well, if he has a good scenario why doesn't he make a film?'

'There is a species of *je-m'en-foutisme* about Godard that I like,' Figon remarked.

The curious thing is that he and Godard were physically and temperamentally not unalike. Godard was also short, dark and given to lashing rages.

Figon had also approached Serge Reggiani, still with star billing after the success of *Casque d'Or*. He described with detestation how Reggiani had given him a public audience in the Coupole and while Figon, drinking a beer, sat at his knee feverishly delivering the plot of the film, Reggiani picked fastidiously at his sumptuous supper, cocking one ear but not deigning to look at his supplicant.

Sitting up on the barstool of the Scotch bar alongside me, Figon's little fists began to pummel viciously into the ribs of an imaginary Reggiani. I tried not to be hasty about finishing my beer, and left early.

I wrote to Losey. He replied promptly. It was not, he said, that he didn't trust French gangsters, he didn't trust French producers.

I tried to cool my relationship with Figon when it was obvious to me that the contact was going nowhere. However, Figon did not appear to notice; he was still working on me to help him get a film project off the ground. Then he began to be more confiding about his activities. I did not mind the yarns of the past, but when it dawned on me that he was giving me information about jobs he was currently planning I decided to back out. My taste for minor anarchy did not extend to becoming an accomplice before the fact in a hold-up.

Less than a year later I picked up a French paper and read that the mysterious third man the police were seeking in the Ben Barka kidnap affair was Georges Figon. The Moroccan opposition leader was lured to a meeting at the Drug Store in St-Germain-de-Prés. There, in full view of passers-by, he was picked up by French police. So confident were they that the most senior authorities were *au parfum* (in the know and approving) that they wore their uniforms and drove a police car. They were kidnapping Barka as a favour to the Moroccans. Subsequently they handed him over to be murdered by the Moroccan Minister for the Interior, General Oufkir.

My heart turned over when I read the details of Figon's involvement. He was sitting at the Brasserie Lipp next door to the Drug Store, ostensibly discussing a film deal with a producer and a French journalist when he fingered Ben Barka for the kidnappers. The film deal was apparently a front for the long-prepared kidnap.

The journalist was arrested a few days later and went through a nightmare of third degree before he was exonerated. I saw myself, his predecessor, in that very hot seat.

Figon went on the run; hunted by police and the secret services, he went on a rampage of spilling the beans in tantalizing morsels to newspapers and television, getting closer and closer at each revelation to the murkier secrets of the Ben Barka affair. He was implicating high-ranking French politicians, among them the Minister for the Interior, Roger Frey, and a shadowy bald character, Jacques Foccart, the Minister for 'African Affairs'.

At one point Figon mocked the authorities – who were not at all anxious to bring him to an embarrassing trial – by calling a press conference in a big store to witness him trying on new hats.

A short time later the apartment block at rue Hoche in which he was cornered was surrounded by police. A mysterious 'press photographer', never later identified, got through the cordon. The street lights went out. There was the sound of shots.

'*Tiens!*' a senior policeman exclaimed with remarkable prescience. 'I think Figon has committed suicide.'

And indeed Georges Figon had been 'suicided'.

Fourteen

The vulnerable and afflicted were always to be found under Beckett's wing – or under his oxter, as Sam would have preferred to put it. On one occasion Jackie MacGowran found protection there and I was, temporarily, cast in the role of villain. I went into the Falstaff one night in February 1964 and there with Sam and Con were Pat Magee and Jackie MacGowran, both superb Beckett interpreters. As I approached the table, Jackie, a famished figure with a head movement like a ferret pushing its face through long grass, rose, raised a voice with a theatrical tremble in it and announced: 'I will not sit at the same table as that man. If that man sits down here, I'm going.'

MacGowran and Magee were over for an English language production of *Endgame* at the Studio des Champs-Élysées. This was a stunt thought up by an Anglo-Irish drama student who had got the financial backing from a couple of friends of mine, Victor Herbert, already planning a tactical withdrawal from Bernie Cornfeld's later bankrupt Investors Overseas Services (IOS), and a drifting Scots engineer named Macdonald Prain. The third investor was a Frenchman, Philippe Staib.

I knew what was ailing MacGowran. At the Dublin Theatre Festival fourteen months before, he had given a shambolic performance of a one-man show, *Beginning to End*, made up of fragments of Beckett's writings. I was covering the festival for the *Guardian* and gave it a panning, in somewhat windy and priggish terms, it has to be said, not knowing then of MacGowran's mental distress; booze and

175

pills were already playing havoc with him. Beckett had a particular tolerant fondness for MacGowran; but desperation sometimes drew MacGowran to disregard this loyalty. He had cobbled together the bits of prose and plays without Beckett's permission, something no one else would have dared to do. Jackie played a little on his misfortunes but, in this case, he was certainly driven by panic about his career.

But now the Falstaff row had to be resolved. It was dealt with in the usual way, by standings up and sittings down, delayed-action eruptions and coaxing interpolations. I hovered around, refusing to be banished from my own pub. Sam did a couple of rounds with each of us in turn, perhaps disturbed at having to take sides. I whispered to Sam that I had had no choice but to do my journalistic duty. 'Jackie's upset,' was all he would say to me, not sympathizing, I got the impression, with my professional candour, despite his own rigorous and meticulous watchfulness when supervising productions of his work. (Later, he took over this compilation, re-edited it and restricted performances.)

Pat Magee did not rise, but, gripping his pint mug as one would a staff, made some judicial pronouncements in that ball-grinding voice of his. The grinding was usually directed towards the balls of the Jesuits, to whom he once served a brief and unconsummated apprenticeship.

There was more than an evening's drinking at stake here: Beckett had agreed that I could attend rehearsals of *Endgame*. But there seemed to be no way MacGowran would accept my presence in the theatre. Late that night a reconciliation was initiated gracefully by MacGowran. Sam had calmed him down by promising to write a play for him and Jackie was magnanimous in his triumph. When this play appeared the first reaction in the Falstaff was that Beckett had played a cruel joke on MacGowran. It was *Eh Joe*, in which Jackie, reckless purloiner of Beckett's texts, was silenced. He had no lines. The words are spoken by a female voice-over. But, knowing Beckett, it was much more likely that he simply followed his own obsessive course and the apparent comment on Jackie was accidental.

When I went in to watch rehearsals it was clear at once there was trouble. The young director who had talked Sam into letting him have the chance was one of those people whose attitude to a work of art is similar to that of a man who ministers to a baby for intellectual reasons; theoretical reverence fogged his brain and did not allow him to give sufficient weight to the fact that in Magee (Hamm) and MacGowran (Clove) he was dealing with a pair of rascals. They made game of his authority and every time he issued a direction they would send a knowing look towards Beckett in the stalls. Sam would give them the nod or a frown as he felt appropriate. It ended with the young director having a kind of nervous breakdown, sitting in a corner of the theatre all day, scribbling, scribbling – 'Like some character out of Beckett,' Herbert said – and Beckett took over the production.

When I went to meet a friend in a café down in Odéon one evening, he turned to an American, a new arrival standing with him at the bar, and, nodding at me, said: 'He's just been to see Samuel Beckett.'

'Jesus Christ,' the American said, 'it's like saying he's just been to see Shakespeare.'

Fame is a tricky, often farcical, element: even by association it can be troublesome. This was the Paris of the 'new wave' in cinema, the 'new novel'; Ionesco and Adamov were at the height of their careers; Jacques Tati had not yet begun to fade, Sartre and de Beauvoir were still considerable figures. You could witness ambulant examples of a wide range of celebrity on every boulevard. But occasionally the mix was dodgy.

One evening after chatting with Ionesco in his apartment on the boulevard Montparnasse I invited him to have coffee in the Falstaff. I had become on good terms with this puckish character after he moved up to Montparnasse from the rue de Rivoli.

I don't know how I got him out to the Falstaff. When he offered me a glass of beer in his apartment on the boulevard Montparnasse, drink had first to be the subject of negotiations between him and his Romanian wife. His mouth rounding in that way it had when tackling the great aesthetic issues of the day, he made a soft-voiced plea on behalf of common hospitality. His wife then stood by on a spring-board of alertness ready to leap on any violation of the terms agreed.

These were that Ionesco could look but not touch. Those doe-sad eyes followed the decanting of beer into my glass with solicitude and a nostalgic tenderness that dampened his expression as he registered the reviving liquid go on its happy voyage down my gullet. By some inexplicable dispensation that night we were allowed out to the Falstaff, probably under precise restraints.

When we went in, Beckett was sitting with Con Leventhal, just inside the door. Observing the usual code, I did not mix guests. Ionesco may have given Beckett a nod, but no more; on the other hand Beckett and Sartre never exchanged a glance.

Sartre was already there with his pretty lip-reader. But, to my astonishment, so was Jean-Luc Godard, who'd never before been in the place, sitting with two friends, paying no attention to anyone. Considering the Falstaff had only about nine tables, and adding Ionesco to the cast list, this was probably one of the greatest concentrations of talent per square foot Paris had ever seen outside the cemetery at Père Lachaise.

Ionesco tottered out into the street convinced he was having another hallucination. 'What is this "*boîte*"?' he asked. 'How could such a place exist a few metres from my home?'

The answer was that the Falstaff wasn't a fashionable nightclub; it was a bar people went to for privacy, not to gawp at the famous. I began to be seriously worried about our unofficial drawing room. In fact Godard never came back; nor did Ionesco.

But one night fame of the uncontrollable variety, Hollywood fame, hit the Falstaff. I had already had a few refreshing jars in the Select before going into the Falstaff one Sunday evening in November 1965. I was in that intoxicated state, impossible to recapture in later life, of extraordinary well-being, its only equivalent that of the athlete at the peak of fitness. I felt capable of dealing with any situation swiftly with competence and indisputable sagacity.

Pierre, the waiter, contorted his face into a conspiratorial rictus: Monsieur Beckett and my friends, he whispered, were upstairs. Upstairs? It was a kind of dusty loft few went near. Sartre was in his place, but there were still plenty of empty tables. What was going on?

The moment my head reached the level of the upper floor I

understood what was up. We had a *film star* in captivity: Peter O'Toole. Although the downstairs section was a bunker secure enough for a Sartre and a Beckett, it was too hazardous exposure for Lawrence of Arabia. There were Sam and Con, and Barbara Bray, a close friend of Beckett, a noted translator who worked for the BBC; my wife, and Peter Graham, translator and gourmet. Beckett sat with his back to the wall, between Con and Barbara. O'Toole faced him, flanked by a silent bruiser who turned out to be his bodyguard and purse carrier. Only I realized we had an awkward situation. Equally, only I did not realize how tight I was. My mood was one in which whatever was on my mind took precedence over whatever anyone else wanted to talk about.

What was on my mind was that Ernie Anderson, a film publicist, had been plaguing me to go out to Billancourt and interview O'Toole who was shooting a film there. I had sidetracked Ernie with an insincere promise of doing something about it that weekend. But being a film buff in those days of the *nouvelle vague* I had no intention of interviewing a bloody film star (except, perhaps, Jeanne Moreau); only directors had status.

I was convinced that O'Toole was aware of this slight and that I must do something to sooth his hurt. I sat down and, leaning across the chunky individual, asked O'Toole what he was doing in Paris; what film he was shooting, was it going well, etc., etc., saving time by answering the questions myself: 'Oh, yes, you're out at Billancourt,' etc.

The chunky individual put his face close to mine and said: 'Don't be bothering Mr O'Toole.'

I was astonished. What could he mean? It was they who were visitors to my bar. No doubt to divert attention, O'Toole ordered a round, in a rather authoritarian manner I felt, which violated our gentler ways. When Pierre brought the drinks he ordered the chunky one to pay.

Undeterred, I embarked on another round of questions with built-in answers for O'Toole.

'Mr O'Toole does not wish to be pestered by journalists,' the chunky one interrupted.

179

Indignation of the purist ilk welled within me. 'Do you seriously think', I blurted out, 'that a journalist would be interested in trying to get an interview out of a film actor when he has Beckett sitting right there in front of him?'

Everybody must have winced.

'If you don't stop annoying Mr O'Toole,' the chunky one said, 'I'll deal with you.'

O'Toole said nothing. I bridled. 'You are not', I informed O'Toole, 'taking responsibility for this man's behaviour!'

Beckett said nothing. But Con Leventhal began distributing verbal ointments around the table like a nurse at the scene of a multiple accident. There was a certain subsidence of tension and I decided it would be diplomatic to turn to a more harmless subject. 'You're Irish, aren't you?' I said conversationally to O'Toole. And then, fatally, answered my own question: 'Oh, no, of course, you're Liverpool Irish.' The relationship between 'genuine' Irish and second generation, particularly Liverpool, Irish is a very delicate one. It can be dangerous for a native Irishman to draw attention to a Liverpool Irishman's second-degree nationality.

O'Toole stood up. 'Come outside,' he said.

I heard my wife cry out: 'Don't go!' But a bar is not a place where one listens to one's wife. Anyway being generous-tight as distinct from rancorous-tight I had got it into my head that I had totally won over this shy man who now wished to apologize quietly and perhaps share with me exclusively some secrets of the film world.

When we got to the head of the stairs O'Toole announced: 'I'm going to throw you down those stairs.'

I looked at him in amazement and then uncomprehendingly at the narrow polished wooden staircase. It was like a scene from a film, I thought. How droll! I must tell the others! I felt no fear, my only consideration was that the moment must not be lost. 'Wait there,' I told O'Toole, and hurrying back to the table I announced cheerfully to the appalled group: 'He wants to throw me down the stairs!'

The unfortunate O'Toole, landed with a man who had a totally cavalier attitude to the rules of bar-room brawling, had no choice but to come back to the table, his honour unsatisfied.

Beckett got up, came around to the front of the table and without a word took the place of danger between me and the chunky one, ranging himself openly on my side. Not since I dreamed as a schoolboy of Henry Fonda standing shoulder to shoulder with me in a saloon shoot-out have I been so thrilled. We faced down the baddies. They apparently decided not to take on the Wyatt Earp of literature. O'Toole, now in a bit-player role, sat subdued on the other side of his bodyguard.

A certain constraint marked the remainder of the exchanges. O'Toole issued an invitation pointedly only to Sam, Barbara and Con to go on to some other place. Sam declined on behalf of everyone, and the two interlopers left soon after.

Beckett preferred to have his social life in cafés. Responding to what he recognized as my need to return the hospitality of having been invited to his home, he agreed to come to my apartment one evening. Entertaining at home was not my style at all and the whole thing had a certain artificiality about it. Sam and Con Leventhal arrived tipsy. They sat together uncomfortably on a narrow divan looking like a pair of schoolboys obliged to perform some social duty for adults. I'm not sure they didn't actually giggle.

Michael Beausang, a young Irish Joyce scholar, who knew them both, was there; my wife, and a Finnish journalist Hilkka Maki, known to Con but not to Beckett. Hilkka was not willing to be as neurotic about protecting Beckett's privacy as I was and straight away began quizzing him about his work, a fatal approach. He fobbed her off with laconic remarks and I put on a Bartók record as a distraction. Sam drifted into the music of one of his favourite composers and forgot everybody.

Next evening I came across him standing alone at the bar of the Falstaff. I chided him on the pair of them having behaved like a couple of truant schoolboys the night before. He looked startled, and then, contrite, began to tell me about James Joyce, his idea of a treat. But his adoration of Joyce at his own expense irritated me.

He told how when Joyce had finished *Finnegans Wake* he was

worried about the ending and rang Beckett from a call-box to ask him what he thought of it. 'Great,' Beckett told him in his laconic way. Reassured, Joyce went ahead with publishing *Finnegans Wake* as it was, getting the go-ahead from a call-box.

When Buster Keaton died in 1966 I got the idea of suggesting to Beckett that he pay a public tribute to this great genius of the cinema, a finer artist, I felt, than Chaplin, although Beckett had only paid one such public tribute – a single sentence salute to Sean O'Casey. To my surprise he agreed to speak about working with Keaton, for publication in the *Guardian*.

Two years previously these great creative figures had had a curious and ultimately barren collaboration. Beckett had always been an admirer of Keaton and when he wrote his first film script, *Film*, he got his director Alan Schneider to offer the main and only role to Keaton. Keaton was already sixty-eight and in bad health but he accepted the part even though it went directly against his temperament, as Beckett admitted. The theme was certainly not Keatonesque. It was a reflection on Bishop Berkeley's dictum 'To be is to be perceived', and concerned a man who has the notion that if he could hide from all human or animal vision he would cease to exist. After much fugitive manoeuvring he is confronted by the inescapable gaze of self-perception. The script required Keaton to be filmed from behind throughout; the great Stone Face was seen only in the final shot, flinching before self-perception.

Beckett told me of how Keaton still smoked from forty to fifty cigarettes a day and had a terrible cough but was still 'extraordinarily graceful'. 'He had enormous body control and his gestures were very beautiful,' Beckett said. 'He made simple gestures such as feeling his pulse or grinding the fragments of a photograph into the floor very significant. He was very interested in the technical problems of film-making, in anything to do with the camera. The extraordinary thing was that even when his back was turned he always seemed to know where he was in relation to the camera.

'He agreed to break his famous mask for that moment,' Beckett added with gratitude.

But he also told me that their relationship was disastrous. This poker-playing addict of TV baseball made it no secret that he felt he was involved in a boring intellectual exercise. He spent most of his free time alone, reading detective stories.

'I never understood why he accepted the part,' Beckett told me. 'It certainly couldn't have been the money.'

Nor was it admiration for Beckett. Keaton had only a sketchy knowledge of Beckett's output and what he knew he didn't like. He had turned down the part of Godot years before.

In fact Beckett was quite hurt by Keaton's dismissive attitude towards him. But this did not diminish his admiration. Typical of Sam, he would not be quoted as saying anything disobliging about a man who had treated him with some contempt.

To my knowledge Beckett had never before allowed himself to be quoted directly about any personal experiences. And here he was talking about working with another great artist. But I was so locked into the idea that I must never report anything Beckett said to me that I completely undermined my own scoop. I phoned in the piece, which hinted at some kind of importance, but I was so reticent in conveying that Beckett was actually speaking to me for publication, so discreet with direct quotes, that even the subs did not grasp the significance of the piece. They gave it half a column on the back page.

But I had remembered an incident of some years before, when an Italian journalist, an old friend from Resistance days, met Beckett again in Paris. They drank together and talked about old times, during the course of which Sam, off guard, gave his opinion of a number of French writers. Everything he said appeared in an Italian newspaper the following week. We met at the Closerie de Lilas the day he discovered this. His distress was so raw, like a child horribly exposed, that I there and then jettisoned whatever scepticism I might have had about the absolute necessity of never betraying his privacy. You were loyal to Beckett not because of his severity, but because of his vulnerability.

Fifteen

The *nouvelle vague* of gifted French film directors who appeared at the end of the fifties was not just a marginal cultural event. It engaged the passions of the entire country; each new French film became almost a national event.

It all had a gratifyingly cheeky beginning. François Truffaut, a young film critic on *Arts* magazine, tormentor of many a Cannes Film Festival, boasted he could do better than any French director (except Renoir, everyone's master). He made *Les Quatre Cents Coups*, and Cannes, the festival he had castigated so often, found itself awarding him the Grand Prix. In the same year Alain Resnais screened *Hiroshima Mon Amour*.

This was a time of great creativity and optimism in film-making. Imagine a thirteen-month period, from the May Cannes festival of 1959 to Cannes 1960, which produced Truffaut's *Les Quatre Cents Coups* and his *Tirez sur le Pianiste*; Chabrol's *Les Cousins*; Godard's *À Bout de Souffle*; Jacques Demy's *Lola*; Alain Resnais's *Hiroshima Mon Amour*; Eric Rohmer's *Le Signe du Lion* and Jacques Rivette's *Paris nous Appartient*. All these directors were under forty; Truffaut and Demy were still in their twenties.

Well, Paris, the university towns and the larger cities, did belong to them and, as happened during the student street debates of '68, the *croulants* (wrinklies) came out to join the queues to see, and argue about, the latest French film sensation.

This movement also had well-nurtured roots; the gardeners were Henri Langois and Mary Meerson who, at the Cinémathèque Française, by the Panthéon, displayed the material, three times a night, seven nights a week, which nurtured a whole new generation of film-makers, and indeed had world-wide influence.

Langois, an ample-bellied man of deep-seated irascibility, started his Cinémathèque in the thirties in his bathroom. In 1944 he was given accommodation at the Institut Pédagogique, on rue d'Ulm, and then in 1960 he was allotted a second splendid cinema at the Palais de Chaillot. Langois was an opinionated and obsessive film collector. It is only a collector's mania, rather than a film critic's judicious appreciation, which could account for his passion for films of any size, quality or provenance. In the fifties, only a collector could be so wonderfully indifferent to the inferior status of American B pictures and treasure them as if they were high art. He enlarged the whole concept of what a film museum should be by not accepting that it should only house 'classics'. 'How are we to know what a film classic will be?' was his argument. 'We are not God!'

His collection grew to over sixty thousand. His success came partly from the fact that he was a great thief – indulged, it must be said, by most of the world's film directors. Once you lent a print to the Cinémathèque it was a hell of a job to get it back. But everyone knew it was in loving hands.

It was in this atmosphere that Godard, Truffaut and Chabrol received their education. Night after night they would sit in the front row of the Cinémathèque at Ulm with their spiritual mother, Mary Meerson, consuming great draughts of mostly American cinema. Meerson was a good-natured woman, as broad as a sail and as benign as Langois was choleric. Since she could hardly see beyond the tip of her nose and the boys knew hardly any English, this led to the most fertile climate of creative tolerance in the history of the cinema. In *Cahiers du Cinéma* the boys wrote about American B pictures like Keyhole Kate on LSD.

It was when Malraux, Minister for Culture, incensed by Langois' holy disregard for accountability, dismissed the founder-director of the Cinémathèque in 1968 that the 'events' really started. It was February, three months before the revolt at the suburban Nanterre faculty which the history books identify as the beginning. But it was on the Cinémathèque issue that student and intellectual first expressed their rage at the high-handed way in which France was being governed culturally. They came out on to the street, Truffaut and Godard linking arms with Bresson and Renoir. From all over the world telegrams of support poured in – from Kazan and Chaplin, Samuel Fuller, Man Ray, Buñuel. The battles with riot police were spiced with the saucy presence of Marlene Dietrich. All this for a man who was not even French. Langois was born in Turkey. This shows how, when it came to culture, the French could not be diverted by irrelevancies. Langois and Mary Meerson were the spiritual parents of a great film movement in France and their pupils were happy to fight for them and for what de Gaulle would have called 'a certain idea of culture'. Langois was reinstated, but the first shot in the '68 revolt had been fired.

Another figure was equally central to a movement which depended on an ability to produce films of high quality without recourse to expensive studios: Raoul Coutard. The young directors would, no doubt, have made their breakthrough anyway, but Coutard was the one cameraman of the time superbly equipped for clearing technical obstacles from their path. His background was perfect for this adventure in film-making. A *Paris Match* war photographer, he became a cameraman for the French army and was parachuted into Indo-China during that war. So, from the outset, it was natural for him to shoot in the worst conditions, in the most unfavourable light without laborious preparation. But he was no hack: he is one of the most creative cinematographers in film history. Coutard was not only the director of photography for Godard's first dozen films, he was also responsible for Truffaut's visually superb *Jules et Jim*, as well as *Tirez sur Le Pianiste* and *La Peau Douce*. And it was he who provided that dreamy romantic look for Jacques Demy's *Lola* (1960).

Coutard was able to light a scene with a few bulbs and silver paper as effectively as any Hollywood cameraman would with a great retinue of assistants. He worked intuitively and often at a speed which astonished other professionals. He said he liked to light a scene quickly to leave the director plenty of time to think about the finished set-up. He had the craftsman's attitude to his role: like a cabinetmaker it was his job to express the director's ideas in superlative design, no more. 'The director is the only one with a total vision of what the film is going to be,' he said. Although superbly confident of his own ability he always did what the director wanted. But he also demanded that the director knew what he wanted; he was not going to give anyone a free ride. This was the better side of film-making demarcation.

Christmas had just passed and I had gone into a slump, tinkering with an intractable short story, when the arrival of Maurice Hatton winched me out on the road again. Maurice had signalled a will to come to Paris and have some expenses paid and appealed to me to provide him with an excuse. So I thought of Godard.

At that time an interview with Jean-Luc Godard was still a novelty in England. By now Godard, a Swiss, was leading the French *nouvelle vague* parade, having followed *Breathless* with *Une Femme est Une Femme* and *Vivre sa Vie*.

The encounter began badly. Godard stood me up. He had given a laconic agreement on the telephone to meet at his office by Étoile, but when Maurice and I arrived there was no sign of him and every sign of concentric prevarication on the part of his staff. One of those handsome middle-aged Parisiennes outfitted like a mannequin, but with the manners of a turnkey, claimed that Monsieur Godard had made no such appointment and he would not make himself available even to two journalists who had crossed the Channel especially to meet him. (I had remodelled the truth a little to make our appointment appear more momentous.) If we did not get Godard it would be disastrous for Maurice who, not being staffed, could not afford to hang around Paris.

In bureaux, public or private, the Parisians' particular fear was to be caught being obliging. They fretted at any transaction calling for routine helpfulness and at any suggestion of making an extra effort they took on a hunted air and plunged into reckless lying. Initially I was taken aback by the breadth and shamelessness of their chicanery. There was no ceiling to it. Unlike normal unhelpfulness their technique stripped you of alternatives to pursue. Rather than tell you someone was away for a few days they preferred to claim he did not exist. If something was temporarily out of stock they opted for impetuously closing down the manufacturers, presumably so you would not bother them again. In offices they banished people from the city who had simply crossed the road to a restaurant. If you persisted they gave vent to outbursts of self-pity. The exchanges rapidly took on the character of a quasi-domestic dispute, achieving the unfairness of a family quarrel in which the background ammunition is withheld from you but copiously drawn on by your opponent. Although you might never have met the person before, your opponent's attitude suggested life-long persecution at your hands.

But there was one advantage: Parisians have no shame. So there is no issue of honour when they are found out. They usually capitulated with minimum rancour.

Soon two young trainee turnkeys in Chanel little-black-frocks joined 'Madame Defarge' to observe the spectacle. They weren't terribly overawed. Just a short time before, in these very offices, Godard himself had knocked a seventy-year-old Paramount producer to the ground and started kicking him so the girls were probably only comparing styles. My bolshie approach was a success. They told us where Godard was working on location, just a few miles outside Paris; as part of the game, they swore us to secrecy about how we found out. We parted quite good friends.

We started off in search of the surly Prince of the *Nouvelle Vague*.

Maurice and I drove for some time through the suburbs, looking for the branch road which was supposed to lead us to Godard and his crew. On its eastern outskirts Paris abandons all pretence of being an elegant city. Frail wooden houses cluster along the road like refugees – cast-off fragments of the metropolis. It was hard to tell whether this was the continuation of a city or just littered countryside.

We turned off the main route and headed off past unused fields, which had the hangdog look of disregarded countryside in the vicinity of motorways. We drove until our instructions ran out. The still fields around had plainly no more information to give us. There was a ramshackle hut in the far corner of one field, but no one stirred.

We parked and pondered. We were both experienced enough in film location work to know that if a film crew was around there would be plenty of signs: a couple of heavy trucks, a generator, cables laid across the field, arc lamps standing by in the open. There would be trailers for the canteen and dressing rooms, limousines for the producers and stars, and a huddle of Deux Chevaux for the technicians.

Nothing. I began mentally to rehearse another jousting session with the female turnkeys back at Étoile. At that point, a slovenly looking youth came out of the hut and trod heavily across the muddied field, followed by a man with a hand-held *éclair*. The radiator of a car poked out from behind the hut. A short man in a fedora, dark glasses, a cigar in his mouth, stood in the shadow of the rickety veranda glancing at scraps of paper in his hand. It was Godard. A moment later they went back inside.

We crossed the field and shoved open the door of the hut which was shrouded inside by a floor-length dirty cloth. A segment of the interior was lit by that curious intense milky white light which declares the film set. The light went cold as we stepped in.

The hut was hardly bigger than a garden shed and it was packed like a Marx Brothers cabin. Godard was there and Coutard, a focus puller, a couple of electricians, two sound-men, a script-girl. There were no arc lamps at all. Coutard had fixed rows of bounce lights around the ceiling, boosted by silver reflective paper. Godard was feeding lines to the actors from the scraps of paper in his hand.

Here was the new genius of the cinema at work on a major film with one of the most renowned cameramen in the world. But if you put this unit and equipment into one of the massive multi-purpose fortresses of creation, which film sets had become, it would have been lost among the tea trolleys.

Godard was keeping his promise of taking film-making back to its ramshackle original innocence. The plot of *Les Carabiniers* – suggested by Rossellini – lent itself perfectly to such a demonstration. Two peasant oafs are recruited for the First World War with promises of spoils and assurances that war will give them freedom to do anything they liked. 'If we smash old people's glasses will no one say anything?' they ask. 'Can we break a child's arm? Two arms? Can we burn women? Can we steal chic trousers? Can we massacre the innocent? Denounce people? Leave a restaurant without paying?' (That last would only be high on a Frenchman's list of advantages.)

'Oui, oui. C'est la guerre!' they are told. Their covetous girlfriends are enchanted.

This small mob, the two barbarians, their girlfriends, and recruiting officer were also stuffed into the hut.

Godard approached us as if we were trespassers, although he knew me by sight. There was no PR on the set, so he had to handle this press problem himself. He spoke to me like a B-picture gangster, a low voice full of soft menace. I suspect that part of his game was impersonation of Bogart. But I found it difficult to take Godard's menace seriously, partly because he had a little whistle in his voice, a form of lisp. I reminded him we had an appointment. He said there was nothing he could do now; he was busy shooting a film. He passed a gang-boss glance over the shambles about him. I said there was indeed something he could do since we had come out so far: we could have the interview when the shoot was over. The sulks rising, but the menace fading, he objected that he did not know when he would be finished. I told him I didn't care when he finished; we were here and we would wait. I made a motion of backing into the only uncluttered corner, an action which contained some of the character of a last stand. Maurice Hatton stood behind me hefting his camera. Then we both tried to adopt a stance of scrupulously non-interfering onlookers. This was as difficult as trying to keep out of the way of a churlish charlady in a broom closet: at every step we were made aware of Godard's smoky glare.

During breaks in shooting, I would attempt to pick up some copy. When I found Coutard on his knees I dropped a question or two on the nape of his neck. But here was a man who knew how to fend off the press. I soon abandoned all attempts to communicate with this monosyllabic man.

When the shooting was over for the day Maurice and I closed in on Godard. We caught him trying to get away behind the hut, his demeanour that of a trapped schoolboy. His excuses were also from the schoolroom. He hadn't time; he had to go home and see rushes, etc. I said he could ride back with us and we could talk on the way. Enfeebled, perhaps, by his long day's work, or impressed by our doggedness, he agreed ungraciously. Off we went, Godard jammed in between Maurice and me in the Land-rover.

I wanted to know did he always improvise like that? It depended on the film. '*Vivre sa Vie* was built up block after block, like a stone wall, in the order it was shown,' he said. There was hardly any editing. The actors did have a script. *Une Femme est Une Femme* was carefully prepared, but he often wrote the dialogue while the actors were getting ready. '*Le Petit Soldat* was improvised a lot.'

'But you cannot completely improvise,' he said. 'It is not improvisation so much as final last-minute focusing, adjustments made when you are in the presence of and reacting to the actors and the décor.'

He made a comparison with a newspaperman writing his article half an hour before the deadline. 'It's terribly exhausting,' he said, 'but what comes out under pressure, while it might not be what you expected, is just as true. Intuitively you can achieve the right atmosphere. It was only when I had finished *Breathless* that I realized it had a breathless quality.'

How did he get away with such small crewing? Didn't he have trouble with the cinema unions? 'They write to me, but I take no notice,' he said. That would be his way of handling tiresome problems – that, or kicking his producer.

He admitted he did need good actors. 'The actors must have it in them. Belmondo is a very good actor, so was Jean Seberg, in her way. My wife Anna Karina', he said somewhat touchingly, 'is a good actress.' (She was not in this film and she was soon to leave him.) But he confessed that his methods created a problem for actors: they never felt that they dominated their character, and they didn't like that.

I told him that people were irritated by the literary quotations he planted like big dumb clues in his films and by the philosophers (notably in *Vivre sa Vie*) giving lectures.

It didn't bother Godard. 'People quote in real life – why can't I? And why not be intellectual?' he demanded.

That wasn't the kind of answer you would get from an English director.

I thought, since he was our prisoner, I would also complain about the private in-jokes and references to fellow directors in his films.

'The ordinary people of Paris are not irritated by that,' he retorted. 'They often don't notice. It is only the critics who spot one or two references and think there are others which they have missed – that's what irritates them.'

I didn't think this was a very convincing defence, but I let it go. My objection was that this nudging and winking was a distracting blemish on the imaginary world he was creating.

He had an interesting complaint about the British censor. At one point in *Vivre sa Vie* a man in a brothel says: 'Why not on the mouth?' The censor cut it to 'Why not?' It was not the truncation but that the censor had put in a fade-out that infuriated Godard. 'It looked as if I had made it that way,' he complained.

For all his apparently haphazard way of working, Godard was always after precise effects. I sympathized with his anger at the censor's high-handed meddling. In the other area of censorship, he told me that the French had finally authorized the screening of *Le Petit Soldat* which had been banned two years previously. It dealt with the OAS and torture. But they had made such extensive cuts, he said, that he had refused to release it. Eventually the full version was shown when the issue of Algeria had gone stale. On the last lap into Paris I came up with the routine question: what did Godard think of English directors? 'I don't like a single English director,' he replied, nicely in character as we dumped him at Étoile.

Sixteen

When I first met Jean Renoir, he said something which still lingers in my mind: 'We are surrounded by screens,' he said. 'Not just bad art. Even in education we are taught to see life in a way it is not. Everywhere there are screens. The artist is the one who pulls them down.'

It is impossible to know how, or to what extent, people influence you. The influence can be no more than gaining courage from someone whose views reinforce your own, whose example demonstrates that your ideals are not foolish and may be attainable. I don't know how Beckett influenced me; perhaps simply, and fundamentally, by being a living example of total integrity. Renoir's films over the years had a direct influence over what I valued in cinema and when it came to my own directorial début I, too, began to try to remove screens (the ones masking Irish religion, politics, education) and got lacerated by my countrymen for my trouble.

Before leaving Ireland I had already begun to transfer my loyalty from film stars to film directors (Henry Fonda retaining a kind of honorary status) and Renoir was one of the first, with De Sica, to seize my imagination. My first encounter was with *The Rules of the Game*, seen in the Theatre de Luxe, the slummy Dublin Saturday afternoon home of the Irish Film Society. Then I saw *Une Partie de Campagne*. It is not sufficient for a young person entering his own world (one still under construction) to know that there have been cultural heroes of the past; there must be some in his own lifetime.

193

There were no film-makers of my generation yet, so Renoir served as my untarnished head of the cinema.

On screen he seemed physically ungainly, almost ugly, a heavy man fairly shorn at the top, overweight below, edging towards a turnip shape. He had played to perfection the porcine farmhouse creature in *Une Partie de Campagne* and somehow it seemed absurd that such a semi-*débile* could be in real life master of the stratagems of *La Règle du Jeu* and creator of the radiant world of *Une Partie de Campagne*.

At the point when I met him, Renoir had just finished his book on his father, *Renoir, mon père*, and was preparing in Paris to shoot his second war film, *Le Caporal Épinglé* with a nervy French actor, Jean-Pierre Cassel, in the lead.

I made the shocking discovery that after forty-three films, many of them masterpieces, one of the greatest film directors in history had serious difficulty in raising money for a film. Indeed, at sixty-seven, he was obliged to take on teaching jobs in America to earn a living. He spent a lot of time then in Berkeley, California, where his son had a teaching post.

The way America could ungratefully discard talent was a deplorable fact of Hollywood life we were well used to, but I had supposed the French film industry operated on a higher plane. In fact it was only the success of the reissued *La Grande Illusion* which brought in enough money for him to finance his new film independently.

Of course, Renoir had had political problems in the past. The producers mutilated *La Grande Illusion* after its first appearance in deference to the rage of the Right. The first audience for *La Règle du Jeu* (1939) tore up the cinema seats and the craven producers mutilated this masterpiece too. I could understand political hostility to his work, but the kind of ungenerosity displayed in the sixties to such a great film-maker – and an admirable person – was acutely depressing. (It was strange that, in Renoir and Beckett, cinema and literature had at this time a benign, totally incorruptible father figure: both genres must feel orphaned now.)

Renoir lived in Pigalle among the prostitutes, the garish lights and the gangsters in a quiet, gated impasse of old, balconied houses. Coming out of the Métro and making my way along by the bars I took a tie out of my pocket and started to put it on in deference to the great man. A tart in a doorway called out to me as I passed: 'Really, darling, you should have finished dressing while you were in there!'

The house could have been transplanted to the southern states of America and served as the home of a Southern gentleman not quite down on his luck but careless about appearances. It was a little ramshackle on the exterior, and exuded cosiness and culture – books, prints, obviously beloved pieces of furniture – within.

Renoir and I entered the large salon simultaneously by opposite doors and started at the sight of each other, like a couple of characters in a farce. He padded towards me and shook my hand warmly, then plonked himself down in a wide, winged armchair and waited.

It would have gone against all my expectations to find Renoir a troublesome man – even troublesome in the licensed way highly-strung creative people can be. But there was nothing highly-strung about him: he radiated an unaffected benevolence with no element of the piety or smugness which often goes with that state. He appeared at ease with the world and lenient towards its people. Close up, the physical impression of pigginess faded – his features were finer than on screen – and the idea of coarseness disappeared altogether once you began to listen to him. As he talked he seemed to assume a physical grace.

A long mahogany table filled the centre of the room which had two high windows looking out on to the dusty tranquillity of the cobbled street. I sat alongside the table.

There was a dramatic contrast between Renoir's periods of repose, in which he sat, chin lowered (looking, I thought, a little like Churchill), chatting away in his throaty, phlegmy voice and the moments of sudden activity when he would jump up and, moving at surprising speed, go the length of the table and pick up a document or magazine to illustrate some point. Then he would settle back into the capacious armchair again.

195

He told me about the film he was making and how it compared with *La Grande Illusion*. 'It takes place in a prisoner-of-war camp during the last war, but it has nothing to do with *La Grande Illusion*,' he explained. 'The characters of *La Grande Illusion* [Pierre Fresnay and von Stroheim] acted according to solid and unshakeable values. But here the people are walking on shifting sands. The world around them is collapsing.'

I asked solemnly if he thought we were heading for the total destruction of civilization.

'Not perhaps total destruction but it's quite possible that we will go into another Dark Age,' he said serenely. 'That could be interesting. The last one produced some great art.'

During a lecture at the Cinémathèque on the rue d'Ulm, Renoir had said: 'It is not with general ideas that you make a film but with details. The details one sees, one feels and senses; there is the sensual joy of sensing forms, colours. We do not make a film with ideas, with the brain. After all, what is the brain, this old prostitute? Why, it profits exactly from what these senses honestly accumulate.

'What is important', he said, in that tranquil room, 'is that a film must have a little bit of human flavour.'

I wondered why he had chosen Jean-Pierre Cassel, at that time an actor only known for flighty roles.

'Because he does not act deep,' Renoir said. 'I would be frightened of an actor who acts deep. It is not true that serious people act deep.'

'You mean, you would not have liked to use Marlon Brando?'

'For instance.'

There was a fashion at the time for adapting the classics to the screen and, recalling Renoir's 1934 film of *Madame Bovary*, I said, 'People complained at the time that your *Madame Bovary* was not Flaubert. Do you think it was?'

'I hope not,' he said. 'Even if you follow the book word by word your personality will come out. But how can you faithfully follow a book with a camera? You cannot copy with pictures what is told with words – or if you try you will get a very poor result. *Madame Bovary* was near enough to Flaubert but *The Lower Depths* [Louis Jouvet] was quite different from the book, yet Gorky liked it.'

'I have always said', Renoir continued, 'that a film must have an author. But people have misunderstood what I meant. I don't mean a script-writer, although a script-writer could be the "author" too. For example, anyone who says that *Les Enfants du Paradis* is Carné's film is crazy. It's Jacques Prévert's.'

I felt a kind of embarrassed pleasure at hearing him endorse a theory I had long held; that Prévert was the genius behind Carné; the latter only made banal films after Prévert ceased to work with him.

'Prévert was the dominant personality,' he continued. 'Not that Carné is not a good director, but I think he was born to be a good director of great writers. Sometimes it can be the actor who dominates. Mary Pickford, for example,' he said unexpectedly.

Had an actor ever dominated one of his films? Michel Simon, for example, I asked, thinking of this hairy, rapacious actor shambling his way through *Boudu Sauvé des Eaux*.

'I don't know. Maybe.' Renoir shifted discontentedly in his chair and made a surprising confession. 'I am easily influenced,' he said.

Had he consciously taught the craft of film-making to Visconti and Jacques Becker when they worked with him as assistants?

'No,' Renoir said categorically. 'I don't believe in teaching. I realized that they had talent so they worked with me – that's all.'

Could films really teach people anything valuable about life? I wanted to know.

'Like any art!' he exclaimed. 'Art teaches you how to look at life. I agree with Oscar Wilde who said that before Turner there was no fog in London. It's true! Now every book and picture you pick up about London is full of fog. The artist teaches you how to see the world. Wait!' He jumped up. 'I was just reading something here by Charlie Chaplin.'

He sped down the length of the room and, bending over the end of the mahogany table, held glasses to his nose and read from an open book: '"I say to people, This is the way you see the world, but it is not like this – it is like that! I show them and they laugh!" That's it,' Renoir said, whipping off his glasses. He became quite excited. 'The artist picks perhaps one tiny corner of life and shows you how life really is. Not', he said picking up a rosy-coloured French Post Office calendar, 'like this! Nor', he said, grabbing a copy of *Time* magazine and thrusting it almost into my face, 'like that.'

He lumbered back to his chair and sat down heavily. It was then he said: 'We are surrounded by screens.'

Did he think the cinema could help pull down some of the screens surrounding sex – in the way *Lady Chatterley's Lover* may have? I had in mind the triumphant outcome, for liberalism, of the *Lady Chatterley* trial that had taken place a short time before.

Renoir thought that a good director could teach you more about sex, that is, about the reality of sexual relationships, just in passing, without trying to make a sexy film, than any of the so-called sexy films. 'Take Pigalle here,' he said. 'All based on sex. But I have never seen anything more unerotic in my life.'

And what about censorship? Could he approve of that in any circumstances?

'I am in favour of censorship,' he said, 'but not against what is supposed to be sexy or dirty, but against what is idiotic. If someone's work shows the leaves of a tree or hunger in an unreal way his work should be banned.'

We spoke about nationalism. Art for Renoir could not be nationalistic. But it could not be 'international' either. 'An international film would have no character,' Renoir said, long before characterless multinational films became current.

I made a curious discovery. Here in his Parisian home he did not have a single still of one of his films. He had them in America, he said, because it seemed appropriate. But here in Paris, not at all. It was as if he had no need of reassurance at home but it was a necessity abroad. Although he now spent long periods in America with his son he had not made an American picture in seventeen years, not since *The Southerner*. 'All my ideas are French,' he said.

I met him again early one morning on location on the Pont de Tolbiac, below the Gare d'Austerlitz. He was supervising a set-up on the bridge with Jean-Pierre Cassel, looking cold in a heavy military overcoat. There was little traffic about and there was the usual lack of animation which is more typical of work on a film set than the supposed show-business frenzy.

Well wrapped up, Renoir exchanged a few cordial words and invited me to dinner in his home when shooting was over. But he had to leave France sooner than expected, to return to his son in Berkeley, so the dinner never materialized.

I next met him at an impassioned gathering of cineastes who were discussing strategy in the protests over the Langois Affair at the Cinema Action in the north of Paris. He had become very much more enfeebled although he lived another eleven years. He only made two more films.

It was March 1968 and the film editor Lila Biro, her assistant Philippe Delsalle and myself were out in the sound studios at St-Maurice, furiously trying to get the dubbing of a film finished in time for it to be shown to the Cannes festival selection committee.

The previous year I had persuaded Victor Herbert (the man who had backed *Endgame*) to finance a feature-length film, directed by me, about Ireland: its political humbug and its obscurantism; its ludicrously patriotic sportsmen who refused to watch 'foreign' games (soccer and rugby), never mind play them; and its spirited people, heartbreakingly tormented by a creepy, oppressive and ignorant clergy.

I told Victor I could get Raoul Coutard, frontier scout of the *nouvelle vague*, to shoot it for me. I, of course, had never succeeded in exchanging a useful phrase with Coutard – but Victor did not know that. What appealed to him was the idea of applying the swingeing new wave to jokey, boozy Ireland. Actually I had another kind of film in mind, more politically committed, more agnostically evangelical.

Victor generously overlooked my never having been behind a camera in my life – it was 1967 so I benefited greatly from the tolerance of the new wave spirit in France. In any event, I had worked myself into such a state about the possibility of making a film about my own country (and possibly winning a few old arguments on screen) that I was able to leap the apparent preposterousness of a tyro asking a world-famous director of photography to pack a handheld camera around Dublin for him.

Peter Graham (my old rival at Cannes) knew Coutard's girlfriend, Monique Herran, and found out for me that he was shooting a film at Tours.

My first sight of Coutard this time was when he strolled into the small local cinema where they were showing the rushes. The moment he walked in, I knew he was the kind of man with whom I could work.

The nonchalant, self-contained demeanour did not sufficiently disguise the John Ford hero: a toughie, I figured, probably with a heart of gold (I got him to work for nothing on his day off). Like the hero of a Western, Coutard came with a team of old army pals. It was comical to see how this group conformed to the Hollywood stereotype. They were the Three Mesquiteers all over again – not Dumas' musketeers, but John Wayne's B-picture mesquiteers. Coutard was the cool, tough, laconic hero; the warm-hearted pal was Georges Liron, who had lost a leg in Indo-China; the droll sidekick was Jeannot, a focus puller, and finally there was the girl, Monique Herran, a Basque continuity girl. Coutard was married to a Vietnamese woman and had a daughter, but some time later he settled down with Monique.

As usual, and wastefully, when it came to the encounter at dinner, I did not trust my own intuition. Wretchedly anxious about my own lack of experience, I felt my only hope was to convince him of the enormous importance of the material. (Without Coutard there would be no backing from Herbert.) I dived into a desperate account of Ireland and its tragical-comical-demoniacal history, leaping verbally like a goosed goat from one pinnacle of Irish political disaster to another, often becoming bafflingly entangled in my own impetuous French. Then in a tone of despair I asked him if he would work with me.

'*Oui*,' said Coutard.

Oui? I had come tumbling down an avalanche of my own making and his '*Oui*' brought me to a skidding halt. My God, it was done!

There was one problem: the first week's shoot – of the two we envisaged – would have to be in exactly four weeks' time; after that he was not free again for six months.

Four weeks! I had hardly a sentence on paper, had made no practical preparations, and within one month I would have to start directing my first film.

This was too much to cope with, but Victor's enthusiasm would never hold for another six months. It had to be now. I blacked out the implications and decided to concentrate on the less intimidating details. To tell the truth, while the project was a frightening one for a complete novice, I knew in my heart it did not matter a toss whether I had ever made a film before or not. It's all in the head; you only need to get locked into an obsession and someone else will work the machines. Coutard knew this too: he hardly understood a sentence of English, yet the supposedly intractable Irish film technicians of the period, the lighting men and sound men, did his every casual bidding – out of admiration, it was plain to see. (It could not have been because of the meagre financial deal, which was all I could afford to offer.)

There was one other moment of pure terror, when we met again in his Vietnamese wife's restaurant to sign the contract which would irrevocably bind me to this financial and technical responsibility. I had a terrified vision of being given all the bits and pieces of a film and then, like someone confronted with a DIY wardrobe, not being able to fit them together. If it turned out a mess I would be humiliated in two countries.

These onslaughts of raw fear are quite distinct from normal attacks of anxiety or apprehension. They are always associated with the moment when you realize you are about to alter your life significantly, perhaps even become a different person. The moment I stepped on to the boat to France, knowing, although not completely consciously, that I was turning myself into an exile, was one. Now I was about to try to turn myself into a film director; to barge, not as a student but as a master, into a world of which I had only the most casual grasp.

Only for that one moment is the fear unadulterated; later, being an exile or a film-maker becomes just part of already accepted behaviour which carries with it the usual diluted rations of anxiety and fear.

I signed, only because it would now have been even more farcical not to.

Four weeks later we went, with Georges and Monique (we could not afford Jeannot on our budget), to Dublin and filmed for five days. Six months later, when Coutard finished working on *La Mariée était en noir* for Truffaut, we went back for the final shoot.

The hubbub this seventy-five-minute *cinéma vérité* film, *Rocky Road to Dublin*, created in Ireland is another story. On *The Late Show* we were accused of making the film with Communist money. It wouldn't have made any difference to them had they known that the backer, Victor, belonged to one of the most notorious bunch of capitalists of the sixties: Bernie Cornfeld's IOS. This was the offshore Investors' Overseas Service which, after Victor had prudently and honourably severed his connection, landed Cornfeld, the rampant capitalist, in legal problems. But as an anti-clerical, anti-patriot I was fair game for TV and newspapers (with the very notable exception of the film critic of the *Irish Times*, Fergus Linehan, who went well beyond the demands of duty in repeatedly defending the film). Then, when it was finally released in Dublin, John Carney of the *Sunday Independent* defended it thoughtfully, which took some courage, considering the then hagiographical slant of that paper.

Sam Beckett did not approve of me getting into this passionate (but also compassionate) confrontation with my countrymen. When he heard in the Rosebud one night that I was going to Ireland to make the film he told me I shouldn't do it.

'Why not?' I asked him.

'Because they aren't serious people,' he said.

He had a point there: when it comes to tough issues, my countrymen can be bafflingly skittish and unreliable. But, for the first time, I was in no way overawed by his opinion. Secretly I decided he didn't know anything about film (as *Film*, his attempt at the medium, I thought demonstrated). Anyway, my own new ambition was powerful and for once I felt it did not matter if I displeased him.

The adventure of getting Irish priests, Christian Brothers, politicians, patriots (not necessarily the same thing) and tentative radicals to co-operate in making the film is outside the scope of this book; enough to say that, the shooting completed and the editing done, we decided to enter the film for the Critics' Week at the May 1968 Cannes festival. We had one day left to get the print to the Cannes committee.

We finished the dubbing at six in the morning and Lila Bird, Philippe Delsalle and I delivered the print to the Drug Store at Étoile. The Cannes committee met there at 9 a.m. We waited, exhausted and rather miserable, in the café.

At ten o'clock Gene Moskovitz of *Variety*, one of the judges, came past our table, raised a thumb and went on. Ours had been one of the eight films selected from around the world for the Critics' Week. My first film was going to Cannes. But the May student revolt did a thorough job of rearranging that commercial triumph.

Seventeen

O n the morning of 25 May 1968, I witnessed a scene in the Latin Quarter which made plausible the students' invitation to 'take your dreams for reality'. On the boulevard St Michel, by the Sorbonne, a student was punctiliously directing the traffic. Queuing meekly to be guided around the debris of the previous night's barricades was a police van, packed with subdued CRS – riot police.

At that point French society was balancing very nicely on its ear. The Government was like a fretful, fearful outsider: nine million workers were involved in a strike that had something of the character of a shambolic holiday. The Parisians had thawed their refrigerated hearts and were publicly experimenting with selflessness.

There was, of course, a vigorous dialogue of truncheon and paving-stone going on at night, but by day the students were preoccupied with the task of reconstructing French society by the only means available to them: talking. The bourgeoisie came on pilgrimages to the Left Bank, prudently on foot (125 cars were burnt during the revolt). They stood about the streets in their hundreds arguing with the young. The adults often became heated. But the students, prettily smoke-smudged from rioting the night before, were patient and tolerant.

There was some perplexity, some anxiety, but overriding all was a curious stillness in the city: the stillness with which we await a great event with secret and slightly fearful joy.

The authoritarian grandeur of France had been brought to an

absolute standstill by a bunch of children. The question was: did they know the Secret of Life – the one we had all fumbled in growing up?

That was what was in the air that cold May morning on the Boul' Mich, that and the lingering tear gas.

The 'Events of May' began on 22 March when a twenty-three-year-old sociology student of French birth but German nationality, Daniel Cohn-Bendit, led the occupation of the suburban faculty of Nanterre and founded the Movement of 22 March. The protest was against the arrest of a Nanterre student following a fire-bomb attack on the American Express office in Paris. French student agitation had until then been directed against American involvement in Vietnam but a profound politicization of youth had taken place, undetected or ignored, and it was now about to swing with startling force against all authority in France.

A focus was provided when Cohn-Bendit and his followers, locked out of Nanterre, came to the city and joined the restive Sorbonne students already demonstrating in the forecourt of the university against overcrowding and unpopular authoritarian customs. On 3 May the rector, Jean Roche, made a fateful decision: against all tradition he invited the police to clear the university. From then on the students, fighting the police with increasing ferocity, attempted again and again to turn the Latin Quarter into a vast sanctuary. Using hijacked buses, parked cars, material from building sites, publicity placards and public benches, they erected barricades often ten feet high. For ammunition they prised up paving stones, thick as plum puddings. During the Events, more than an acre and a half of the Latin Quarter was dug up.

In the early hours of the morning the *agents* and CRS would rush the barricades and track the students through the narrow streets, clubbing them, often refusing to allow Red Cross ambulances to get to the injured. Unresentful of their own discomfort, local residents dropped sandwiches down to the trapped students and poured out buckets of water to dilute the saturating tear gas. In revenge the CRS often fired gas grenades through apartment windows and into crowded cafés which gave shelter to the insurgents.

Twenty-eight students were arrested the first night, on the second

495 and on 25 May a total of 805 students and police were injured. 'Mort à Grimaud!' roared the students. (Maurice Grimaud was the Paris Prefect of Police.)

Three figures emerged as leaders of the students: Jacques Sauvageot, twenty-five, acting president of the student union; Alain Geismar, twenty-eight, a lecturer in physics, president of the Higher Education teachers' union; and Danny the Red, Daniel Cohn-Bendit.

Sauvageot, grave as a deacon, handsome as a film star, was considered by the authorities to be the stable force in the leadership; Geismar, tubby with a webbed emotional voice, had a way of transforming himself into an incandescent sphere of passion and reproach; Cohn-Bendit, carrot-haired, gap-toothed, had the heavenly blue eyes and suspect candour of a nursery favourite.

If President de Gaulle, Prime Minister Georges Pompidou, and Minister for Education Alain Peyrefitte were visibly at a loss to understand the revolt, these three *enragés* could not, on the other hand, be said to be leading it in any formal sense. They rode the waves of an apparently inexplicable outburst of exasperation.

The Communists, fearful of losing control of the young workers, criticized Cohn-Bendit for his German background in veiled anti-Semitic terms. In a moving response thousands of students marched through the Left Bank in sombre procession chanting: 'We are all German Jews!' The crucial divide between the young and adults in France was demonstrated at that point not only by the readiness of students to call themselves Jews, but especially the willingness of the new generation to call themselves German.

The day before *Rocky Road to Dublin* was to be screened at Cannes I set off alone for the Gare d'Austerlitz with the film cans in a suitcase. We could not afford to pay Coutard's train fare. As the taxi headed towards the rue du Cherche-Midi we ran into a crowd of chanting students blocking our route to boulevard Montparnasse. We did a fast reverse, shot back to Duroc and tried to come back up the boulevard before the students flooded into it. But they were already there, leaving only a narrow opening into the avenue du Maine which leads away up towards the Porte d'Orleans. I was in a panic: if I missed the train to Cannes there would be no screening for us next day. Our chance for world renown would be scuttled by banal unpunctuality.

Even the narrow gap into the avenue du Maine was not easy to penetrate: a fiddly barricade had been erected by the students. There was also a tractor abandoned on the pavement. The world was topsy-turvy and a misplaced tractor or two was a detail hardly worthy of remark. But as we fretted a young man in his holiday best detached himself courteously from his girl, took off his jacket, folded it on a bench with care and got up on the tractor. With a few deft manoeuvres he uprooted a tall tree from the pavement and dropped it on top of the puny barricade. He got down off the tractor to a scattering of cheers, put on his jacket and strolled off with his girl.

We had no choice. My taxi had to nudge its way through the tree's topmost branches; it was like going through a crazy car-wash. I kept mouthing, 'Press', through the closed windows and flapping my press card. The students let us through grudgingly.

To avoid Montparnasse we had to do a huge arc by rue Froi-deveaux around the cemetery, across boulevard Arago and back down by the Sante to boulevard de Port Royal. I got to Austerlitz with five minutes to spare.

When the lights went up after the projection of *Rocky Road* in the Petite Salle at Cannes, Jean-Luc Godard, François Truffaut and a temporarily revolutionary Claude (*Un Homme et Une Femme*) Lelouch, who had arrived in his private yacht, came into the cinema and announced that they were closing down the festival. *Rocky Road* was the last film projected at that historic festival – the Grande Salle had already been shut down. The prize-giving ritual was scrapped.

Louis Malle, Monica Vitti and Milos Foreman resigned from the jury in solidarity with the students. Nice airport was closed. Foreign critics fled to Monaco or Italy. On the terrace of the Carlton a normally rapacious waiter refused to accept a tip from me. The adult world came panting humbly after the students, but neither generation knew precisely what was going on.

The students, cineastes and film buffs began a debate on the film

207

industry, the theory of authorship, the purpose of culture, the bankruptcy of politics, the ideal of freedom, which lasted three days and two nights. It was non-stop. At various times we would go and have a meal or even go to bed and, coming back, the debate was still on.

Anybody could get up on the stage and hold the couple of thousand spectators with wit or ramblings. There was courtesy and tolerance towards all. The only element of duress was that film-makers had no choice but to address the multitude. Although I was unknown to probably nine-tenths of the audience I was commanded to speak (I think it was Comrade Godard who issued the order, taken up by the revolutionaries). I have no idea what I said, nor had I while I was saying it. Addressing all these people, double parked in the seats and packing the aisles, scattered one's sense of reality. Denunciation of the obstacles organized life puts in one's path must have been one of my themes. And watch out for the clergy!

With incredible dispatch the students set up a parallel exhibition and distribution system stretching from the university at Nice to Paris. Only revolutionarily appropriate films were put on the circuit. A delegation of grave young students from Nice came to see me: their attitude embodied concern for the world, tenderness towards mankind, a readiness to invite sacrifice – a state of mind of which only youth can be the custodian.

They now had a grave responsibility: they were running the world. Their first concern was to educate. *Rocky Road* was too pointedly close to the psychodrama they were enacting to be left out: The film asked, 'What do you do with your revolution once you've got it? – Give it back to the bourgeois and the clergy,' was its disenchanted response. They asked me to donate a print to their distribution system. It was about the only viewable one we had, but they were so touching and we were all in such a glorious state of generosity that I think I would have given them the negative, if they'd asked for it.

I was invited to the first revolutionary screening at Nice university that evening. Milos Foreman and Louis Malle were on the platform. Louis Malle, whom I had not met, insisted that I be brought out of the audience and up on to the stage with the other representatives of world cinema. It is extraordinary how a tiny gesture of goodwill can work in a man's favour for decades. I have never been able to think ill of any of his films since.

I left Cannes for Paris at dead of night in what was rumoured to be the only transportation available: an old provincial bus. Through the night we passed garages with forecourts full of stalled cars. Signs everywhere: '*Panne d'essence*'. No petrol. Mentally we were already refugees, huddling in the freezing bus. Passengers stood on seats and stuffed newspapers into gaps in the sun-roof to keep out the bitter draught. Revolution had engulfed the whole of France, even under-mining the heating mechanism of buses. Something odd about this reflection made me go up to the driver.

'Oh, you want the heating?' he said, and switched it on.

The Gare du Nord was like a great, slumbering *clochard*, rubbish piled around its limbs. Virtually nothing was working. No left-luggage service and no one I knew had enough petrol to cross Paris and pick me up. I hired a hotel room for my suitcase, put it to bed and began the walk right across the city to Montparnasse. It took me a while to realize that the bolshie Parisians were so humbled: their cars were at the disposal of everyone. You only had to flag down a Deux Chevaux or Mercedes to get a lift. This was truly revolutionary; France had been the least obliging country in Europe for hitch-hikers.

I was soon being chauffeured around Paris by a great variety of strangers. One of them turned out to be a plainclothes policeman, more than a little nervous about his future.

Rocky Road had been sent ahead to Paris and I was asked to address a screening in the Sorbonne. The Latin Quarter was strewn with carcasses of cars. Routine life was completely unravelled. We wandered the dishevelled streets, discussing with strangers what would happen next. While the world was in turmoil it was also, in a curious way, standing still. We were exonerated from the responsibil-ities of daily drudgery, punctuality or any kind of overbearing organization.

I forgot to write for the *Guardian* for a couple of weeks. What England might require did not seem essential. I was not troubled. There had been another, frictionless change-over in *Guardian* features: Peter Preston was now features editor. He made no changes so far as I was concerned.

The first Paris projection of *Rocky Road to Dublin* took place on rue de la Sorbonne in a university amphitheatre, which was jammed. We were below street level and from the ventilation shafts came a gentle prickling of tear-gas flavoured air.

I took questions afterwards. A man at the back stood up and challenged me on some aspect of Ireland's political history. It was Tony Geraghty of the *Guardian*. 'He's just an Englishman,' I told the students. He was wiped out by their laughter. Tony, in fact, is an Irishman, but a certain cheekiness was part of the style of the times.

Life magazine took an interest in this Irish revolutionary film that had been adopted by France's revolutionary students. The American woman reporter who came to interview me had trouble getting the hang of our crosshatched Celtic history. I gallantly offered to write the piece, for which she was grateful. We got a two-page spread under her byline.

Now the film was invited to the Faculty of Law on rue d'Assas. This was a different proposition from the Latin Quarter faculties. The law faculty was notoriously right-wing, a nest of Jeune Nation, the group who had battled with the students occupying the Sorbonne.

The amphitheatre here was huge, like an old Odeon cinema. This time I sat in the equivalent of the upper circle. Suddenly in the middle of the film a great wodge of the audience started to cuff and belt each other. 'What exactly are they fighting about?' I wondered to my neighbour, Joe Carroll of the *Irish Press*.

'They're fighting about your film,' he explained helpfully. I could not quite grasp this: it was all completely unreal. I thought that perhaps in decency I should also take part in this fighting, but they did not seem to have any need of me. (In any event, no one recognized me.)

Although the Socialists, and particularly the Communist Party, worked resolutely to keep the workers from co-operating with the students or joining in any demonstration, we made the leap with the film. The men occupying the Renault car factory at Billancourt sent out a request to see *Rocky Road*. A couple of days before, I had watched the students calling from the road to workers up in the factory windows to come out and join them. But while the exchanges were friendly if guarded, the trade union line was rigidly kept: none of the workers would come out. Official trade unionism abhorred the maelstrom created by middle-class *fils de papa*.

When we arrived one evening with the film and a projector, the Renault factory was surrounded by CRS, but the laxness of the times had infected them too and they made no fuss about letting us in (and letting us out without a clout on the head). There was just a skeleton staff of occupying workers in the huge shed.

'Where's the screen?' we asked.

For some reason we assumed they would have a screen.

Fortunately I had brought Lila Biro with me, who happened to live nearby in Billancourt. She went home and got a bedsheet.

Half an hour later the sentinels of the French automobile industry were acquainting themselves with Ireland's woes. Their seriousness was moving: I remember one man sucking on his pipe and attempting to offer a solution for Ireland's endless troubles. With the CRS outside he was not in a comfortable position; his own future did not look too secure. But he considered many options to save Ireland from itself.

On 24 May de Gaulle, now aged seventy-eight, finally faced the nation on television in an attempt to reassert his authority. But all the students saw was a grotesque old man with the dislocated gestures of a marionette. That night tens of thousands of them took to the streets in a candlelit funeral cortège, chanting, '*Adieu, de Gaulle! Adieu, de Gaulle, Adieu!*' Seventy barricades went up in the Latin Quarter and students and police fought until five in the morning. The next day I wrote a piece for the *Guardian*, published on 29 May:

These past few weeks have witnessed the truth of what the poets have been telling us since the beginning of time: there is no adult world. Youth is reckless, generous and valuable, but the world of wise, mature and organized adults for which youth is supposed to be a preparation does not exist.

The morning it appeared de Gaulle helpfully fled the country, escaping to the French army stationed in Baden-Baden.

France was stunned. Name of God, were they going to have to take their dreams for reality?

No one would have believed that, at that moment of shocking triumph for the students, the spirit, the intoxicating freedom of May '68 had less than 48 hours to live.

The May revolt was unique among the worldwide student unrest of 1968 because it succeeded in paralysing an entire country and ultimately brought down a head of state. President de Gaulle retired after the failure of his 1969 referendum. The students had widespread public support. On 19 May a poll showed that 53 per cent of those in the Paris region believed the students' revolt was justified. This approbation, even from the older generation, may be partly explained by the fact that, unlike in London and Los Angeles, obscenity was not regarded as an appropriate weapon by the students and there was nothing of a drug culture about the revolt. Although revolutionaries, the French students were respectable, and set alongside the manoeuvres of conventional politicians, their aspirations had a touching disinterestedness.

'*Chienlit!*' (*Chie-en-lit*: shitting in one's own bed) was how de Gaulle on 18 May unwisely described their behaviour. '*Le chienlit, c'est encore lui!*' retorted the students in a celebrated poster and it was de Gaulle's support which collapsed.

But on 29 May, returning to the Élysée Palace from Germany, de Gaulle astutely rejected television and used the radio to speak to the nation. A mythical voice, belligerent, inflexible, called on the faithful to flood the streets. A tidal wave of Gaullists, more than half a million, flooded the Champs-Élysées next day, led by the writer and former radical André Malraux.

All through May the students had chanted a slogan with a peculiar rhythm which still brings a shiver to those who lived through the revolt: 'Ce n'est / qu'un début / continuons le / COM-BAT! (It's only a beginning / continue / the Fight!) Now came the turn of Gaullist golden youth: they raced around Paris in open coupés trailing giant tricolours, honking a signal with a three-two beat. It was the beat of the old *pieds-noir* anti-de Gaulle slogan: '*Al-gér-ie / Fran-çaise.*' It was the only slogan they could think of.

The Sorbonne was not 'liberated' until 16 June. Demonstrations, rioting, occupations continued sporadically throughout that month and later. But everyone realized the spirit of May was extinguished.

On the day following de Gaulle's radio appeal, petrol magically reappeared. Now a dying man couldn't hitch a lift.

The leaders of the May revolt have an unstable status in the political history of their country. It is not just that their movement did not have the kind of conventional programme which lends itself to scholarly annotation. It is difficult to remain an authentic representative of an historical event whose achievements are either impalpable or camouflaged by the political and commercial forces which later appropriated them. (Already by June the damaged Drug Store at St-Germain-des-Prés was selling souvenir rubber paving stones.)

But the relationship between teacher and pupil, employer and employee – above all, youth and the adult world – was crucially changed by the events of May and not only in France. It is only necessary to remember how backward were these relationships before 1968, despite the splendid liberal image of de Gaulle's and Malraux's France.

These young insurgents presided over a time when instead of a society being swept by that truculent fever called patriotism, which catapults a country towards suffering, a not dissimilar force carried France towards joy. To anyone who lived through those weeks the experience was as triumphant as that of any great battle and lies much more comfortably in the memory.

I always wondered why there were so few deaths during this prolonged revolt: none in May, three in June, two accidental, one when a student drowned fleeing from the riot police into a river. It became clear that despite the students' hostile slogan the Prefect of Police, Maurice Grimaud, must have been exerting extraordinary control over his men.

Years later I met him and asked what he had felt at that time.

'A kind of joy,' he replied. 'I do not say that lightly. I was interested to live an event which at every moment I had a feeling was important. Government had broken down; I found the experience invigorating, a tonic.'

I looked at him in silence. How had such a man become Prefect of Police?

'You know,' he said. 'I never understood why they made me Prefect of Police.'

During the four-week run of *Endgame* we had noticed a remarkable development in Sam Beckett. The companionship, even rascally, cheered him up and his salvaging of a production gave him greater confidence in directing his own work. He became so relaxed that for the first time, to our knowledge, he allowed himself to be photographed during rehearsals and permitted Clancy Segal of the *Observer* to write an impressionistic account of the proceedings. (I did not feel I wanted to alter our agreement about total confidentiality.)

But in 1969 the Nobel Prize put Beckett in retreat. Con came to the Falstaff and told us Sam was going to get the prize. Sam had already made it plain he did not want it in 1964. It was then offered to Sartre, who turned it down. In 1969, submitting to his publisher's (Jerome Lindon) ambition for him, and realizing that open refusal would expose him to even more publicity than acceptance, he agreed at last. But he would not go to Sweden: Lindon went in his place.

The next time we met alone was in his apartment on the boulevard St-Jacques. I asked if he hadn't been tempted to go to Stockholm. Like a scientist producing some bizarre specimen he took a colour photograph out of a drawer and handed it to me. It showed Jerome Lindon climbing a staircase towards what looked like a Ziegfeld Follies tableau of ambassadors and sages.

'If I had to walk up those stairs, I'd faint,' he said.

He showed me what he had bought with his Nobel money (what was left of it after he gave away most of what he referred to as 'the loot' to indigent writers). It was a telephone with a little red light instead of a bell. He expressed great satisfaction that this way he would no longer have to endure its constant ringing. But he'd have to keep his eyes peeled if he were expecting a call.

It has been well documented that the Nobel Prize dislocated the careers and undermined the creativity of the majority of writers and scientists who have been burdened by its notoriety and its consequences.

A short time after the announcement I met Beckett walking past the old Gare Montparnasse. He did not even have time for a drink at a counter. He showed me his diary: virtually every hour of every day and week was taken by publishers, translators, theatre producers. Those who had supported him for decades now naturally wanted to cash in on the prize. He did not blame them, he said, but they wanted to mount new productions of his work, publish new editions, bring out fresh translations, all of which required his supervision or involvement.

'It has wiped out any possibility of work for at least a year,' he said, distraught.

There was a kind of freemasonry among those who were friends of Beckett but had little in common with each other. I am certain that for most of us the core of the relationship was not pride in knowing a world-famous figure but an extraordinary pleasure in being a friend of such a genuine and heroic human being.

For many the mystery is, how is it possible to have a normal relationship with a literary genius? This may be difficult in the case of the writer who is barker of his own wares, the common stance of celebrated authors. In less pejorative terms, the writer is also expected to appear as a public authority on his own subject, delivering lectures or engaging in literary controversies ostensibly central to his profession but essentially irrelevant to his creative activity, which is always private. Beckett, quite unaffectedly, had no truck with any of this, neither in self-advertisement nor in participating in occasions which reinforce status . . . and increase sales. Because he never flaunted his fame, and because he was not as Sartre was, in a position of publicly

– or indeed privately – defending a philosophy, it was possible to have a relationship with him based entirely on simple human companionship.

There is no disputing that Samuel Beckett was an anguished man and never attained consistent social ease. Late one night in the Falstaff, he stopped paying attention to us; as was our way we left him to his silence. Then quite deliberately he raised his mug of beer and poured it slowly over his head. That seems like ammunition for another anecdote about Irish writers' buffoonery – but with someone you know you can tell the difference between clowning and private distress. It was a gesture of desperation. There was a quality in it, too, of spreading ashes on the head, or of dousing an intolerable pain. No one made any comment and, shortly after, we walked him part of the way home.

On another occasion after a performance of *Endgame* when we were having a drink in a terraced café by the Studio des Champs-Élysées, Pat Magee turned to Victor Herbert and in his grinding voice enquired: 'Victor, why are you always so happy?'

'Because nothing ever troubles me,' Victor said, not entirely truthfully.

'Did you hear that, Sam?' Magee said.

Beckett looked at them: 'I have never', he said, 'had a single untroubled moment in my entire life.'

If Beckett was a tormented man it never led you to regard him as an invalid or to treat him like one of the confused, neurotic creatures of which Montparnasse had plenty. What you sensed in him was an inability, or more likely a refusal, to turn from an unblinking confrontation with life. So that they may function in some sort of comfort most adults set up in their minds series of screens and distractions to dim the intolerable consciousness of the reality which confronts us all, the painful maze that is human relations, inexorable, humiliating decay, and the final insult that renders life meaningless: death. Not only in work but in his daily life Beckett refused protective screens. He seemed to stand and stare it out.

*

There was pathetic fallacy in the way everything seemed to disintegrate after May '68; France, de Gaulle, our bar in Montparnasse and my relationship with the *Guardian*. De Gaulle was mortally wounded by the student upheaval and when in 1969 he lost his referendum on constitutional reform he resigned and retreated to Colombey-les-Deux-Églises. Many of the British newspapers closed their Paris offices, considering the place now only worthy of a stringer.

My laid-back, long-distance relationship with the *Guardian*, which involved no supervision and spared me the chronic disquiet of too close intimacy with office politics, was no longer working in my favour. There was now serious office politics (earlier the *Guardian* had been almost obliged to merge with *The Times* for survival) and I had only the most distant knowledge of it. Hetherington's new economy measures lopped me off.

The Falstaff changed hands in 1969. The new flashily waistcoated young owner posed by the bar at night, flanked by a couple of hard men and permitted a guitar player with the touch of a navvy to solicit money from us. We abandoned the Falstaff.

Harry Evans invited me to join his *Sunday Times* in London (and become embroiled in a decade of high-class journalistic lunacy).

I left Paris for London in 1970. I kept in touch with Beckett on occasional trips back to Paris or meeting him at the Hyde Park Hotel on his infrequent visits to London for rehearsals at the Royal Court or Riverside theatres.

But time, absence and separate preoccupations eroded a friendship finally sustained only by New Year cards. Even that became irregular, and stopped.

Index